The Church

*To John Baker + family
with warm nostalgia
for days of youth!
God Bless
John Bergman
Easter 2014.*

The Church

Defining Moments in Its Western Tradition

John Berryman

Copyright © 2010 by John Berryman.

Library of Congress Control Number:		2010913572
ISBN:	Hardcover	978-1-4535-7464-5
	Softcover	978-1-4535-7463-8
	Ebook	978-1-4535-7465-2

All rights reserved. No part of this book may be reproduced or transmitted in any form or by any means, electronic or mechanical, including photocopying, recording, or by any information storage and retrieval system, without permission in writing from the copyright owner.

By the same author:

'The Bahamas: A Social Studies Course for Secondary Schools (2nd edition).
ISBN 0 333 46120 7

'The Bible: A Helping Hand'.
ISBN 1 85776 509 5

This book was printed in the United States of America.

Rev. date: 05/20/2013

To order additional copies of this book, contact:
Xlibris Corporation
0-800-644-6988
www.xlibrispublishing.co.uk
orders@xlibrispublishing.co.uk
300455

Contents

Acknowledgements 9
Foreword 11

Chapter 1: On This Rock 13
Chapter 2: Conquer by This 23
Chapter 3: Take up and Read 33
Chapter 4: To Work Is to Pray 41
Chapter 5: Not Angles but Angels 51
Chapter 6: Hail August Emperor 59
Chapter 7: Anathema 66
Chapter 8: The Aid and Consolation of Apostolic Mercy 72
Chapter 9: God Wills It 85
Chapter 10: Rome Away from Rome 94
Chapter 11: Rather the Turkish Fez than a Cardinal's Hat 106
Chapter 12: Here I Stand 117
Chapter 13: The King's Great Matter 130
Chapter 14: How Angry Is Heaven 144
Chapter 15: But It Does Move 153
Chapter 16: My Heart Strangely Warmed 168
Chapter 17: Vive l'Empereur 181
Chapter 18: Prisoner in the Vatican 194
Chapter 19: Windows Opened 206
Chapter 20: Black Christmas 218

MM+ 233
Selected Reading List 235
Appendices 247
Index 271

To David and Barbara Wilson: In Friendship.

Acknowledgements

It is a cliché, but a valid one, that our interests and insights are stimulated and cultivated by those at whose feet we have sat. Prof. Jack Scarisbrick was my inspiration to look deeply into the philosophical and theological bases of my faith at Queen Mary College, London, by introducing me to the works of Aquinas and Maritain. I have drawn on his own scholarship as upon that of Prof. S. T. Bindoff and Prof. R. F. Leslie under whom I studied. To my tutors, Dr Kevin McDonnell and Dr Humphrey Fisher (at the School of Oriental and African Studies, London), I owe a personal pastoral debt and to Prof. Roland Oliver and to Mr John S. Brown for giving me a chance; to Mr. Roger Perrin, founding Headmaster of Bede's School for giving me more than one, and whose influence upon so many has been meaningfully profound. At St Edmund Hall, Oxford, I was privileged to have been tutored by the Medievalist Rev. Dr H. E. J. Cowdrey at the time when Rev. Dr J. N. D. Kelly was principal, both of whose work on the church I have consulted in this study.

To my students and colleagues at Wesley College, Belize City; at H. O. Nash High School, Nassau, Bahamas, and latterly at Bede's School, Hailsham, I owe a tremendous debt of appreciation for their rapport, wisdom and warmth. In particular, my heads of faculty in the religious studies and history departments, Rev. Simon Morgan, Mr Marc Rattray, Dr John Oliphant, Mr Richard Frame and Mr David Bowden have facilitated a most congenial working fellowship; the technical expertise of Mr Guy Cleverley and Mr Martin Costley has been invaluable.

Mrs Daniele Martinez has been of unstinting support, having spent many hours of her time typing and retyping the material, giving of her skills liberally. I thank her. Mr Ashley Evans, a former student, was of kind assistance in this regard during the early stages as were Mrs Freda Head and Mr Ron Lucas of Hailsham Methodist Church; I extend my appreciation to them.

I am truly mindful of those seeking Christian perfection and scriptural holiness within the Methodist societies in whose fellowship I have lived, worked and worshipped: in West Africa, Belize, Turks and Caicos Islands (British West Indies) and the Bahamas as well as circuits in south-east England, where the influence of Rev. Dr David Dunn Wilson as tutor to local preachers has been particularly meaningful. They have exhibited the power of the Spirit. I am indebted to Hugh and Barbara for accommodating 'the church that meets in their house', which facilitates that spiritual link with the supportive fellowship of those first Christians in the 'province of Asia' (1 Cor. 16:19); we share with them the presence of Christ when 'two or three are gathered in His name' (Matt. 18:20).

Naturally my wife Isabelle and my family have been sufficiently tolerant in allowing me 'time out' to complete this enterprise and whose forbearance has helped to keep me going. Mr Vincent Morre at Xlibris publishing has been tremendously helpful; all these and many others have been the enablers to see this project through.

Catsfield, Sussex, 2013.

Foreword

Continuity and change are the essence of historical investigation and analysis. The perennial debate relates to the extent to which iconic moments are themselves defining moments in time, suggesting, as they might, a radical departure from the path that has gone before or simply as significant episodes within the context of a predetermined process. Historians tend to be wary of making too much of the discrete event as a moment of pivotal import in the shaping of future developments. Their preferred position is to adopt the approach that would rather emphasise the inexorable evolution of human development, punctuated by highlights of drama, which coincidentally might well infuse the ingredients of interest and spice to the ongoing story. Nonetheless, it cannot be denied that such definitive events may well be identified in the human perception as more than that. To those with vested interests, they serve as catalysts promoting proactivity, to retrenchment or to reaction; to advance, or to impede, a progression already set in train; to provide a satisfying mental highlight by which eras or epochs may be conveniently packaged and contained, artificially or otherwise. It's what the human mind makes of such instances and the interpretation they afford, which renders them worthy of recall and of an import worthy of reflection. In recent times, few could but be moved by the oration proffered by Martin Luther King in the shadow of the Lincoln Memorial during the high summer of 1963: his 'dream' so eloquently articulated and which by any measure scales the sublime mountain top of inspired imagery paved the way for the historic Civil Rights Bills of the Kennedy/Johnson presidencies and in the longer term for the advent of President Obama himself. Similarly, 1066 remains a date forever etched in the psyche of many an English person as a turning point in the island's history. The fact that Anglo-Saxon Britain was in any case experiencing inexorable decline, it is nonetheless the popular perception that the bloody encounter at Senlac on the outskirts of Hastings, on 14 October of that year, which proclaims its definitive denouement.

The advent of millennium number three invites us to examine the continuity that has characterised the Western Church whose very existence is virtually coterminous with it; moreover, it is the traditional birth of its founder that defines it. Twenty defining moments, perceived as pivotal to the development of the church, have been identified to symbolise the summation of the centuries representing the passage of the Christian era. The employment of secular incidents to identify some of these occasions is a recognition of the human factor, as it plays upon the fortunes of the Holy Church. Christ Himself seized upon some very human circumstances in order to trigger some of His most memorable and recordable pointers to abundant living (Matt. 9:14-17; Mark 4:35-41; Luke 10:25-37; John 4:4-26, for example). He recognised that the art of communication is founded upon a recognition that people respond when one's starting point is at their most meaningfully personal. Thus with the church; frequently, its only too human response to the secular world in which it is called to operate is but an acknowledgement of the very nature of our fallen nature in whose service the Lord called it into being in the first place. In this world, the profane and the sacred coexist, and church history is testimony to this. Yet the church remains, and for this reason, its record, its tenacity and the defining moments with which it is punctuated suggest that its purpose and its spiritual import will continue to meet human yearnings, as it responds to changing environments, into eternity.

Chapter 1

Banyas Pan Cave and Spring, near Caesarea Philippi

ON THIS ROCK

The conceptual foundation of the church and its eternal authoritative focal reference point resides exclusively within the person of Jesus Christ.[1] Scripture is very specific about this and the New Testament must be our starting point. As the organism that Christ was to love and for which He was prepared to die; indeed as His bride,[2] the church is the human expression of His message and promise to succeeding generations across two millennia.

The church, then, is the embodiment of Christianity. The church, its fragrance—warts and all—is Christianity's distinguishing corporate feature, with local, universal and mystical dimensions, embracing the living and the dead.

Paradoxically—to some, frustratingly and tantalisingly—Jesus Himself was apparently somewhat coy and unspecific about the nuts and bolts of the earthly component of His church, preferring to leave others to formulate its structure.

---

[1] Ephesians 5:23; Colossians 1:18.
[2] Ephesians 5:23-25; Colossians 1:24.

14
On This Rock

Of the canonical Gospel writers,[3] only Matthew makes any reference at all to any opinion that Jesus had on the matter, just twice—but what significance in these few verses![4] Those who claim membership of the church in any of its multitudinous manifestations must be drawn to the former of these two utterances[5] and incontrovertibly this leads us to the first of our defining moments in the history of the church.

Matthew's account takes us to the northern extremities of the Holy Land, to the then Roman province of Ituraea and Trachonitis where Philip (c.4 BC-AD 34), as Tetrarch,[6] ruled in the name of Emperor Tiberius (AD 14-37). Into this stunningly beautiful, yet sparsely populated area, Jesus and His small band of associates had withdrawn to find respite from the dramatic spiritual climate He had unleashed in His Galilean homeland. There, the one-time carpenter had taught and healed, challenged and provoked. He was becoming big news and recognised that decision time as to the direction His future ministry should take was fast approaching. He needed tranquility and solitude, with His small assorted band of followers to assure Himself that those whom He had

---

[3] We must be very careful here. Many accounts of Jesus's life have been hidden for centuries, as well as other material pertinent to His life and times as some have suggested, either by chance or deliberately obscured. The *Dead Sea Scrolls* progressively discovered between 1947 and 1956 reveal something significant of an isolated Jewish community at the time of Christ and contain many Old Testament texts and commentaries. The discovery in 1945 at Nag Hammadi in Egypt of the so-called Gnostic writings containing such tracts as the *Gospel of Philip*, the *Gospel of Thomas* and the *Apocalypse of Peter* are quite revealing, although they self-evidently belong to a later period than the canonical accounts, and in any case, they are written in Coptic not Greek. It must be remembered, therefore, that what constitutes the Holy Scriptures—the Canon—is in no small measure a compilation by Ireneus, bishop of Lyons, and others, between AD 180 and 240, of sources either available to them and/or which fitted their own, and their paymasters' preconceptions; nevertheless, rigorous tests *were* applied of which 'eye witness' accounts and 'divine inspiration' are key.

[4] Matthew 16:18-19; 18:17-18.

[5] Matthew 16:18-19.

[6] Philip was the son of Herod the Great (c.40-c.4 BC), ruler of the Roman province of Palestine, at the time of Jesus's birth. After Herod's death, the province was split, Ituraea and Trachonitis ultimately falling under the sway of Philip and recognised as such by Caesar Augustus (29 BC.-AD 14). Tiberius was Roman Emperor at the time of our defining moment.

attracted, by the sheer force of His personality, were further prepared to suffer with Him, to share in His victory and to expand the kind of kingdom He had in mind. Quite probably, Jesus was conscious of the significance the area to which he had now led them, a region penetrating deeply into the history, heart and soul of the Jewish people. Within the sight of the majestic, snow-capped Mt Hermon, its lower reaches playing host to a woodland of resplendent oak and almond trees, the Hebrew tribe of Dan had settled nearly half a century after the dramatic Exodus from Egypt with their fellow Israelites.[7] It was the emergent springs from these slopes that the sacred river Jordan derived its sustenance. Yet the Jewish culture had been undermined by the Assyrian invasions between 600 and 500 BC, which in turn had been largely superseded by a Greek civilisation centred ultimately upon the metropolis of Caesarea Philippi.[8] This Gentile city, at an elevation of fifteen hundred feet above sea level, dominated on three sides by mountains and on the fourth by a lush plain, which was, according to Josephus,[9] named by Herod the Great to honour his overlord and benefactor Caesar Augustus to whom a white marble temple had been dedicated. Tetrarch Philip developed the city, significantly appending his own name, in order to distinguish it from the seaport otherwise similarly called. Amidst scenes of commercial activity in the forum and the broad avenues where the wealthy resided, the Greek God Pan[10] was pervasive. Its hinterland was pockmarked with grottoes dedicated to other deities—Zeus, Aphrodite, Artemis and the like—cut into the cliff face close to the roadside through which Jesus and his entourage would have passed. Whether or not the party actually visited the city we are not told. The alien environment was quite possibly a deliberate move on the part of Jesus in order to prepare His followers for a wider ambience than that of the Orthodox Judaism in which most had been raised.

It was here, in its scriptural context, that Jesus, having sensed the 'tide in the affairs of men which, taken at the flood, leads on to fortune . . . and taking the current when it serves',[11] seized on Simon Peter's unique public recognition and acclamation of the messiahship of Jesus: 'You

---

[7]   Joshua 19:47-48; Judges 18:11-31.

[8]   Today, the Arabic town of Banyas.

[9]   Josephus: *Antiquities of the Jews*.

[10]   Pan—the god of shepherds, huntsmen, and country folk, the protector of herds and flocks.

[11]   Shakespeare: *Julius Caesar*, IV. iii.

are the Christ: the very Son of the Living God'.[12] This, then, was the time and place for the Lord to single out Simon Peter from disciples John, James, Andrew, Judas, et al. in order to capitalise on this man's particular insight and character, and to charge him with something big: . . . 'I tell you Peter, you are a rock,[13] and on this rock foundation,[14] I will build my Church . . . I will give you the keys of the Kingdom'[15]—terse as pronouncements go, yet sufficiently inscrutable, perhaps, to give rise to the plethora of interpretations that have activated subsequent verbal spats, disaffection, division and bloodletting.[16] Such would grieve the Spirit of Christ, whose most earnest desire for his followers was 'that they may be one'.[17]

Yet if anything can be said about this passage with any certainty, we can say three things: the church, as envisaged by Christ, was to be a gathering of people responding to his call;[18] it was to be guaranteed by

---

[12]   Matthew 16:15-16.

[13]   Matthew uses the Greek *petros* to describe Peter, the word meaning a detached stone or boulder, possibly derivative of the immovable foundation stone, *petra*

[14]   We must note the distinction here. The rock foundation is denoted by the Greek *petra*. This *petra* (unmoveable and enduring) does therefore appear to be of a different nature than the (mobile and itinerant) *petros* applied to Peter. See footnote 13.

[15]   Matthew 16:19.

[16]   Barclay, W.: *The Gospel of Matthew*, vol. 2, The Saint Andrew Press, 1967.

Barclay suggests several interpretations here. The (foundation) rock according to Augustine could mean Jesus, who promises Peter that the reward for His insight would be greatness in the church; alternatively, the rock is the *truth* that Christ is the son of God upon which the church is founded *or* the faith that Peter demonstrated is the symptom of the faith of the church.

Perhaps Peter is being seen as the foundation stone of a fellowship, which declares its own acclamation of Christ as Lord, but that the *true* rock is God Himself—it might not be limited to one denomination. The Catholic interpretation would imply that Simon Peter himself is the 'rock' upon which the church was to be built.

[17]   John 17:11.

[18]   From the Greek *ekklesia*—an assembly, specially called, originally not a religious term at all, but a gathering of citizens for civic purposes and used in translation from the Hebrew to denote in Old Testament terms a congregation of the Israelites (Deut. 23:3).

The Church 17

Christ[19] as permanent and secure as the Rock of Gibraltar and sustained by Peter's brand of granite-like faith as the first to share his recognition of Jesus as Messiah. 'Some are born great, some achieve greatness', but here Simon Peter, the common or garden Galilean fisherman, was being challenged to live out the meaning of His new name to be counted among the number of those having had 'greatness thrust upon them'.[20]

Peter, it seems, was being chosen—for the moment, at least—as chief minister of Christ's Spiritual Kingdom: the steward, according to William Barclay,[21] whose qualities were such as to unlock the doors and to reveal the liberating and fulfilling opportunities the crucified and risen Christ was offering to all people,[22] despite evidence suggesting shared insights and that his *powers* were to be distributed among other disciples also.[23] It is the *precise* role intended for Peter that has led to such intense debate, and in any case, no direct mention is made of 'successors'.

Certainly, further New Testament scriptural evidence points to some sort of leading position for Peter in the embryonic church; despite Peter's all too human failings, Jesus in His resurrection encounters made it clear not only to rehabilitate him, but also to single him out for the very specific task of feeding the flock.[24] For his part, the apostle's zealous sanguinity in promoting the cause of Christ was not going to allow his sometime matrimonial status to cramp his style![25] Peter was in the thick of it from the outset. It was Peter who, as Luke recounts, boldly took on the cynics in Jerusalem by expounding upon the international, multiracial and enabling significance of the Holy Spirit experience at Pentecost: the church *Born* now and *Alive* . . . sleeves rolled up and ready for action.[26]

---

[19]   Matthew 18:18-19.

[20]   Shakespeare: *Twelfth Night*, II. v. It was on this occasion that Jesus formally confirms the name of Peter, to reflect his quality, in contrast to his given Jewish name of Simon.

[21]   Barclay, W.: *Gospel of Matthew*, vol. 2, St Andrew Press, 1967.

[22]   Ephesians 4:4-8; Colossians 3:11.

[23]   See Matthew 18:18; 28:19-20. It is apparent that Jesus is addressing His disciples en masse here.

[24]   See Matthew 26:69-75; Mark 14:66-72; 16:7; Luke 22:54-62; John 18:25-27; 21:15-18; Galatians 2:11-14.

[25]   See Matthew 8:14; Mark 1:30; Luke 4:38. Peter seems to have been married at some stage; also 1 Corinthians 9:5.

[26]   Acts 2:1-42. Herein is contained Luke's account (he wasn't there) of Peter's masterly sermon on the theology of the early church: the proclamation of

18 On This Rock

Peter evidently led by example by embracing non-Jewish believers within the Christian fold, forging them with a Christian identity, defending his actions before church leaders in Jerusalem[27] and advocating this cause successfully at the first recorded church convention or council, which later met there.[28] This council was apparently chaired by James,[29] suggesting his primacy in the city that must have been regarded, still, as the focal Christian community where Christ around AD 30, had crowned His ministry. Significantly the council was not summoned at Peter's behest, casting some doubt on subsequent Catholic claims on his unquestioned primacy.

Nevertheless, Peter was almost certainly active in the early church fellowship at Jerusalem, pooling individual property and chastising hypocrites,[30] personally performing acts of healing,[31] being forced to endure imprisonment[32] and to suffer scourging[33] for his pains at the hands of the authorities. Miracles are attributed to his person.[34] We read about the beginnings of some form of church administrative deacons in the Jerusalem congregation with the appointment of seven lay assistants taking on some practical responsibility—the business side—as the church grew in numbers and complexity.[35] While Peter's name is not

---

the Kerygma, the definitive message of God's purposes: the dawn of the messianic age, as fulfilment of prophecy; Christ's assumption into glory, His eventual return, divine judgement and the need for repentance; the offer of forgiveness, the Holy Spirit and eternal life.

[27] Acts 9:1-18, despite Galatians 2:11-14 (as above).

[28] Acts 15:1-21.

[29] James, sometimes referred to as 'the Lord's brother' (Matt. 13:55, Mark 6:3 and Gal. 1:19), is generally regarded as the leader of the Jerusalem Church. The term *brother* has been debated hotly among Catholic and Protestant scholars, with the obvious allusion to the status of the 'Virgin Mary'. Josephus in his *Antiquities of the Jews* relates how this James was martyred on the orders of the Jewish High Priest in AD 62 and not to be confused with James, brother of the Apostle John (Matt. 17:1) or another Apostle, James, son of Alphaeus (Matt.10:3).

[30] Acts 4:32; 5:3-11.

[31] Acts 3:1-10.

[32] Acts 12:1-5.

[33] Acts 5:40.

[34] Acts 5:15-16; 12:6-10.

[35] Acts 6:1-7: traditionally, the first *deacons* although the word itself is not used in the text. See also chapter 20.

The church at Jerusalem, according to Eusebius,[36] escaped the destruction of the city by the Roman General Titus in AD 70, at the behest of Emperor Vespasian (69-79), by fleeing en masse across the Jordan to the Greek city of Pella. In advance of this calamity, Christ's warning might well have been heeded.[37] The church for a moment was severed from its earthly roots, and the Jewish Diaspora had begun and Christianity was to take on a Gentile Persona. Christianity found its way, early on, to Ethiopia, and Thomas allegedly sowed the seeds of the church in South India. Yet while Peter himself went off on missionary work of his own,[38] it is Paul and his companions who appear to steal the missionary limelight, being the first to take the Gospel to Europe—into Macedonia, no less![39] It was Paul, the former pharisee, not Peter, who was to shape so much of Christian doctrine, describing the church as 'the Body of Christ',[40] His 'Bride',[41] His 'Temple'[42] and as the 'New Israel',[43] the commissioned organ of Christ,[44] not a voluntary association. Indeed, he appears to make much of the non-hierarchical character of the church, suggesting a partnership of functions in its members: apostles, prophets, teachers, miracle workers, helpers, advocates and interpreters.[45] In New Testament terms, the offices of presbyter and bishop seem to have been used interchangeably[46] although the deacon was held to be more concerned with the practical side of things (only later, during the second century in the writings of Ignatius does the

---

[36]   Eusebius (c.260-c.340): *Ecclesiastical History.*

[37]   Luke 19:41-44.

[38]   Acts 9:32; Galatians 2:9-21. Evidently Peter was actively engaged in pioneering work in Antioch (Syria), where Paul suggests Peter hadn't quite jettisoned his Jewish preferences, and that there's a hint, in 1 Corinthians 9:5, Peter's wife accompanied him in his missionary endeavours. Sometimes Peter is referred to as Cephas (meaning 'rock'—a direct translation into Greek from the Hebrew word *Kephim*). Simon was probably his given name; the name *Peter* being given to him purposefully by Christ, as above.

[39]   Acts 16:6-15.

[40]   Colossians 1:24.

[41]   2 Corinthians 11:2; Ephesians 5:25.

[42]   Ephesians 2:20-22.

[43]   Galatians 6:16 (implied).

[44]   Matthew 28:16-20; Acts 1:1-11.

[45]   1 Corinthians 12:27-30. See also chapter 20.

[46]   Philippians 1:1; Titus 1:5, 7; 1 Timothy 3:8. See also chapter 20.

distinction of hierarchy evolve). Furthermore, the idea of a personal concept of a sacerdotal priesthood seems to belong exclusively to Christ Himself[17]

Be that as it may, Peter apparently ended up, like Paul, in Rome, whence he wrote pastoral letters traditionally bearing his authority to fellow Christians ('the church') in which he modestly describes himself 'an Apostle',[48] 'a Servant'[49] and 'an Elder' among many[50]—positions of themselves not indicative of supreme status; significantly in one such letter which, coming from the thoughts of the supposed 'Supreme Priest', certainly casts some doubt on his own perception of such an office, he clearly testifies to the priestly nature of the church *as a whole*.[51]

Much of the New Testament is devoted to the establishment of Christian communities throughout Asia Minor and the Mediterranean lands (not all of them flattering[52]) in response to the great commission of Christ:[53] the evolution of a variety of church offices[54] such as those mentioned above, though as yet utilising Jewish centres of worship, and more latterly personal homes for their meetings.[55] Yet the ultimate triumph of the true church is proclaimed and prophesied in the revelation to John,[56] in the face of existing persecution,[57] heresy[58] and division[59]—even then!

Tradition has it that, like Paul, Peter fell victim to the scapegoating of Christians in Rome at the behest of the Emperor Nero (AD 54-68)[60] in AD

---

[47] Hebrews 5:6, 10; 6:26-27. See also chapter 20.

[48] 1 Peter 1:1; 2 Peter 1:1.

[49] 2 Peter 1:1.

[50] 1 Peter 5:1-3 emphasises the pastoral rather than the authoritarian role of an elder. See also chapter 20.

[51] 1 Peter 2:9. See also chapter 20.

[52] See, e.g. 1 Corinthians 1:10-13; 5:1-13; 11:17-34.

[53] Matthew 28:19-20.

[54] 1 Corinthians 12:27-31; 1 Peter 1:1; 5:1; 2 Peter 1:1.

[55] Acts 2:46; 20:7; Romans 16:5; 1 Corinthians 16:19; Colossians 4:15; Philemon 1:2. No specific church buildings are mentioned in scripture.

[56] Revelation 7:9-17. See also 1 John 3:2.

[57] 1 Peter 1:6-7.

[58] 1 Corinthians 11:19.

[59] For example, 1 Corinthians 11:17-22, Acts 15:1-21.

[60] According to John 21:18-19, Jesus anticipated Peter's violent death, albeit not specifically in Rome. The two New Testament letters ascribed to Peter could well have been written from Rome, though this is supposition. The legend of Peter's martyrdom in Rome is not to be traced to any of the

The Church 21

64, according to Tacitus, the Roman historian, when they were blamed for the city's disastrous fire: wrapped in the skins of wild beasts, 'torn by dogs... nailed on crosses... burned to serve as a nightly illumination... for the glut of one man's cruelty'.[61] Close to the alleged site of his martyrdom in the Circus to the west of the Tiber, Peter's relics are said to repose, jealously guarded by successive popes, many attempting to outdo their predecessors in surmounting them with evermore grandiose schemes for the basilica raised in his name. What began as a single shrine marking the traditional site of Peter's grave evolved a motley edifice constructed initially from decadent monuments, resonating with Rome's pagan past. A fitting focus for pilgrimage, its elegance was enhanced by the accretion of precious stones and metals until neglect during the Avignon exile of the fourteenth century reduced it to a pale shadow of its honoured past. Considered by now unworthy of the dignity of Peter, it was replaced at the renaissance papacy's instigation throughout the fifteenth, sixteenth and seventeenth centuries. The familiar domed construction of today bears testimony to the work of Bramante, Michelangelo and Bernini. As asserted during excavations initiated by Pope Pius XII in 1939, the high altar symbolically surmounts the traditional spot of Peter's final resting place many feet below. Here in the crypt, his alleged sarcophagus is to be found, accessible by a tortuous venture into the subterranean world of an ancient necropolis, a privilege itself only accorded to the most highly regarded and intrepid of the faithful.

Thus has the martyred Peter attracted a kind of cult status, the Semitic icon of an increasingly Eurocentric Church: Peter, a participant in the life, death, resurrection and spiritual experiences of Christ himself.

From this starting point, the Roman Church codified its 'four notes': each note combining to justify its unique role and status; each designed to counter heresy and especially schism. Because of its divine origin, its nature is inherently 'holy'; by virtue of Christ's intention, it would be incontrovertibly 'catholic' or universal; its discreet 'unity' was to be a reflection of Christ's clearly expressed view and it must, by extension, be bound in its doctrine by its 'apostolicity', as derived from the teaching

---

canonical gospels, but found in a tract *The Acts of St. Peter*, written towards the end of the second century, in which Peter is said to have been crucified upside-down after fleeing Rome and being confronted by Christ on the Appian Way: the 'Domine, Quo Vadis?' ('Lord, where are you going?') incident. This was reiterated by the early Father, Ambrose (339-397), presumably to lend credence to Peter's Roman connection.

[61] Tacitus: *Annals* 15:44.

of the early Fathers and those of their successors in the apostolically constituted church.

Such human interpretations were bound to be susceptible to challenge, especially when the organic church and its representatives were deemed to display certain features at variance with the scriptural admonitions and personal example of Christ himself. Significantly the church throughout its history of two thousand years has had to face and cope with issues that have resulted in schism and fragmentation: the *nature* of the church whether visible or invisible; relations between church and state; the validity and interpretation of the sacraments; the quality of those called to high office; the apostolic succession itself.

Yet more than that, Peter himself, as we have seen, had received some apparently unique, intimately personal assurance from the hands of Jesus: that the stewarding of the very early church was destined to be bound up with his personal response to the awesome commission. This was the defining moment, already described, upon which the church in Rome and its succeeding bishops, benefiting indirectly by the fall of Jerusalem in AD 70,[62] would controversially claim the Papal Tiara and ultimately justify its monolithic pre-eminence for over one thousand years: *Ubi Petros ibi ecclesia*,[63] the source from which the sheep will be fed.[64]

Love it, loathe it, like it, lump it or leave it, the Roman Church was destined to provide the framework for the religious, political and social evolution of Western society and even beyond.

---

[62] Josephus: *The Jewish War*, Penguin Classics, 1969 (Tr. Williamson, G.).

[63] Latin: Where Peter is, there is the church.

[64] John 21:17.

Chapter 2

Milvian Bridge, near Rome today

CONQUER BY THIS

What is astonishing is not so much that the church sustained its hold over the Western world for well over a millennium, but that its tender shoots survived the upheavals in its Mediterranean nursery over the first 250 years or so of its existence.

The death of a Roman emperor was always the trigger for court and military intrigue, and in 306, Co-emperor Constantius had passed away, while serving with the legions in York. There his son, Constantine, also on duty as an army officer, was acclaimed as his successor. Proclamation, however, was one thing, general acceptance another. To make good the claim, it was necessary to see off one's ubiquitous contenders for the post. Six years were to elapse before Constantine was to confront the challenge of his most serious rival, Maxentius, just outside Rome itself, at the Battle of Milvian Bridge.

The military victory Constantine secured in 312 must be regarded by any calculation as a watershed—a defining moment in the fortunes of the church—decisive! This result sewed up the empire in the west in Constantine's favour and served as his springboard to acquire all of it by 323.

The precise circumstances of this historic encounter between the two Caesar wannabes have been clouded, perhaps by a somewhat romantic or liberal perception of its spiritual dimension. According to Eusebius, Constantine's biographer, the pagan Constantine confessed to having sought some kind of divine assistance prior to the clash of arms, which was followed by the apparition of a Cross etched against the sky, accompanying the inscription 'In Hoc Vinces'.[65] Lactanius, a Christian convert, asserted further that Constantine encountered a vision of Christ, who suggested that military triumph might be facilitated by replacing the Roman Eagle on the army's shields and standards by the well-known chi-rho symbol of Christianity.[66] Maxentius had been able to make good his claim to the sole imperial title by virtue of his presence at the heart of things in Rome when Constantius had died. As the man on the spot, the Roman patricians recognised in Maxentius their best chance of sustaining some measure of peace and stability in the face of a political vacuum, which had the potential to spin out of control. Constantine, unsurprisingly, would have none of it and prepared to beat a long, drawn-out and tortuous path southwards with his faithful army in tow: across the channel and over the Alps to stake the claim he believed rightfully his. In contrast to some rough encounters in Gaul, Northern Italy was quickly subdued and the Via Flaminia facilitated his progress to within a stone's throw of Rome. Having assembled his forces at Saxa Rubra, some nine miles to the north of the river Tiber, Constantine was preparing for the final showdown. In response, Maxentius moved his own troops forward to meet the challenge, opting to defend from a distance the ancient and venerable stone structure of the Milvian Bridge

---

[65] Latin: *Conquer by This* (loosely translated): Eusebius, *Life of Constantine.*

[66] The symbol of chi-rho, representing the first two letters of Christ's name in Greek, XP, superimposed thus ☧. The precise occurrence of these apparitions has been open to debate. Eusebius suggests that the emperor spotted a cross superimposed on the sun, in juxtaposition with the chi-rho symbol, at an unspecified time before the battle, under which floated the *Conquer by This* inscription. The other account, ascribed to Lactanius, suggests the vision came to Constantine in a dream during the night preceding the battle. Gibbon, E., in his *The Decline and Fall of the Roman Empire* (abridged by Low, D. M.), Pelican, 1960, is characteristically sceptical of the veracity of these mysterious assertions, in so far as the source of any such information could only have been that of Constantine himself; the intervention of the cross, a device by which the Roman Church could in due course advance the cause of its veneration, as well as giving Constantine heavenly backing for his victory and imperial title.

The Church 25

straddling the river and possession of which was crucial if Rome were to be denied to Constantine.

On 28 October 312, the two protagonists unleashed their forces, and despite inferior numbers, Constantine's strategic precision forced his rival back towards the bridge itself. Maxentius had hurriedly prepared a pontoon of linked boats across the river to augment the bridge facility in any rapid retreat, should worst come to worst. Even so he hadn't bargained for such a rapid retreat on the part of his depleted manpower, given the numbers involved and the weakened condition of the old bridge. Unfortunately, for him, the wooden pontoon itself wasn't really up to the job and it collapsed under the weight in the confusion, propelling many hapless soldiers to certain death, swallowed up by the swirling drink, leaving those stranded on the northern bank abandoned to their fate. Maxentius himself drowned in the midst of it all and his duly severed head was paraded as part of Constantine's victory statement as he entered Rome in triumph.

Touché! Rome now belonged to Constantine and the new emperor was allegedly convinced that it was the Christian God who had made it possible. The outcome for the church: a phenomenal turnaround in its worldly fortunes.

Since the journeyings of Paul[67] and the fall of Jerusalem in AD 70,[68] Christianity had spread widely, albeit thinly, across the Mediterranean world and beyond, but what a fragile sapling it seemed. Local churches had sprung up, nurtured by the heroic and tenacious exploits of their pioneer leadership. They were sustained and encouraged by itinerant storytellers of the work of Jesus by the receipt of apostolic letters, and by written fragments of the Gospels as they were being copied and circulated. Inevitably, authentic accounts of the life of Christ were disseminated alongside the more fancifully dubious and apocryphal, and who could tell the difference? Attempts by Apostolic Fathers—the 'Apologists'—to articulate the significance of the Jesus phenomenon often clouded the issue rather than resolve it. The heresies of Gnosticism[69] were rife and

---

[67] Acts 13 ff.

[68] Josephus: *The Jewish War*, chapter 22, Penguin Classics, 1974, is a valuable source on the details of this.

[69] The broad, loose term *Gnosticism* actually predates Christianity; it attempts to synthesise oriental cults with Greek philosophy—maintaining a strict dualism between the spiritual and material dimensions of existence. By around the second century, many adherents attempted to bolt Christ onto its beliefs. In their view, Gnostics believe the material world to be the evil creation of a perverse lesser god—the demiurge—into which humans are

26 Conquer by This

demanded a robust orthodox response in the course of which Greek philosophy was invoked by such thinkers as Justin Martyr,[70] Clement of Alexandria,[71] Origen[72] and, despite his protestations, Tertullian.[73]

---

unfortunately born to inhabit. Yet people are blessed with an inner soul, capable of divine insight or esoteric knowledge (the 'gnosis'), which by means of arcane ritual allows the ultimate deliverance from grim mortality into their true spiritual home with the ultimate divinity. To many Gnostics, Jesus *was* the incarnate gnosis from the Supreme God, who temporarily inhabited an ephemeral body for that purpose. This idea of an elite divine circle is alien to orthodox Christian belief, which teaches the 'all inclusive', 'all embracing' nature of God, as expressed in Christ. The so-called 'Gnostic Gospels' discovered at Nag Hammadi in 1945 referred to in chapter 1 are seen by many as evidence for a different style of Christianity from that taught by the mainstream church.

[70] Justin Martyr of Palestine (c.100-c.165): saw in Christ the fulfilment of Greek and particularly Platonic thought. In this, he links the Greek idea of the 'Logos' ('word' or 'reason') as used in John 1:1, with Jesus (the unknown God of Acts 17:22-34) as the explanation of all things and communicating between God and Man. Justin firmly believed *all* to be capable of discerning God in Christ and was therefore a strident opponent to the Gnostics.

[71] Clement of Alexandria (c.150-c.215): He regarded the 'Logos' as the second strand of the Holy Trinity (again as expounded in John 1:1). As such, Christ *is* the Logos—the origin of human reason and therefore God's supreme revelation to humanity, leading thus to immortality in the Divine Being.

[72] Origen of Alexandria (c.185-c.254): a truly Greek thinker whose debt to Plato and influence on Christianity have been immense, although he himself verged on Gnosticism by distinguishing between the 'ordinary' Christian and the 'knowledgeable' Christian, who sees *beyond* the 'material' Jesus to the 'Logos' (John 1:1 again) and that by contemplating Him, the 'enlightened' one can achieve salvation. His theory, however, of a three-tier Trinity—with the son at a lower level than the father was to further distance himself from mainstream Western thought and to sow the seeds for the subsequent Arian controversy.

[73] Tertullian of Carthage (c.155-222): Very 'Western' and 'Roman' in his background and thinking. He claimed that Greek philosophy was the antithesis of the Christian faith. For him, faith in Christ is enough; his take on Paul's encounter with the Athenian philosophers in Athens (Acts 17:22-34) was the sheer *pretentiousness* of human wisdom: *possessing* Christ is the ultimate; the resurrection is *certain* because of its apparent incredulity; the hallmark of a Christian is nothing less than a morally changed, disciplined life.

The Church

It was clear that if the church were to exercise anything more than purely local significance, some form of central direction was necessary and this was patently lacking. The bishop of Rome could not take for granted the status he felt his, due simply as the guardian of Peter's relics, nor indeed was his own position internally unchallenged.[71] In the Eastern branches of the church, the bishops of both Alexandria and Antioch had their own reasons to claim equality with Rome, if not outright supremacy. Each could draw upon doctrinal issues in the name of Christianity as a lever against the other if the need arose and there were plenty from which to choose. If this were not bad enough, the church was having to face up to seemingly attractive pagan philosophies in a region awash with fertile minds. Greek ideas were certainly not dead and were indeed infiltrating Christian thinking. Even the Persian teachings of Zoroaster were being embraced by not a few.

To cap it all, the Roman State had been notoriously selective and inconsistent in its attitude towards the different sects within the imperial fold. For the first 250 years of its life, Christianity, a minority belief, despite gaining adherents as far afield as the fringes of Gaul and Britain, existed in a state of perpetual insecurity and uncertainty.

The fortunes of the church were essentially dependent upon the whim of whoever happened to be Caesar at the time, and the will and capacity of the local authorities to execute his policies; it was a bit of a lottery as to whether the local Christian community be accorded grudging tolerance or be thrown to the lions.[75] The names of Justin, Polycarp (c.69-155), Ignatius (c.45-110) and Alban (around the third and fourth centuries) during these frenetic times lend some credence to the view that 'the blood of the martyrs is the seed of the Church'.[76]

---

[71] For example, in 251, Novatian, a schismatic, proclaimed himself as anti-pope in opposition to Pope Cornelius (251-253) over the general practice of forgiveness being offered to the 'Lapsi' (Christians who had weakened and who had acknowledged the divine status of the Roman Emperor), during the persecutions. Novatian and his followers were opposed to this.

[75] Persecutions during the reigns of Caligula (37-41), Nero (54-68), Decius (249-251) and Diocletian (284-305) were traumatic periods for Christians. It was Decius who intensified the demand for citizens to worship the Imperial Office as divine. Refusal to publicly recognise this status—technically impossible for Christians—was death.

[76] Tertullian 'Apology'. For details, see Foxe, J. *History of Christian Martyrdom*, pp. 11-31, Spire Books, 1973.

The Battle of Milvian Bridge was destined to change all that. Constantine had long recognised that Christianity was resilient: There was an inner strength there which, as Gibbon vehemently asserts, could be cynically employed. Might not he now harness the qualities he discerned in the church for himself in order to set the seal on his authority? It had already helped him to become master of Rome and to become the sole, undisputed Caesar in the West. At the very least he felt he owed it one!

Within a year, in 313, Constantine and his co-ruler in the East, Licinius, had issued the so-called Edict of Milan,[77] under the terms of which Christianity and its church were to be accorded not only tolerance and recognition but also little short of state sponsorship. At a stroke, Christianity became 'respectable'. The church could now worship and proselytise without let or hindrance; state funding was made available to reinstate church property damaged or destroyed during the Diocletian-inspired persecution of but very recent memory (300-305); tax relief was to be enjoyed by the clergy; newly enacted imperial laws were to bear the stamp of Christian principles. Even Helena (c.260-330), Constantine's mother, was reputed to have converted and sacrificially made pilgrimage to the Holy Land, where she founded churches at the sacred sites in the saviour's name. By 321, Constantine had decreed that the Christian propensity to observe Sunday as a day of rest be officially enjoined upon all the peoples of the empire; something of a moral fudge on his part, really, dovetailing as it did into his known practice of sun worship.[78]

Such a profound change in the fortunes of the members of the church could probably be equated with the effect that the fall of communism had upon the peoples of Eastern Europe in the late 1980s or the final collapse of the apartheid regime in South Africa in 1994 on the oppressed majority there. The Edict of Milan transformed the face of Christianity—but it was a mixed blessing.

---

[77] The edict of Milan was not so much an edict or law, but a statement of intent.

[78] It is indeed doubtful whether Constantine himself was committed to the personal embrace of Christianity. It would seem as though he was a fully paid-up member of the prevalent cult of 'Sol Invicta', the sun god. This cult was, however, monotheistic and it was not difficult to synthesise elements of its beliefs with Christianity. Its festival on 25 December of the rebirth and regeneration of the solar force—a recognition of the winter solstice—for example, provided fertile soil upon which to graft the celebration of Christ's birth.

On the one hand, membership of the church increased by leaps and bounds: no longer any need for covert operations nor for the more robust to resort to heroic stands against state power. With it, superficial adherence accompanied a compromise in moral principles and a tolerance of pre-Christian standards and superstitions. To belong to the church now offered a path to status and material advancement; for the first time, the widespread and systematic construction of purpose-built places of Christian worship increasingly capacious and grandiose became necessary in order to accommodate the growing number of converts. Doubtless, the building trade itself was now anxious to establish its Christian credentials in order to secure lucrative contracts: not least in the construction of the first Christian basilica erected over the shrine of Peter, from plundered monuments of pagan Rome and purportedly commissioned by Constantine himself. More worryingly, the church had been transformed from representing a persecuted minority to privileged dignity with authoritative and persecution potential of its own[79] and the as-yet still pagan emperor as its patron.[80] Certainly Rome's bishops were quick to seize on their newly acquired kudos with incipient pretensions towards civil authority as well.

Not all followers of Christ *were* happy with the changed circumstances. Fearing that the church was being seduced into the structures of the world, some hardy souls set up shop in the Egyptian desert, where a life of disciplined contemplation, the performance of basic agrarian and domestic tasks, and the meticulous copying of sacred texts shielded them from the increasingly secular infusion: the genesis of *Christian* monasticism.

Now that the church was in Constantine's debt, he was, of course, determined to ensure that it danced to his tune. With some validity, it could be argued that the church was now compromised. Certainly the emperor was determined to weld the church into a cohesive force, and to do this, it was important to iron out damaging theological dissension and division within it; not much use to him if the nexus lacked cohesion. His defeat of Co-emperor Licinius in 324, granting Constantine sole authority throughout both Eastern and Western portions of the empire, strengthened his hand in dealing with potential schism.

---

[79] Gibbon, E. in his *Decline and Fall* comments acidly on the evolving 'boundless intolerance (whereby) credulity (was) taught as a virtue, and all conclusions . . . dictated by authority', leading to a dulling of the human mind for centuries.

[80] Constantine, reputedly, was neither baptised nor received into the church until on his deathbed (337).

One particular controversy was especially disturbing during Constantine's reign and it had the potential to tear the church apart. In Alexandria, an erudite theologian, Arius, expounded the view that the *nature* of the person of Christ was *similar*[81] in substance to God, the Father, but was *not the same*.[82] Athanasius, later to be bishop of Alexandria, disputed this: how could anyone be *saved* by Christ's merits, he argued, if Jesus were not totally of *one* substance with the Father—'consubstantial, co-eternal' as one hymn-writer puts it?[83] This difference of opinion had led to an unholy row with the various churches in the East at each other's throats.

Now for Constantine, this was all a bit technical, but wildly embarrassing, not to say inconvenient, for his protégé to seen to be splitting at the seams over a theological nicety. Something had to be done. Constantine, seeking to access the resources of the Middle East as well as to escape the factious unruly political atmosphere in Rome, and by completing the process of shifting his capital to Byzantium,[84] ordered the gathering of a council of the church at Nicaea in Asia Minor, in 325.[85] At this august assembly of bishops and other ecclesiastics, the majority came down on the side of Athanasius. The final communiqué incorporated the creed of Nicaea, which essentially resolved into the Nicene Creed[86] and as such remains the orthodox statement of Christian belief—the theological strand that has been passed on through mainstream Christianity to the present.[87]

---

[81]   Greek: homoiouson.

[82]   Greek: homoouson: one 'iota' of difference.

[83]   Hymn: *Blessed City, Heavenly Salem,* as translated by J. M. Neale, volume 5, from an early source.

[84]   See Gibbon, E.: *The Decline and Fall of the Roman Empire,* chapter 17, Pelican, 1931.

[85]   Interestingly, the bishop of Rome, Pope Sylvester, was not present and in fact just sent two priests to represent him. As in the case of the Council of Jerusalem (Acts 15), it does seem to counter the Roman Catholic claim that only the Pope can call a general council.

[86]   The Nicene Creed, as we now know it, was refined and formalised at subsequent councils: Constantinople (381) and Chalcedon (451). The later insidious addition of the 'filioque clause' in the West was divisive. See chapter 7.

[87]   For a full résumé of the theological complexities of the so-called Arian controversy, see Lane, T. *The Lion Concise Book of Christian Thought,* pp. 28-30, Lion Publishing, 1956.

The Church 31

Nevertheless, the Arian position, as it is known, has been tenaciously preserved by sects of believers—Gothic/Visigothic converts, the Merovingians, Unitarians and Jehovah's Witnesses among others—down the ages, who regard Constantine's accommodation of the church as a flaw and distraction rather than a blessing.

Even so, it may have been fortuitous for the church, whatever his motives, that Constantine ordered the Nicene Council, out of which emerged some kind of credal statement. The Nicene Creed in its final form did provide the church with a touchstone of belief. Certainly it was vital if the church were to retain its universal dimensions. Perhaps, therefore, this episode did afford the church an identifiable catalyst, without which it could have fragmented and its corporate image lost; Constantine, in the manner of a latter-day Jehu,[88] an unlikely instrument of God's will, or as Christopher Hitchens sees him, a fortuitous facilitator of a megalithic institution spawned of dubious traditions.[89]

It is perhaps not without significance that agreement on what books should constitute New Testament Scripture (the Canon) followed hard on the heels of Nicaea—variously at the Councils of Rome (382), Hippo (395) and Carthage (397),[90] and Bishop Basil's doctrine of the Trinity confirmed (395).[91] Jerome's commission (late fourth century) by Pope Damasus (366-384) to produce the definitive Latin translation of the Bible advanced the cause of a united Christendom still further. This, in itself, was for its time, a remarkable feat of scholarship, despite being limited by the unavailability of sources not discovered until much later. Nonetheless, many of the sixteenth-century reformers saw the influence of Rome's patronage of the enterprise as an exercise in self-interest.

It could be argued, therefore, that these developments would have been impossible had not that defining moment at Milvian Bridge in

---

[88] See 2 Kings 10:28-31. An errant king of Israel who nevertheless executed God's will.

[89] Hitchens, C.: *God is Not Great*, Atlantic Books, 2007.

[90] Already Rome had made a start to select what constituted scriptural canon and what did not merit inclusion. Ireneus, bishop of Lyons (c.180), is reputed to have classified the sixty-six books of the Bible as we now know them. Many scholars again suggest that herein lays a selectivity based upon Roman preconceptions rather than objective or even spirit-inspired wisdom. Nevertheless, the accepted canon has stood the test of time and provided further evidence of a touchstone for faith.

[91] The Trinity: One substance (ousia); Three Natures (hupostatis), as implied in Hebrews 1:3.

312 apparently directed the course of a young man's thinking. For the church, it certainly created as many problems as it appeared to solve; nevertheless, it helped to consolidate its defences. Since the emperor subsequently ruled from Constantinople, the Pope's authority in Rome was enhanced. Significantly when, in 410, Alaric's Visigoths sacked the shadow of once-almighty Rome abandoned by its emperor in 410, they left intact its bishop with his prestige barely sullied, the self-proclaimed successor of Peter, the Holy Father—the Pope.

The thorny issue of the future relationship between church and state was therefore not going to go away.[92] Augustine of Hippo, the pre-eminent theologian of the time, proclaimed it the duty of the church to preserve much of what was good in Roman culture while reassuring the faithful of the transcendental spiritual permanence of the Kingdom of God (the church), even to the extent of advocating the use of force in order to preserve its unity, as David McIlroy wryly observes.[93]

Under these circumstances, the see of St Peter could not have been more secure. 'Conquer by this'—our defining moment—had fundamental secular and spiritual implications for the church, and the significance for Europe and the West in particular could not have been starker.

---

[92] Of interest, here is the now-discredited document known as *Donation of Constantine*, which purported to surrender some of the emperor's civil power in Rome to its bishop (the Pope) when the capital was moved to Byzantium. It served as the basis for subsequent popes to claim civil authority, bolstered particularly by the actions of Pope Leo the Great (440-461), who persuaded Attila the Hun to vacate Rome (452) and who persuaded a damage limitation exercise in the city on subsequent Vandal depredations in 455. The original document was exposed as a forgery in the fifteenth century.

[93] McIlroy, D.: *A Biblical View of Law and Justice*, Paternoster Press, 2004.

Chapter 3

Saint Augustine by Sandro Boticelli

TAKE UP AND READ

Since Constantine's 'Edict of Milan' in 313, the fortunes of the Roman Church and the temporal imperial state were increasingly perceived as being mutually bound. It would come as no surprise, therefore, that, by the end of the fourth century, with the foundations of the empire in self-evident decline, questions were going to be raised as to the efficacy of the Christian faith, which was supposed to undergird it. Gibbon[94] records how many Romans, indeed, for whom the tenets of the religion had been only skin-deep, or blatantly opportunistic, openly suggested that Rome's misfortunes owed much to the vengeance of the former pagan deities who had apparently served them so well for centuries and who were now marginalised or supplanted.

Our defining moment takes us again to Milan, described even by outsiders as a place of warmth and inspiration; a city founded in AD 222 by the Romans, its strategic location on the plain of Lombardy had ensured its importance and prosperity, at the confluence of great trading routes just to the south of the Alps. Here the beautiful octagonal Basilica Church

---

[94] Gibbon, E.: *The Decline and Fall of the Roman Empire*, abridged by Low, D. M., Pelican Books, 1966.

of San Lorenzo had been built during the course of the fourth century, over the ruin of a Roman amphitheatre; here the redoubtable Bishop Ambrose[95] held considerable sway in respect of his spiritual influence and political instincts. It was thither that a brilliant young academic from North Africa had resorted in his search for religious assurance. Born at Tagaste in the Eastern Maghreb, in 354, Augustine, the son of a Christian mother, Monica (c.331-387), and a pagan Father, Patricius, had dallied with various beliefs, including for a while the Manichean variant on the scriptures,[96] as well as the more orthodox Christian beliefs. At the age of thirty, he had been appointed a teacher at Milan's Academy where his fertile mind was recognised in equal measure with his fondness for the satisfaction of carnal desire. Greatly influenced by the preaching and example of the saintly Ambrose, he was increasingly convinced by the claims of Christianity, although his proclivity for the sensual—he had maintained a mistress and fathered a son by her—prevented him from taking the final step into baptism. 'Lord', he is reputed to have petitioned, 'make me chaste . . . but not yet!' Notwithstanding, Augustine's intellectual curiosity and his fundamental integrity would not allow his soul to rest there. The defining moment comes during an introspective period of profound self-analysis[97] probably during the year 386. In sombre mood, Augustine, reflecting on his own emotional disaffection from the cerebral acceptance of the truth of Christ, fled into the garden of his Milanese lodgings. Here, beneath the shade of a fig tree, and in the depths of near despair, the ethereal voice of a child wafted into earshot. With soothing urgency, the words *Tolle legere* (take up and read) came with such compelling insistence that he immediately resorted to his copy of the scriptures 'to read the first passage on which my eyes should fall'. The passage thereby revealed were some words of Paul to the Romans: 'Clothe yourselves with the Lord Jesus Christ and do not think about how to gratify the desire of the sinful nature . . . '[98]

---

[95]   Ambrose, bishop of Milan, 374-397.

[96]   Manichaeism reputedly originated in Persia, which taught that Jesus, among others, was sent to assist in the release of light into the world, which the Creator of darkness and evil had imprisoned, redolent of Gnosticism. See chapter 2.

[97]   Our knowledge of this defining moment comes from the account penned by Augustine: *The Confessions of Augustine in Modern English*, translated and abridged by Wirt, S. E., Lion Publishing, 1978.

[98]   Romans 13:14.

The Church 35

In an instant, as Augustine himself testifies, 'The light of confidence flooded into my heart and all the darkness of doubt vanished'.

This epiphany experience of Augustine cleared the final obstacle to his baptism—in 387—and doubtless to the eternal joy of his long suffering mother, who died shortly afterwards, her mission having been apparently fulfilled.

From such beginnings evolved the witness and thinking of the man commonly regarded as the 'Father of the Western Church', whose shrewd interpretation of his times, in the light of the Gospel, has determined its theology for posterity. 'In the Fifth Century, at the hour that the Church inherited the Roman Empire, she had within her a man of extraordinary genius; from him she took her ideas, and to this present hour she has been unable *to break away from them*'.[99]

On his return to his native North Africa, Augustine was initially attracted to a solitary, hermitic existence, but his credentials preceded him and he was lured into priestly ordination and subsequently as bishop of Hippo (in modern Tunisia) in 396, by popular demand. Here he was to make his mark as a legendary son of the church—an ascetic administrator, preacher, pastor and writer. North Africa, at the time, was alive with dissident religious groups, which presented him with the opportunity to confront them; the result of his reasoned responses has seen Augustine acclaimed as the articulator of the doctrine of the Western Church: a proto-scholastic who recognised human wisdom as derivative from faith, which in turn proceeds from the eternal truth latent in the God-given human soul.

The Donatists[100] were an essentially widespread North African community founded in reaction to the apparent decline in moral leadership by the church in Rome. They presented the bishop with the potential for schism and that they had to be dealt with. Sensitive, no doubt, to his own erstwhile shortcomings in the morality stakes, as well as his in-built conviction of the sanctity of the universality of the Catholic Church, Augustine dismissed Donatist claims with a mixture of cogency, popular propaganda and, where necessary, the exercise of state power. Scriptural justification was cited for such heavy-handed

---

[99] Von Harnack, A., (1851-1930), a prominent Protestant theologian writing around the turn of the twentieth century. The words in italics are those of the present writer.

[100] Donatists refused to accept the validity and efficacy of those baptised by priests considered unworthy of Christ's calling. It was largely a North African phenomenon although such ideas have never been totally eradicated.

policies with perhaps questionable regard to the wider textual context of Christ's injunction to 'compel them to come in'.[101] For Augustine, the prime principle was that there could be no personal salvation *outside* the Catholic Church and that the administration of the Holy Sacraments is both valid and efficacious, ignoring the personal integrity of the ordained celebrant. The mass, argued Augustine, is Christ's personal offering through the due process of the apostolic succession, thus rendering the individual foibles of the priest irrelevant.

The Donatists had made much of the distinction between what they termed the Church Visible and the Church Invisible. For them, it was the Invisible Church that really mattered. Quite logically, they argued that only God, who knows the hearts and minds of His people, and not man, could ultimately determine who constituted the sincere, genuine members of His church: who might, or more probably might not, be coterminous with the Visible (or structural) Church of Rome. Up to a point, Augustine agreed with the *principle* of the distinction between the Visible and the Invisible concept of the church—'we must consider the position of the heart, not the body',[102] but with obstinate consistency argued that the *Invisible* Church could only be found among adherents to the Roman Catholic Church of his day, not *outside* it, as the Donatists had tried to argue. Thus Augustine reinforced the exclusive nature of the Roman Church, its monopoly of the sacraments, as such representing the sole route to individual salvation, and by implication its assertion as the one true church—a persistent claim by Rome through the centuries.

Another theological challenge tackled by Augustine was the alleged heresy perpetrated by the Pelagian sect,[103] which, in his eyes, was in effect trying to dilute God's size and power. For the Pelagians, the Christian was to find fulfilment simply by embracing, by human effort, the undeniable precepts and example of Christ, the Son of Man: do your best, basically; humble effort, and striving, will see you through. In Augustine's eyes, this negation of God's power to work *within* and *through* the believer was to ignore His inherent loving nature. Thus Augustine came round to articulating the theology of grace, which still underpins mainstream Christianity today. As he saw it, the indiscretion of Adam and Eve in that

---

[101] Luke 14:23.

[102] Augustine: *Baptism, against the Donatists.*

[103] The Pelagians were similarly an early fifth-century sect, mainly centred on North Africa, although owing its origins to one, Pelagius, from the British Isles. Pelagianists believed that it was the human being who initiated the process to individual salvation.

The Church 37

earliest of plantations[104] has afflicted humankind with what he called original sin—we have no choice in the matter. From the moment of conception, we are all tainted.

'In Adam', wrote Paul, 'we all die'. Nevertheless, in God's *mercy*, and through this *grace*, by means of Christ, one can 'be made alive'.[105] By this means, God chooses to save His elect from the *consequences* of original sin.[106] The point is that salvation does not come by a person's unaided efforts, as the Pelagians taught, but by means of God's freely given *love* and *mercy*, and the capacity of human beings to respond to it in *faith*. 'God', he says, 'extends His mercy . . . not because (people) already know Him, but in order that they might know Him'[107] or as Paul wrote, 'What do you have that you did not receive?'[108] Here, Augustine was exercising his pure 'God-given' logic to sustain his case and this, not surprisingly, led him to exalt God to incomprehensible heights so as to argue the case for predestination. Ironically enough, such themes as those he identified as grace, mercy, faith and predestination were to be taken up with vigour by the Protestant reformers over one thousand years later and for them to marshal Augustine's own theological premises to tear apart the one Western Church by which he held so much store.

We have already noted that Augustine had dabbled in the Gnostic esoteric realms of Manichaeism—the belief in the existence of both a Creator of light (God) and a Creator of darkness (the evil one). Augustine now countered this dualistic argument, by upholding the view that the existence of evil does not preclude the ultimate creation by one loving and merciful God. God, Augustine maintained, has indeed made all things 'good',[109] but the free will which in His love He bestowed upon mankind has been responsible for its own corruption. As one commentator puts it, 'Evil is something good that has been spoiled'. Augustine, then, by employing contemporary neo-Platonist concepts,[110] reinforced the Judaeo-Christian belief in one God, while reaffirming, at the same time, the exclusively Christian doctrine of 'a Trinity of Persons mutually inter-related and a unity of equal essence'.[111]

---

[104] Genesis 2:4-3:24.

[105] See Romans 5:12-21.

[106] Romans 9:16.

[107] Augustine: *The Spirit and the Letter.*

[108] 1 Corinthians 4:7.

[109] Genesis 1:31.

[110] Ed. Lane, T. *The Lion Book of Christian Thought*, Lion Publishing, 1992.

[111] Augustine: *The Trinity.*

The Roman State, as we have seen, was teetering on the brink when Augustine became bishop of Hippo in 396. Alaric and his Visigoths saw to the denouement of the Eternal City in 410, whose Emperor Honorius could only watch on from a distance as the splendours of past centuries were violated in sorry spectacle. This event, in itself, presented Christian apologists and Augustine, in particular, with fresh challenges. On the one hand, Christianity had, for many, allegedly undermined the traditional beliefs of Roman society and so they were all now paying the price; to the Christian faithful, the security that had been offered to them by the imperial state was, in their eyes, now unravelling and to herald a new era of perplexing uncertainty yet again.

It was Augustine's masterly analysis of this pivotal event that set the seal on his overall contribution to Christian theology and doctrine. This was his *De Civitate Dei* ('the City of God'), a monumental work that took him over a decade to complete. At root, his was an attempt to unscramble the intricate web of relationships between church and state, which had arisen since Constantine, and to counter the charge that the empire's demise was Christianity's fault. Augustine cut through the church/state relationship with ruthless mental efficiency. The two 'kingdoms'—the temporal state and the spiritual pre-eminence of Christ—are discreet and differentiated. Certainly the existence of the church must in no way be regarded as being dependent on the state. After all, had not Christ asserted that 'the Kingdom of God is within you',[112] proclaiming that 'My Kingdom is not of this world'?[113] It was precisely this line of thought that Augustine pursued. Augustine tried to assure the faithful that it is in the nature of the Kingdom of the Gospel for the individual to experience the *inner* peace and the certainty of an external destiny, which transcends in both spirit and temporality the pretension of earthly empires. Augustine was surely mindful of Paul's words to the Romans of an earlier epoch, 'Who . . . can separate us from the love of Christ . . . neither death, nor life . . . neither the world above or the world below',[114] when he wrote in a succinct statement of his theological foundations 'Citizens are born into the **earthly** city by a nature spoiled by sin, but they are born into the **heavenly** city by grace freeing nature from sin'.[115] As Roberts has commented, Augustine demonstrated that 'Christians and the Church could transcend history, because (the very

---

[112] See Luke 17:20-21.

[113] John 18:36.

[114] Romans 8:35-39.

[115] Augustine: *City of God.*

The Church 39

meaning and significance of the Church) is to be sought elsewhere'[116] as he postulated the transient shallowness of human time by invoking God of the eternal present: beyond mortal cognition—timeless. As the nineteenth-century hymn writer poetically captures the sentiment in his words as follows:

> So be it, Lord, Thy throne shall never,
> Like earth's proud empires, pass away;
> Thy Kingdom stands, and grows forever,
> Till all Thy creatures own Thy sway.[117]

In a withering coup de grâce against the alleged cynical and faint-hearted supporters of the pagan deities of Rome, Augustine challenged them head-on 'to produce some similar example of (any) town taken by storm in which the fabulous gods of antiquity had been able to protect themselves or their deluded votaries'.[118]

Augustine died, with ironic symbolism, during the siege of Hippo by the invading Vandal forces, in 430; within the year, the city was to fall and the background around which he wrote was to pass away forever; yet the spiritual legacy he left behind lives on. Canonised by the Catholic Church, revered as one of its 'four doctors',[119] Augustine's tradition has been claimed by all shades of Christian opinion. In the mainstream traditions, his exposé of the true nature of the inward experience of Christ's Spiritual Kingdom, his interpretation of 'original sin', his emphasis upon the love and saving grace of God, in Jesus, and the precept of the Trinity of the Godhead are regarded as axiomatic. His insistence that authoritative dogma derives from scripture as interpreted by the 'one and only' universal (Catholic) church, and as a model bishop in the execution of his duties, assure Augustine of Roman Catholic patronage. Yet his teaching on the supremacy of God's *grace*, rather than upon human *effort*, as a route to salvation and his related inclination towards predestination were later to be seized upon by Protestants. Despite the reservations that liberal theologians might harbour in regard to Augustine's justification of official persecution to ensure the application of religious orthodoxy, they are heartened by his prescience when he observed that 'We must be on our guard against giving interpretations (of scripture) that are

---

[116] Roberts, J. M.: *The Triumph of the West*, B.B.C., 1995.

[117] From Everton, J.: *The Day Thou gavest, Lord, is ended.*

[118] Gibbon, E., op. cit.

[119] The others are Jerome (c.340-420), Ambrose (c.340-397) and Gregory (c.540-604).

hazardous or opposed to science, and so exposing the word of God to the ridicule of unbelievers':[120] an early manifestation of the theologian attempting to synthesise faith with reason.

Augustine's inspiration derived almost exclusively from the practical need to respond to his personal circumstances and the times in which he lived. The nagging search for the truth experienced by this self-acknowledged dissolute youth climaxed in that defining moment in a Milanese garden—'Take up and Read'. The political, religious and social uncertainties of the Roman world of North Africa, the wider Mediterranean ambience and beyond, resulted in the outpouring of his spiritual and intellectual spirit to reinvigorate the church for survival and mission; he provided it with a theological touchstone upon which to build and a set of beliefs with a capacity for sustaining power.

---

[120] Augustine: *Commentary on Genesis.*

Chapter 4

Monte Cassino today

TO WORK IS TO PRAY

The Middles Ages (c.500-1450) witnessed the heyday of the monastic orders that served to vitalise the church, both East and West. From these religious communities emerged many of the church leaders, their ideals, direction and spiritual flavour. 'Monks', declared the respected ninth-century monastic activist, Theodore, 'are the sinews and foundations of the church'.

For an appreciation of the development of a coherent monastic concept in the West, we must retrace our steps to the turn of the sixth century—to the valleys of Central Italy—and to the yearning of one man to experience the profundity of God through solitary detachment from the compromising stance adopted by the church towards the world, the state and their seductions since Constantine's patronage of the faith. The name of Monte Cassino, eighty miles from Rome, at a height of nearly two thousand feet on the western fringes of the Apennines will forever symbolise the stubborn German resistance in World War II, as allied forces made heavy weather of their advance northwards up the Italian Peninsular. In February 1944, the later version of the large-scale monastery above the town of Cassino was reduced to rubble by sustained allied bombing and its shell occupied by Polish troops in May.

It is to this region that we shall repair, albeit some fifteen hundred years earlier, to focus upon our defining moment within the context of the evolution of the church.

Benedict was born around 480 in the ancient town of Nursia, nestling in a valley cutting into the mountains not far from Rome; his association with the city, as a young man, led him to reflect upon its spiritual decadence and worldly pretensions, concluding with the sentiments attributed to Solomon, in another context, how its vanity induced 'vexation of spirit'.[121]

Thus disaffected, this erstwhile well-to-do young man withdrew into the mountains to assume the life of a hermit. This was around the year 500. The cave in which he reputedly sought spiritual repose is now incorporated into the eleventh-century abbey of San Benedetto overlooking a deep gorge; a stairway carved into the rock face facilitates access. Yet if personal solitude was his objective, then he was to be distracted; his life was to be channelled into a different path as a result of his chancing upon a small group of men eeking out a communal existence in limestone caves, in the hills close to the small settlement of Subiaco, sharing similar ideals to his own. Enthusiastic and hard working, this group nevertheless lacked Benedict's organisational skills and intellect. In short it needed him to lick them into shape. Benedict's reluctant decision to accept their invitation to lead them must mark as a defining moment, for herein lay the seeds of the profuse expansion of Western Monasticism. It slowly dawned upon Benedict that communal living, rather than solitude, more adequately reflected the spirit of the early disciples of Christ, who shared all things in common.[122] Already his newly found acquaintances had appropriated caves for use as individual cells, had adapted larger caves as a chapel and communal refectory, respectively. As Benedict warmed to his task and the responsibility of moulding his community, with the customary enthusiasm of a new convert, it became apparent that his rigorous, authoritarian and puritanical regime was not quite what the monks had in mind and resentment built up to the point whereby the inmates conspired to poison him. Pope Gregory (590-604) to whom we owe the accounts of Benedict's early life and whose observations must be treated with some circumspection relates that Benedict was miraculously spared, but not surprisingly he recognised the time to move on. A further spell 'in solitary' was short-lived: the monastic ideal of communal living had bitten deeply into Benedict's soul; furthermore, his fame had spread. Others sought him out in the mountains and he organised twelve

---

[121] Ecclesiastes, 1:14. (A.V.)

[122] Acts, 2:45-47.

communities each containing twelve monks, representative of Christ's apostles, with himself as roving counsellor and guide. Ultimately, around 525, Benedict recognised that something more concrete and permanent was needed if his monastic ideal were to be sustained. Perched amidst the hills above the town of Cassino, midway between Rome and Naples, he saw potential in a disused fortress.

In his forthright manner, Benedict took charge of the heavily wooded mountain. With a band of faithful followers, he defied the odds. A gently winding road was constructed to the summit, land was cleared, a water supply laid on, fields were ploughed and the remnants of statues of pagan gods destroyed. The old fortress was refashioned and Monte Cassino became established as the template for Western Monasticism.

The idea of an ascetic withdrawal from the world was not new.[123] We have seen that the hermit lifestyle was not unique to Benedict, nor indeed was the idea of a religious community his.[124] What is significant about Benedict's experiment is that what was initially envisaged as a retreat from the world, and a tacit rejection of a church tainted by it, evolved into the medieval powerhouse of the church. It was the 'rule of Benedict' that was to become the plumb line of the Medieval Monastic

---

[123] We have already noted, in chapter 2, how men had taken to the desert in response to Constantine's nationalisation of the church, early in the fourth century and even before. Tradition refers to Antony, born in Egypt towards the close of the fourth century, who sought hermitic solitude, but who, like Benedict, attracted followers, out of whom a quasi-monastic existence evolved.

[124] Of course, Christianity is not unique in the establishment of monastic regimes, nor can Benedict claim to have initiated the concept. Buddhism has had a long tradition of monastic observance while the pre-Christian Essene community at Qumran, made famous by the discovery of the Dead Sea Scrolls, had been existing at the time of Christ. Monasticism in the Eastern Orthodox traditions is alleged to have been founded upon the tradition of Pachonious (290-366) whose monastery at Tabernisi on the banks of the Nile is supposed to have served as inspiration of Basil of Caesarea (c.330-379) whose 'rule' has formed the basis of Eastern monastic observance. Such monks as were attracted to this order were similarly bound by the constraints of poverty and chastity as well as the injunction to care for the poor. Closer to home, Celtic Christianity tended to be centred on the monastic ideal rather than the apostolic tradition. This tended to give way to the Roman concept, established at Whitby, as outlined in chapter 5.

dynamo whose influence upon Western society has been incalculable.[125] It is to that 'rule' that we must now turn.

In establishing his 'rule' at Monte Cassino, it is clear that Benedict had learned the art of sensitivity to the human weakness present even within a community of dedicated monks, and the excessive rigour he had imposed on the Subiaco congregation was softened both in theory and in practice.

The underlying philosophy of the Benedictine Rule is *Laborare est Orare* ('to work is to pray'), the regime revolving around a composite of study, teaching, sacred reading, prayer and manual labour. All activities of the community were to be determined by the prior demands of the Divine Office[126]—the seven set hours of communal prayer from 'Matins'/'Lauds' first thing to 'Compline' at night. Within the framework of Benedict's Rule, the abbot, as head of the community, was to exercise unilateral authority against whom 'let no one boldly dispute' (rule 3). In keeping with the spirit of the early apostles, *all* property was to be held in common,[127] 'for indeed it is not allowed to the monks to have bodies or wills in their own power' (rule 23). As such, individual needs such as clothing, bedding, handkerchiefs, pens, etc., were to be furnished by the abbot at his discretion. Meals were to be taken in silence although wine was permitted 'sparingly', consumption being limited to around a pint per monk by day (rule 40): not a bad concession to human weakness. As stated, Benedict had obviously learned. Work was to be shared out according to capacity, there being no quarter given for the sin of idleness; the monks would be well cared for in time of sickness and guests were to be welcomed as if they were Christ Himself.[128] For full membership of the community, a structured, intensive programme was instituted from novitiate to the taking of vows as 'the professed'—essentially those of poverty, chastity and obedience; at first the acceptance of 'stability'—a life-long attachment to their abbey—was a condition of profession.

---

[125] Roberts, J. M. in *The Triumph of the West*, B.B.C., 1985, goes so far as to suggest that Benedictine monasticism is the foundation of much of Western European civilisation.

[126] The 'Divine Office' of prayer established fixed times of prayer throughout the day as follows: Lauds; Prime; Terce; Sext; None; Vespers; Compline. This observance was sacrosanct among Benedictines and remains the basis of their religious observance.

[127] Acts 2:45-47.

[128] Matthew 25:40.

The Church

Hence, in establishing his community, Benedict had come a long way from his hermitic presuppositions. However, the seeds for a kind of universal monastic order might never have germinated. For Benedict, the Monte Cassino experience was a one-off and that the movement spread is due to an ironic circumstance. Around 550, Benedict died, his remains being interred at the monastery. Shortly afterwards, in 581, the Lombard invaders sacked the place, the Cassino monks fleeing to Rome for sanctuary. They took with them Benedict's Rule and great interest was shown in it by Gregory, later to become Pope (590-604) who presumably was responsible for popularising the regime. In 817, at a church synod at Aachen, Benedict's Rule was officially recognised as the accepted rule for all Western Monks, with scope, as we shall see, for both modification and expansion.

It was to the north of the Alps, and particularly in France, where the great flowering of Medieval Monasticism was destined to flourish. At Cluny in 910, a Benedictine order was founded, which aimed to reverse the growing tendency for existing monasteries to become somewhat lax and complacent. These were the Cluniacs,[129] who despite their original profession to return to the simple, untrammelled lifestyle of the earliest followers of Benedict evolved, by the sixteenth century, into a hierarchical, centrally directed structure controlling some two thousand houses throughout Europe, including the priory[130] at Lewes in Sussex. As with so many orders, the Cluniacs benefited from the endowments of wealthy patrons often in return for their offering of the mass for specific souls of the benefactor's family, or for the benefactor himself, to ensure minimal aggro in purgatory and ultimately a felicitous afterlife. It is scarcely surprising that this trade-off gradually clouded the pious intention of the order's foundation. Ornate abbey churches, with chantries[131] vying with each other in their splendour, coupled with their

---

[129] So named after the town or village in which the order first appeared.

[130] The distinction between priories and monasteries is, at best, very fluid. However, for our purpose, a priory was a dependent 'house' upon an established abbey. Battle Abbey in Sussex, for example, would in due course superintend the activity of Michelham Priory, some fifteen miles distant. Alternately, in a large monastery, a prior might signify a monk who deputised for the abbot in times of sickness or incapacity. By the late Middle Ages, a priory signified a 'small' monastery.

[131] Technically, a chantry was the support of a benefice, which was maintained for the purpose of the celebration of Holy Mass on behalf of the benefactor, his family or friends. This usually took the form of an endowment to the establishment of a special chapel in an abbey, priory or parish church,

mellifluous liturgy, increasingly characterised the order. The Cluniacs' organisational skills were to prove very useful as Catholicism 'reclaimed' much of Europe from Islam. The larger abbeys were very much organised on business lines. The cloister was the centre of a Benedictine's focus where he wrote, copied and studied when not at prayer or required in the fields, cellar, schoolroom, pharmacy or the kitchen.

Less controversial, perhaps, was the Carthusian order, founded in 1084 at Chartreux[132] in the Dauphiné Alps by St Bruno. The Carthusians, from the outset, were committed to a purely contemplative regime, demanding from the professed strict personal privation and renunciation of the world: the eremitical cell, its distinguishing feature. Thus the members were vowed to observe utter silence[133] and mental prayer, meeting each other only for the Divine Office and for communal meals on feast days alone. Practical chores were frequently carried out by lay brothers who tended to the material needs of the monks. Their 'houses' are known as 'Charterhouses', from which the English Public School derives its foundation, inspiration and name.

Of tremendous influence were the Cistercians, founded, significantly, at the dawn of the Crusading era in 1098 at Cîteaux in Burgundy and as reinvigorated by the redoubtable Bernard[134] from his abbey at Clairvaux from 1115. Again, their origins were benign enough—to return to the simple ways of the earliest Benedictines, but their vulnerability to wealthy patronage followed a typical pattern. Identifiable by their white habit with black cowl and hood, the Cistercians must be credited with advancing the cause of agricultural development throughout Europe. They hewed out of lonely moorland and hill country as a wealthy, arable and pasture economy, thereby regenerating vast areas of neglected acreage. Like the Cluniacs, the Cistercians were ideal tools for Catholic aggression. They went: in the words of Trevor Roper 'wherever there was land to clear and waste to cultivate'.[135] Wealthy indeed they became and particularly

---

    dedicated to the memory of an individual or his family or in some cases to the 'sponsorship' of a clerical ordinand set aside for that purpose.

[132] So named after the town or village in which the order first appeared.

[133] The Trappist Monks, a variant on the Carthusian model, is nevertheless an expression of this tradition, as recognised by Pope Innocent XI (1676-89) in 1678.

[134] See chapter 9.

[135] Trevor-Roger, H., *The Rise of Christian Europe*, The History Book Club, 1965.

The Church 47

ripe for the picking at the time of Henry VIII's reformation to which the remarkable ruins of Tintern,[136] Rievaulx and Fountains testify.

The crusades, as we shall see, provided the stimulus for a further development of the Benedictine concept. Jerusalem, once taken, must be defended, its Christian ethos guarded and its pilgrims protected. Thus were founded in 1113 the knights of the order of St John of Jerusalem (the Hospitallers)[137] whose triple role was both monastic and social as well as military. This composite feature was the pattern adopted by the sinister Knights Templar founded by Hugues de Payens and eight French associates from their headquarters at a house near the site of Solomon's temple, in 1118, whose activities in the Holy Land, at the time of the crusades have been the source of intense interest, suspicion and speculation. Suffice it to say that despite their vows of chastity, poverty and obedience, this dynamic order characterised by the stereotypical crusading white habit surmounted by the Red Cross, peaked at around fifteen thousand members by the year 1300. Their legendary wealth, their arcane rituals, their heretical tendencies, their influence and power excited both the jealousy and the fear of many—not least Popes Boniface VIII (1294-1303), Clement V (1305-14) and King Philip the Fair of France (1285-1314). The order was suppressed in 1312 on the alleged grounds of immorality, superstition and heresy, their Grand Master, Jacques de Molay executed in cruel circumstances a year later. The ruins of their richly endowed Temple Churches can be found scattered around Europe, typically round in construction, on the model of the Church of the Holy Sepulchre in Jerusalem. On their demise, many of their assets were transferred to their contemporaries and rivals, the knights of St John.[138]

---

[136] See especially, Wordsworth, W.: his poem 'Tintern Abbey' reflects upon the material and spiritual aspect of the Cistercian foundation, one of the wealthiest houses in the British Isles. The ruins of the abbey stand in the Wye Valley amidst a landscape spellbinding in its numinous beauty.

[137] The orders of St John exist to the present day, albeit in modified form and expectation. On the victorious reclamation of the Holy Land by Moslem exploits in 1291, the hospitallers retreated to the islands of Rhodes, and subsequently to Malta, having been assigned a fair proportion the material possessions of the Templars in 1312. They retained possession of Malta until 1798, succumbing to Napoleon's expansionist policies. Subsequently the order has been dedicated to the civilian relief of suffering. See also chapter 9.

[138] See also chapters 9 and 10. A footnote, here, must be spared for the Teutonic Knights, formed as a result of the desire of pious citizens of Bremen and

It seems that by the beginning of the thirteenth century, the Monastic orders generally were evolving in a spirit in stark contrast to original ideal. Abbots became chief executives of a flourishing business enterprise, often obscuring the spiritual catalyst of their foundation. Even at the time of the Norman conquest, according to the Domesday Survey (1086-87), the abbot of Ely's holding of the Hatfield Estate was assessed at '40 Hides. There is land for 30 plough teams . . . yielding 47s and 4d . . . wood for 2000 swine . . . worth £30'.[139] Yet while the church still found them of use, a new dynamic was needed if heresy were to be tackled and regeneration fostered. Enter the era of the friars. If the church were to reach out to folk at the grass roots, the monastic orders, for reasons outlined earlier, were increasingly less well suited. During the papacy of Innocent III (1198-1216), two men, one Italian and the other Spanish, established the orders of Mendicant Friars—people, yes, bound by the monastic rules of poverty, chastity and obedience, but *freed* from the constraints of lifelong communal residence. In short, the philosophy of the friars was to be free to exert their influence by means of itinerancy and the seeking of prayerful and material support from the faithful as the spirit moved. Such is the basic distinction between monk and friar. Both adhere in principle to Benedict's Rule, yet the latter do not subscribe to the vow of stability.

For the Italian Francis of Assisi (1181-1226), founder of the Franciscan order (the Friars Minor) and recognised by Innocent III in 1210, the essence of Christ could best be sustained by spreading joy and by sharing their experience of the spirit through service to the poor, the sick, the needy. A corresponding order for women, the 'Poor Clares', was formed in 1213. Dressed in a simple habit, a cloak, the Franciscan order is frequently referred to as the Grey Friars. It is probably to that order that the legendary Friar Tuck of Robin Hood fame belonged. By contrast, the Black Friars, or Dominican order (the Preaching Friars), similarly itinerant, appealed to the mind, rather than the heart. Dominic de Guzman, the Spaniard (1170-1221), its founder, believed firmly in the process of education in order to sustain orthodoxy and faith within the church: that people could be won over by means of reason and argument. The order was recognised in 1216 and its members were used to mastermind the first serious inquisition (against the heretical

---

Lübeck, who wished to alleviate the suffering of Christian forces defending Acre, 1290-91. Subsequently the knights exercised political, social and economic influence in Northern Germany throughout the Middle Ages and into the Modern Era.

[139] Quoted in Wood, M.: *Domesday: A Search for the Roots of England.*

The Church

Cathari (Albigensians) in Southern France). Less well known, but equally effective were the Carmelite Friars (the White Friars) and the Austin Friars who claim to trace their origins back to a rule attributed to St Augustine in the fourth/fifth centuries although this provenance is questionable.

The orders, then, have played an immense role in the evolution of the Western Church throughout the Middle Ages. The papacy in Rome, distracted as it so frequently was, by political and social considerations closer to home, could not hope, by virtue of its embryonic structure alone, to sustain any kind of inherent spiritual momentum. It was the orders upon which it was to increasingly rely and which were to provide to the church with the back-up needed for its self-preservation. Separate from the world, yet officially sanctioned by a church that was very much part of it, the monastic regimen became for Rome a source of strength as well as a potent force for its own decline. To the monastic orders, Western Civilisation owes a great deal:[140] to its painstaking transmission of the values of classical civilisation and to the preservation of scripture itself; to the concept of spirituality, self-denial; to the invaluable benefits of literacy; for the care of the poor, the sick, the needy, the traveller; and for the benefits of community. Yet they remind us of the dangers of complacency and of a failure to keep a watch on our ideals. The orders have given us the opportunity to appreciate the contribution of both genders to humankind's spirituality and to the development of women's orders and to Mother Theresa's Sisters of Charity.[141] They were the inspiration for a new generation of orders during the Catholic Reformation.[142]

---

[140] Roberts, J. M. op. cit.

[141] The role of women's orders has been recognised from early times. The feminine focus of Christianity has been researched by such writers as Pickett, L. and Prince, C: *The Templar Revelation*, Corgi Books, 1998, who present a cogent, if debatable thesis, on the role of women in the evolution of the Christian Church. Whatever, the female contribution to church evolution must never be underemphasised. See ch. 20.

[142] The Catholic reformation of the sixteenth century led to the formulation of many distinctive orders: the Oratory of Divine Love, the Ursulines, the Theatines, and the earlier foundation of the Brethren of Common Life. All of these orders testify to the variant strengths of local Catholic feeling and influence during the Late Medieval Period. Their direct descendants, the Society of Jesus, or Jesuits, recognised in the 1540s, are a significant development of the Benedictine principle. See ch. 14.

Our defining moment, when Benedict responded to the call of the troglodyte monks at Subiaco in AD 500 and his rebuilt monument at Monte Cassino, has left the Western Church and its civilisation an indelible legacy.

Chapter 5

The Forum in Rome today

NOT ANGLES BUT ANGELS

To a church whose heartland was the Mediterranean, the islands of Britain during the first five centuries of the Christian era must have seemed a world away. To the Roman civil and military authorities, the sometimes truculent, rebellious Britons posed an endemic challenge. Hadrian's Wall, built around AD 120, and the fourth-century earthworks of Severus stand as monuments to the failure of the imperial legions to consolidate a meaningful foothold in the northern extremities, while the Irish Sea shielded the warring tribes of Ireland.

Nevertheless, hand in hand with Roman rule and the Pax Romana, Christian activity, for example, unquestionably featured among those in Britain who cared and dared to embrace its precepts. Alban, reputedly the first British Christian martyr, was beheaded for saving the life of a priest and refusing to offer incense to the gods or to the Emperor Diocletian allegedly in 303.[143] After Constantine's decrees in the fourth century,

---

[143] Bede: *The History of the English Church and People*, Penguin Classics, 1964, pp. 44-47. Bede (c.673-735) is an invaluable source for the Early Medieval Period of English history. It must be born in mind of course that this undoubted scholar wrote in an ambience totally monastic and Roman;

there is some evidence of the embrace of Christianity among the upper classes. The Roman Villa at Lullingstone in Kent has been instructive in that there is evidence of a chapel for family use containing plastered walls with robed figures painted in an attitude of prayer and with the Christian monogram clearly visible. Given this, Christian influence and structure appear thus to have been variously heroic, factious,[144] spasmodic and piecemeal.[145]

Imperial Rome was in gradual decline, the Eternal City itself finally succumbing to the barbarians in 410. Already the legions had left Britannia for the last time. To the hapless Britons, this spelt disaster. The vast majority, unskilled and untrained in either the political arts or the military acumen of their Roman Overlords, now lay exposed and vulnerable to the unwelcome incursions from the perennial thorns in the flesh from the north—the Scots and the Picts—and from the east—the invasive Continental pagan tribes known to history as the Jutes, the Saxons and the Angles. These latter, coveting the natural wealth and resources of the island, were intent on establishing their authority, their imprint to be formalised in the emerging kingdoms, such as Mercia, Deira, Kent, Wessex and Northumbria.

It appears that those Christians unwilling to submit, yet again, to pagan pressures and influences hived off into the western fringes of Britain—into Cornwall and Wales—only to be harassed from the sea by pirates from Ireland.

Thus tormented and effectively cut off from its umbilical cord in the Mediterranean, this was scarcely promising for the development of the Universal Church in the British Isles, hardly the later sanctified 'blessed plot . . . renowned . . . for Christian service and true chivalry' of John of Gaunt; much more apposite his assertion that 'England . . . hath made a shameful conquest of itself'.[146]

Yet as so often happens in the course of history, when an apparently casual encounter mutates into a herald of destiny, sometime during the 580s, an acute observation by a senior ecclesiastic in the marketplace in

---

his perceptions therefore reflect his circumstances, wherein even in our account of the defining moment, historical veracity might well be flavoured with the overwhelming desire for moral precepts. See also Foxe, J.: *History of the Christian Martyrs*, Spire books, 1973, pp. 25-26.

[144] The Pelagian and Arian theological controversies affected English Christianity. For an account, see Bede, 'op cit', pp. 48, 49.

[145] Bede, 'op. cit', p. 42, refers to one Lucius, a 'British' king seeking to be made a Christian and writing to Pope Eusebius in 156 to that effect.

[146] Shakespeare: *Richard II*, II. i.

Rome was to lead to a remarkable change in the fortunes of the English Church, and it is this incident, recounted by Bede, to which we owe our consideration of this defining moment.[147]

The abbot of St Andrew's monastery in Rome, presumably taking time out from his obligations around the cloisters in favour of an excursion downtown, stopped in his tracks as he passed through the local market, probably the impressive brick edifice adjacent to the forum in the city as renovated by the Emperor Trajan (AD 98-117) during the early part of the second century, in the shadow of the illustrious coliseum and the triumphal Arch of Titus. There among this several storeyed labyrinth of bustling humanity haggling over the choicest pepper, spices, vegetables, fruit, wine and oil worthy of Harrods to the assorted flotsam and jetsam of a boot fair, Abbot Gregory's attention was drawn to an enclosure harbouring young men of fair complexion, well-defined facial features and blond hair—human merchandise on offer to the highest bidder: captives from Rome's far-flung conquests. Upon enquiry as to their origins, Gregory was apprised of the fact that these young men were Angles, the subjects of King Hella of the province of Deira on the island of 'Angle-land'.

'How sad', Gregory is reported to have remarked, 'that such handsome folk are still in the grip of the author of darkness—"non angli, sed angeli" ("not Angles but Angels")—whose province, Deira, was appropriately named, for they shall indeed be "de ira" (saved "from wrath") and called to the mercy of Christ . . . Then must "Alleluia" (as befitted the name of their king) be sung to the praise of God, our Creator, in their land'.

Gregory vowed to initiate a conversion programme—an action plan—to transform in Bede's words 'our still idolatrous nation' into a Church of Christ as part of his vision 'to convert raving barbarians and to form a Christian Commonwealth led by the Holy Father'. Before Gregory could realise his romantic vision, however, he had been elevated to the bishopric of Rome itself, in 590: a highly significant tenure of fourteen years as it turned out.[148]

---

[147] Bede: 'op. cit'; see pp. 66-83, 98-99, for his full account.

[148] In fact, Pope Gregory I (590-604) is so revered by the Catholic Church as the spiritual and temporal ruler of Rome, as the promoter of the Gospel and for his care for the less fortunate that he was canonised shortly after his death. Subsequently, he has been accorded the status of 'the great'. The Gregorian chant is associated with him. He is one of the four honoured 'doctors' of the Catholic Church along with Ambrose of Milan (c.340-393), Jerome (c.340-420) and Augustine of Hippo (353-430). Gregory's pontificate was pregnant with implications for the future of the church. He established

In the course of time, he prevailed upon the prior of the monastery to which he had been attached to head up a missionary delegation of some forty prelates and make contact with people of influence among England's barbarous tribes: a daunting prospect, by all accounts, and a challenge that the papal delegate, Augustine (c.530-604), would face with a degree of reticence, bred, one imagines, by a level of trepidation marginally greater. As the laconic Anglo-Saxon Chronicle prosaically presents it, 'In this year (596), Pope Gregory sent Augustine with very many monks to preach the word of God to the English people'.[149]

Crossing the channel from the by-now relatively civilised and Christianised kingdom of Gaul, Augustine's party landed in Kent in 597, ruled by King Ethelbert (c.585-616), arguably the most powerful potentate in England at the time, with nominal suzerain authority extending as far north as the Humber.

Gregory's strategy was simple: win over the prince and mass conversion will follow; Augustine's opportunity, in fact, could not have been more favourable. Although a pagan himself, Ethelbert was, in fact, married to Bertha, a Christian princess from Gaul and a woman, it seems, of character and influence. This doubtless facilitated a rendezvous between the papal emissaries and the king, and accounts for the apparent cordiality of their reception as they 'approached the king carrying a silver cross as their standard and the likeness of our Lord and Saviour painted on a board'.

---

an administrative machinery in Rome, which virtually ignored the authority of the emperor in Constantinople, thereby advancing his own claims to temporal authority and advancing the cause of Rome's primacy within Christendom. As administrator, he firmed up the role of bishops while at the same time influencing the development of the Parish concept. He articulated the seven deadly sins: pride, covetousness, lust, envy, gluttony, anger, sloth. He refined the doctrine of purgatory and encouraged the veneration of relics. So powerfully did Gregory's office evolve during his fourteen-year pontificate that Thomas Hobbes was to acknowledge that the papacy had become 'the ghost of old Rome sitting crowned upon the grave thereof'.

[149] The *Anglo-Saxon Chronicle* was traditionally initiated at the behest of the court of King Alfred the Great, around 890. It is in fact a compilation of works chronicling significant events dating from the turn of the first millennium based upon various traditions and continued in various guises until 1154. The year 595 is the preferred date of this event according to the *Parker Chronicle*. In this respect the 'Laud Chronicle's' date as used here is more likely to be accurate: Garmonsway, G. N. *The Anglo-Saxon Chronicle*, Everymans University Library, 1972.

Favourably impressed by the occasion, the king granted them a dwelling in Canterbury, his administrative centre. Evidently moved, subsequently, by what Bede describes as the attractive lifestyle of Augustine and his companions, the king and his household were duly baptised into the faith and the old Roman Church of St Martin in Canterbury was placed at their disposal. Work permits thus secured, missionary activity proceeded apace, Paulinus (c.575-644) ministering to much of the territory adjacent to the north-eastern seaboard, then under Ethelbert's nominal overlordship.

Back in Rome, Gregory was ecstatic! On learning of such progress, his policy and strategy were apparently vindicated. 'Britain', he asserted, 'now lies quiet before the feet of (Christ's) saints, and its ungovernable savages . . . are now quelled at the simple word of His priests in the fear of God . . . and . . . restrains them of their former wickedness . . . '[150]

Advice to Augustine from the Holy Father followed to ensure the first flush of success was sustained. He urged that the missionary approach be one of pragmatism: that the Christian observance be grafted onto local custom and tradition; pagan sites and Saxon burial grounds were to be respected and where possible metamorphosed for use as places of Christian worship; the observance of Christmas was to be bolted on to the existing revelries enjoyed as an integral ingredient associated with the Yuletide Festival around the December Solstice, while it was felt appropriate to superimpose the celebration of Christ's passion and resurrection upon the springtime observance of Eostre,[151] the goddess of fertility.

To some this has been seen as a sensitive and essentially pragmatic device to secure adherence to the truth; to others a devil-inspired compromise, a watering down of the true message and a sell-out of Christian principles.

Whatever be the case, the tradition established by Augustine has survived in the established church to the present.

In order to reinforce Augustine's authority in such matters, Gregory formally bestowed upon him spiritual supremacy authority 'over the whole nation', recommending that Augustine appoint a superintending bishop for the north to be established in York in order to complement his base at Canterbury in the south: Augustine, then, the first archbishop of Canterbury and the establishment of England's two ecclesiastical

---

[150] Pope Gregory, 'Commentary on Job'

[151] From which, of course, the English term 'Easter' derives. There is no biblical injunction upon Christians to 'celebrate' the resurrection nor Christmas for that matter. Sects such as Jehovah's Witnesses take exception to such festivities on these grounds.

provinces—Canterbury and York—officially sanctioned by the Holy Father at the end of the sixth century.

In point of fact, Gregory's sanguine assessment of the state of play on the ground was somewhat premature. General acceptance of the faith was by no means universal nor was it a one-way process. While, for example, King Edwin of Northumbria (588-633) had married Ethelberga, the daughter of Ethelbert and Bertha, and embraced Christianity himself, the kingdom suffered a reverse when it fell to the pagan king of Mercia in battle. To the west, as we have seen, an isolated remnant of Christian civilisation had survived (it had, in fact, already been revitalised by the work of Patrick (c.387-c.461)—an erstwhile Romano/British aristocrat). He, in his own words,[152] converted and baptised thousands of people and ordained many clergy from the seemingly implacable people of Ireland and established his own missionary centre and see at Armagh by the middle of the fifth century.

While still retaining at least a nominal loyalty to the papacy in Rome, the Celtic Church (as the church in Ireland became known) on the edge of the so-called civilised world had developed idiosyncratic features of its own. Communal life was to centre around the spiritual landlords, in a quasi-feudal monastic fashion, springing from the third-century tradition of Celtic monks clustered in wooden huts and protected by earthworks. This was the catalyst for considerable learning, scholarship and illuminated texts, such as the *Book of Kells*, and the springboard for a spiritual assault further afield. These influences were destined to play their part in the revival of Christianity in the north of England.

Just thirty-four years prior to Augustine's mission to Canterbury in 563, Columba (521-597) and a number of his fellow monks from Ireland had established their distinctive brand of Celtic monastic life on the island of Iona, just off the west coast of Scotland. No mere reflective, introverted retreat this; Iona became the 'generating powerhouse of missionary enterprise throughout northern Britain, the islands beyond and indeed into Europe'. Convergence and possible conflict with the officially sanctioned Roman-based Christianity centred on Canterbury was almost inevitable.

Oswald, king of Northumbria (634-642), anxious to re-establish his independence and the observance of the Christian faith, had been temporarily eclipsed by the Mercians (as we have seen) and now sought spiritual help from the monks on Iona. Ever happy to oblige, Aidan (c.600-651) was despatched to the east coast in 635, where he established a monastery on the peninsula at Lindisfarne (Holy Island), whence a

---

[152] Patrick: *Confessions.*

The Church 57

wide acceptance of the Celtic brand of Christianity spread across swathes of the north.

Some of the more ecumenically minded souls were expressing their misgivings at the threat to the cause of Christ that this increasingly apparent division occasioned. It was clear, for example, that, in their isolation, the Celtic faithful had not kept pace with developments in the wider Catholic community.

Bede identifies three significant areas of disagreement: the shape of the monks' tonsure (not such a big deal, perhaps); the format of the baptismal service (much more worthy of theological debate) and the precise dating and observance of Easter:[153] a cause for confusion, to say the least, so that in Kent both Celtic and Roman observances were practised in one royal household, and when the king had ended Lent and was celebrating Easter, the queen and her attendants were still fasting and keeping Palm Sunday![154]

King Oswy of Northumbria (655-670) decided to grasp the nettle. In 664, he convened a council of church leaders from both traditions—the decisive Synod of Whitby. As expected, the arguments were heated, but at the end of the day, the Roman and Catholic standpoint prevailed and effectively England (followed more reluctantly by Ireland, Scotland and Wales) accepted the decision.

Henceforth the British church was to remain loyal to the Roman connection down to the sixteenth century, and the close links between church and state as established by such as Augustine, Aidan and Cuthbert (c.634-687) down to the present survived the Viking destruction of the Lindisfarne and Iona monasteries and long outstripped the survival of Bede's cloistered workplace at Jarrow and Wearmouth.

Their monument survives, then, not in wood and stone, but in the inspired missionary efforts of Alcuin (735-804) and Boniface (680-754), the production of the Lindisfarne Gospels (c.680), Bede's own pioneering work on English history, the pious work of Alfred the Great (871-899) and his translation of the Psalms into Anglo-Saxon—to name but a few. The educational and teaching tradition of the English Church was well founded.

So the story of the beginnings of Christianity in England is complex, but basically two-pronged. From the vantage point of history, we can now see the outcome of the decisions taken at the Synod of Whitby. The Roman pattern of the English Church as established by Augustine in 597—its structure and traditions—was that which was destined to

---

[153] Bede: 'op. cit', chapter 25, pp. 182-188.
[154] Bede: 'op. cit', p. 182.

prevail. Only thus can the significance of Gregory's inspired vision, hard on the heels of his encounter with those tall, blond, blue-eyed 'Angels' in the Roman marketplace, be appreciated as a defining moment in its ongoing story.

Chapter 6

'Coronation of Charlemagne' (Raphael)

HAIL AUGUST EMPEROR

On Christmas Day in the year 800, Charles, king of the Franks, was kneeling in appropriate solemnity at the altar dedicated to St Peter in Rome when mass had been celebrated. While presumably reflecting on the beneficence of administering the Blessed Sacrament, the Pontiff Pope Leo III, from whose hands moments before Charles had ingested the Holy Mystery, positioned a crown upon the royal head in an act of pure theatre and knelt in homage to a now duly sanctioned emperor, known to history as Charlemagne (Charles the Great) (king of the Franks, since 768, and emperor, 800-814).

According to Norman Davies, Einhard, Charlemagne's biographer, asserts that this apparently spontaneous action on the part of the Holy Father prompted the assembled company of Rome's great and good to acclaim its new sovereign 'Imperator, Augustus'[155] in terms redolent

---

[155] Davies, N.: *Europe—A History*, Pimlico Press, 1997. The actual term, 'Holy Roman Empire' was never formally used to denote this entity until the thirteenth century and indeed its temporal effect fluctuated over the centuries until at the end its heartland was essentially Germany. Charlemagne himself was content with the title 'August Emperor'. It was

59

of the Roman Empire of old. Once more Rome was acknowledging an emperor of its own for the first time in over three and a half centuries,[156] in defiance of the whim and caprice of the increasingly alien authority established by Constantine in the Byzantine[157] capital that bore his name. How spontaneous, or indeed surprising, Leo's apparently precipitous action was on this occasion is a matter of serious conjecture; whatever be the case, the circumstance must qualify for inclusion as one of the defining moments in the history of the church.

The coronation of Charlemagne does not, in fact, mark the beginning of his illustrious career; rather, this practical gesture with profound symbolic overtones was a recognition of the remarkable achievements of this archetypal representative of the Frankish Carolingian dynasty and his predecessors.

More to the point, it could be seen as a calculated move to clear a path for the papacy and for the church, which had become increasingly muddied in the domestic politics of Rome and instability on its frontiers.

Certainly Charlemagne himself was known to be uneasy with his newly acquired dignity and the relationship that it implied—perhaps conscious of the possibility that he had fallen victim to a shrewd exercise of papal guile.

Pope Leo (795-816), while inwardly self-assured as the successor of St Peter, not unusually for a pontiff had found himself in a certain amount of difficulty. On a personal level, he had fallen foul of the Roman establishment, members of which had proceeded to humiliate him verbally and abuse him physically. In desperation, he had repaired to the Carolingian Court of Charlemagne where, for reasons that will become apparent, he was assured of sanctuary.

Charlemagne had persuaded Leo that a melange of humility and a strident denial of the more serious allegations levelled against him, before a solemn convocation of the Roman aristocracy, might result

---

Otto II (973-983) who was the first to be styled 'Roman emperor', while the term *holy* was not used until even later. Whatever the style, it's the concept that remains significant.

[156] In 395, the eastern and western sections of the empire were split. Rome had its own nominal emperor down to its fall in 476 when Romulus Augustulus was effectively deposed.

[157] For practical purposes, the Eastern Empire is commonly referred to as the Byzantine Empire, ruled from Byzantium (Constantinople).

The Church

in the reinstatement of his papal dignity. It worked and this was the immediate catalyst precipitating the events of Christmas Day, 800.

However, there were wider, more long-term concerns with which the papacy and the church had to contend and that are directly relevant here. On a wider front, relationships between the traditions of Leo's Western (Roman Latin) Church and the Eastern (Greek) Church of Byzantium had deteriorated dramatically during the course of the eighth century. Not only was it irritating to Rome to be, at the very least, nominally subject to a secular (and Byzantine) Caesar, who was wont to interfere in matters of church doctrine and practice as affected the Eastern Church, but it compromised Rome's own claim to speak for the Church Universal.[158] In short, it was insult added to injury to accept that, even by the dubious standards of Rome, the Byzantine court was a regime sustained by cruelty, inconsistency and madness.[159]

Further afield, the Persian armies had posed a threat to the Eastern Church since the middle of the sixth century, but it was the meteoric rise of Islam, dating from the flight of Mohammed (570-632) from Mecca in 622, which had forced Christendom and the church onto the back foot.

The simple Islamic creed enjoined upon all Moslems ('There is no God but Allah and Mohammed is his prophet') certainly had an appeal to those confused by the complex doctrinal disputations over which the church seemed to expend so much energy. Thus, helped along by the evangelical zeal of a jihad, mass conversions to the Moslem faith eliminated the Christian monopoly of the Mediterranean world.

Westwards, from its Arabian heartland, crossing the North African littoral, the Moslem warriors carried all before them. Bastions of Christian civilisation, tradition and learning, such as Alexandria and Hippo, fell to the onslaught of the Koran and the scimitar. Kairuan and Carthage succumbed and Europe's doors had been prised open with the capture of the Gibraltar toehold in 711.

There followed a relentless push and consolidation northwards, embracing much of the Iberian Peninsula, then over the Pyrenees; the Arabic Ummayad forces were into Gaul and at the gates of Tours.

---

[158] The conflicts over clerical celibacy, the dating of Easter, monastic tonsures and the iconoclastic controversy are evidence for this.

[159] E.g. Irene, mother of Emperor Constantine VI (780-797), blinded her son, deposing him in 797.

While the Moslem invaders were thus engaged, other Islamic zealots had been advancing into Holy Land itself: Jerusalem and Damascus in 636, with Asia Minor and Constantinople next on the hit list.

By the eighth century, then, the European Church was bracing itself for the logical outcome of a movement bent, it was feared, on its destruction. It marks the beginning of, at worst, a bloody conflict of arms and at best sullen mutual suspicion between the practitioners of Christianity and Islam of which modern society is all too painfully aware.

In the year 732, with the Moslem armies already into Central Gaul, the hapless Duke of Aquitaine had appealed to Charles Martel, leader of the Carolingian branch of the Frankish tribes (714-741),[160] themselves increasing their stranglehold in the north of the country to come to the rescue of Christendom. In response, Martel ('the Hammer') with his army of mounted stirruped warriors saved Tours and recaptured Poitiers, stemming once and for all, as it turned out, the Moslem advance into Western Europe, pursuing them back into Iberia.

Fortuitously for Charles Martel, his victory over the Islamic Crescent in 732 enabled him to assert his authority over southern Gaul at a stroke. It fell to Martel's son, Pepin (741-768), to cultivate a positive relationship with the Roman Catholic Church in order to legitimise his authority; mere military supremacy, he recognised astutely, is tenuous and ephemeral in an ambience of instability—Caesar today, Antony tomorrow! He appreciated, as had Constantine before him, that the spiritual cement supplied by a pervasive church would help to consolidate his material

---

[160]   The Franks, originally from the region of the Danube had been led by the Merovingian branch, headed by Clovis (481-511), who had been baptised in 496. In fact, his career represents a sort of prophetic preview to the more lasting accomplishments of Charlemagne. In 496 Clovis, already master of much of Gaul, had signed a pact with Rome, whereby Rome's authority over other competing bishoprics could be reinforced militarily, while anointing Clovis with spiritual armoury to enhance its legitimacy—the prototype for the arrangement made with Charlemagne in 800. It was only when his successors seemed to lack the kind of spiritual zeal, as woefully apparent in the effete Dagobert II (674-679), for example, that Rome later reneged on their deal with the Merovingians and backed Pepin's coup d'état in 751, deposing Childeric III (743-757) in favour of the Carolingian line that appeared a safer bet than the ailing Merovingians. For a fascinating discussion of the significance of these events, see Baigent, L., Leigh, R. and Lincoln, H., *The Holy Blood and the Holy Grail*, Arrow Books, 1996, pp. 254-274.

The Church 63

gains. Accordingly, Bishop Boniface, the English evangelist to Germany, was commissioned by Pepin to effect positive and radical reforms within the Frankish Church. In 751, as legate of Pope Zachary (741-775), Boniface anointed Pepin as *king* of the Franks, recognising him and his descendants as 'the protector of the Romans'. This symbiotic relationship between the Frankish king and the papacy had been further enhanced by the so-called 'Donation of Pepin', whereby lands Pepin had seized from the troublesome Lombard warlords of North Italy were transferred to direct papal administration—the basis of the Papal States and with the pontiff as a secular prince in consequence.

Thus the coronation of Charlemagne—Charles Martel's grandson and the son of Pepin—in 800 was the culmination, part fortuitous, part calculated, whereby the Roman papacy could with greater confidence assert its independence of the Byzantine emperor. Conveniently, there surfaced—at the same time—a now discredited document, the *Donation of Constantine*, by which the legendary emperor was purported to have surrendered considerable secular authority to Rome's bishop when Constantine had decamped to Byzantium in the early part of the fourth century. A minor inconvenience that the document was suspiciously fraudulent, it served its purpose. In sum, the bishop of Rome had broken loose from Constantinople and almost by default had assumed the status of a secular prince in his own right; moreover he had become 'de facto' the creator of emperors.

In so far as the Carolingians had played their part in stalling Moslem ambitions upon Western Europe, the papacy presumably angled for their continued support; hence the assertion of one controversial historian, Henri Pirenne, that 'without Mohammed, Charlemagne would have been unthinkable'.[161]

As Alcuin, Charlemagne's spiritual confessor and chancellor, was later to enthuse, his master was 'designed to keep the Church of God inwardly pure . . . to protect it from the doctrine of the faithless, as to defend it outwardly against the plundering of the heathen'[162]—sentiments more akin to Alcuin's own pious predilections than a true reflection of the more reserved opinions of Charlemagne himself.

At root, then, the coronation of Charlemagne signified that in return for his enhanced status as a papally endorsed Christian ruler, approved as such by God at the very hands of a successor to St Peter, the beleaguered Roman papacy was pinning its hopes upon the greater protection, which the most prestigious and powerful military potentate in the West

---

[161] Pirenne, H.: *Mahomet and Charlemagne*, English Translation, 1939.

[162] Quoted in Deanesly, M.: *A History of the Medieval Church*, Methuen, 1947.

might afford. A potentially cosy relationship such as this had never been conceived, even by such luminaries of the past as Constantine, Justinian or even Pope Gregory the Great himself.[163] Now the church was being brought into a partnership, giving legitimacy to the feudal structures the Carolingians were in the process of establishing. At the same time, the church in the West had been freed from the resented secular empire in the East, albeit at the cost of hastening the process of ultimate schism.

Charlemagne's Frankish Empire notionally extended from his capital at Aachen (where he died in 814) into much of Modern France, Northern Spain, the Low Countries, the Germanic lands and part of Italy. The tradition if not assurance that Germanic kingship led to the imperial title had been established. However, this temporal power was more apparent than real and its political substance did not long outlive its mentor.

What is important, though, is the symbolism—the more long-lasting features of our defining moment and the signals it sent out. The spiritual renaissance initiated by Charlemagne is a feature of his reign, even allowing for his own ambivalence and his cynical use of church patronage to secure political objectives.

Alcuin's students, capable and intellectually prepared, encouraged and sponsored by the emperor himself took hold of individual monasteries throughout the Carolingian Empire, where rigorous standards were enforced and precious manuscripts scrupulously copied. Theological debate was encouraged, schools were attached to many monasteries, cathedrals established and Latin promoted as the vehicle towards a common format for worship. Such is the spiritual legacy of Charlemagne, which extended far beyond his dominions.

Despite the fact, as Norman Davies points out,[164] that 'Pope Leo had no recognised right to confer the imperial title and Charlemagne had no right to receive it', the coronation on the day when Christ's Nativity is celebrated established an enduring concept and principle, namely the twin pillars of Western Christendom—papacy and empire—the sacred and the secular working in tandem to secure a civilisation whose spiritual base was to be anchored in the patrimony of St Peter.

This relationship was to be tested to its limits throughout the Middle Ages and beyond, but was to continue, theoretically at least, until Napoleon (1804-15) put the ailing office of Holy Roman emperor out

---

[163] Roper, H. T.: *The Rise of the Christian Europe*, p. 100, The History Book Club, 1965.

[164] Davies, N.: op. cit., p.302.

of its misery by bringing down the metaphorical guillotine upon it in 1806.

Yet the legacy lives on: the Charlemagne prize awarded periodically to those who actively and significantly promote the ideas of European unity. To some, this is seen as symbolic of a systematic, insidious and conspiratorial movement towards a European Superstate. To others, it points to a political, economic and perhaps spiritual destiny of European consciousness, as tentatively conceived by Charlemagne, but which has so frustratingly over the centuries been punctuated by the endemic propensity to civil war. Whatever the future of the continent, our defining movement gave the Western Church, if not to Rome itself, beset as it was throughout much of the Medieval Period by unprepossessing intrigue,[165] a shot in the arm.

---

[165] In fact, Charlemagne could offer little practical and ongoing assistance in respect of the squalid conditions prevalent in Rome nor could his successor prevent the city and its treasures from being raided by Saracens in 846.

Chapter 7

Hagia Sophia, Constantinople

ANATHEMA

Despite the tensions, the mutual jealousy, heresies, recrimination and a distinct lack of Christian charity, the church at large, throughout the first millennium, took seriously the axiom of Christ that 'It might be One'.[166] The church, after all, was the assumed human expression and embodiment of Christ's ideal: the vehicle by which 'whosoever believes in Him might be saved'.[167]

Thus, ideally, spiritual unity was presupposed and sustained. Heresy and schism, actual and potential, account for the many councils called throughout Christendom during this period to preserve it. Yet in some ways the church was to be the victim of its own success. As its missionary effort gathered momentum into Scandinavia, the British Isles, the Balkans, Africa, and significantly into Russia, so the occasion for cultural and linguistic diversity—not to mention political opportunism—were to widen the gulf between the two main streams of Christian tradition, the Latin West and the Greek East. Our defining moment recalls the event

---

[166] John 17:11.
[167] John 3:16.

when these two strands were duly and irrevocably severed, played out before the high altar of the Church of St Sophia in Constantinople.

St Sophia was the spiritual heart of Byzantium. This edifice, conceived initially by Constantine and perfected in the sixth century under the auspices of the Emperor Justinian (527-565), would have rivalled any such ecclesiastical structure in terms of its meticulous design, sensitive detail and monumental proportions.

Hagia (St) Sophia loomed high over Constantinople's other churches, and to the faithful, its immense array of domes symbolised Christianity's all-embracing heavens: 'Solomon', Justinian, is reputed to have boasted on its completion, 'I have outdone thee!'

Some 450 years later, on 16 July 1054, the interior of St Sophia, an ornate blend of porphyry, ivory, marble, silver and glass would have been shimmering responsively to the myriad diffusion of candlelight; beneath the heavenly dome, 180 feet high, Michael Cerularius, patriarch of Constantinople (1043-59), was celebrating the divine liturgy at the high altar. Above, mosaic seraphim that embellished the huge dome's supportive pendentives could but resign themselves as passive participants in the proceedings leading to the decisive act of schism, their faces overlaid with stars as if to shield them from the unfolding drama of the betrayal of Christ's Universal Church.

Beneath, an incredulous congregation of the faithful was about to witness the ultimate confrontation. Doubtless, emerging from the comparative security of the colonnades, in an act of apparently calculated defiance, Cardinal Humbert, papal ambassador to Byzantium, and his retinue paraded into the full spectrum of the vast nave. Purposefully advancing towards the high altar itself, the cardinal flung down the gauntlet: nothing less than the Roman pontiff's bull of excommunication levelled against Constantinople's patriarch. Cerularius's response was swift and to the point; a tit-for-tat excommunication of Pope Leo IX (1049-54).

Thus, in a dramatic and symbolic gesture, perhaps the inevitable outcome of Constantine's shift to the east some six hundred years previously, the final split had occurred: the consequence of the evolution of two traditions, the complex power struggles and shadow boxing, waged between Rome and Constantinople.

Constantinople, of course, had been an unashamedly Christian foundation from the outset, the proud advocate and defender of Orthodox doctrine. Its missionary exploits in Eastern Europe and Russia had borne considerable fruit. Byzantium's proximity to the holy places afforded it a kind of proprietorial sense of sanctity, ever the more acute since its co-patriarchates in Jerusalem, Antioch and Alexandria had been subsumed during the Moslem onslaught.

Its emperors, of wide-ranging diversity and quality, the successors of Emperor Constantine, notably Justinian and Basil (976-1025), enjoyed their presumed status as the church's earthly arbiter and guarantor.

Emperor and patriarch were not renowned for getting the harmonies right, let alone checking to see that they were singing from the same hymn sheet! Indeed, the Byzantine court could seldom have been regarded as a consistent model of divine inspiration; in fact, in relative terms, it would rival the social arrangements of the young Windsors as the embodiment of moral rectitude.

Further, internal doctrinal disputes effectively drove those of the Monophysite persuasion[168] within its ranks into ecclesiastical isolation, while the external threat posed by militant Islam had become a more serious endemic anxiety.

Rome's claim upon the world's spiritual focus, as we have seen, was based upon its traditional association with the last known movements of eminent apostles. The city itself could not assert a Christian basis for its foundation as could Constantinople; indeed, had not the great Constantine effectively deserted the conurbation, leaving it prey to unsolicited visitation by Visigoth, Norman and Saracen?

The papacy then tended to rely on its international standing as the supposed repository of Peter's relics and its largely misplaced dependence on the successors of Charlemagne to defend it. Such was the calibre of so many of the incumbents of the Roman see during this first millennium that they preferred to retreat behind a security fence indulging themselves periodically in the sins of the flesh behind closed doors. Nevertheless, with an authority in Rome with priestly/monarchical assumptions, its bishop could make out a case for a wider secular jurisdiction than that of the patriarch of Constantinople.

---

[168] The Monophysite or Coptic Tradition, which affirmed that Christ incarnate was in essence a *single* Divine Being. This counteracted Chalcedon's conclusion (451) that the person of Jesus is a seamless fusion of the human and divine. Largely prevalent in the Eastern Empire, the Monophysite churches sympathised with the iconoclastic position. After Theodora's concession to the iconodules (843), the Monophysites effectively detached themselves from their Byzantine roots. As it turned out, their prevalence in Egypt, Syria and Byzantine frontier areas were overwhelmed by the Moslem advance, yet remain as significant religious minorities in such regions down to the present.

The Church 69

Just occasionally did the pontiff emerge from his seclusion to assert his authority in the simmering dispute with Constantinople. Whenever he did so, it was destined to prove ironically detrimental to the universal calling of the church.

The coronation and recognition of Charlemagne as a rival western emperor in eight hundred had been scarcely calculated to reconcile such difficulties between east and west. Theological disputes, contrasting the Latin and Greek positions, theoretically resolved at Nicea and Chalcedon in particular, continued to be a running sore and tended to inflame passions already ignited over rival claims about political jurisdiction. Two such issues would suffice to identify the nature of the disputes responsible for the increased tension between the two traditions.

The first relates to the use of images (or icons)[169] as an aid to worship. Between 746 and 843, the battle lines were clearly drawn in what became known as the iconoclastic controversy. The Eastern emperor, Leo III (717-741), declared war on religious imagery in 726: a common, albeit inconsistent, strand in imperial policy for over one hundred years. Citing the second commandment,[170] he had concluded that icon worship contravened Old Testament law, demeaned the Divinity of Christ and represented a concession to pagan practice. Predictably Gregory II, the Roman Pontiff (715-731), had registered his strident objection to what he regarded as the emperor's unwarranted interference in religious matters, more especially as the decree provoked attacks of such violent dimensions as would do credit to Kristallnacht[171] on religious icons; the wholesale smashing of relics, the burning of religious vestments and the wanton desecration of any pictorial representation of the deity and His saints. Indeed, Iconoclasm (as this movement is known) went further; its radicalism extended to an attack on monasticism. Those under discipline—monks and nuns—went in fear for their lives. The church in the Eastern dispensation was being tested 'in extremis' with the Roman pontiff powerless to intervene. Ecumenical councils were indeed summoned periodically in an attempt to resolve the issue and

---

[169] Broadly speaking, an icon is a depiction of a holy personage—our Lord, perhaps Mary, or a significant saint of the church. These images constitute to this day, in the Eastern Orthodox tradition, a special vehicle to grace. The danger has always been that the icons represent the *end* of devotion, rather than an aid to it.

[170] Exodus 20:4-5.

[171] Kritallnacht: The night, in November 1938, when the Nazi faithful in Germany went on systematic rampage in the course of the destruction of Jewish property.

the balance between iconoclasts and their adversaries, the iconodules (supporters of images), swung both ways. Ultimately (and ironically) at the ecumenical council of Constantinople, in 843, the Eastern regent/ Empress Theodora finally restored the rite of iconography to the Eastern Church—the end of an ironic affair in so far as the icon has become synonymous with the Orthodox worship tradition; divisive in so far as the iconoclastic controversy had further exacerbated tensions between East and West.

The second bone of contention was a theological dispute, which spilt over into the realms of 'realpolitik'. The pretensions of the Eastern emperor to ecclesiastical authority were a constant thorn in the side of the Western papacy. At the height of the iconoclastic controversy in the eighth century, the Byzantine emperor had unilaterally realigned certain bishoprics in southern Italy and the Balkans from Roman oversight to that of the Constantinople Patriarchate, while the subsequent appointment by the emperor of one, Photius, a layman, as patriarch of Constantinople had not been recognised by Pope Nicholas I (858-867).

However, it was in Bulgaria that matters took a decided turn for the worse. Originally evangelised by missionaries from Byzantium, its king, Boris I (852-889), around 864, sought what he considered a better deal for 'his' church from Pope Nicholas in Rome over the head of Photius, concerning the appointment of a local bishop. This not only elicited a howl of protest from Byzantium by virtue of 'poaching' on an Eastern patch, but the theological approach adopted by the papal legates in Bulgaria excited doctrinal scandal. They were insisting that the controversial Latin 'filioque' clause form part of the official creed of the Bulgarian Church as the price of Rome's patronage.

To modern minds, this was but a subtle addition to the definitive Nicene Creed (325), but the latter's reaffirmation at the council of Constantinople in 381 was considered inviolable. Effectively the offending additional phrase explicitly recognised that the Holy Spirit proceeds from the father *and* the son (filioque) in equal measure and not from the father *through* the son, as Nicene purists would insist. Thus, in Byzantine eyes, the papists were adding insult to injury. A charge of heresy against the culpable pontiff, Nicholas, was sufficient to secure his deposition by the emperor in 867—a somewhat toothless gesture given Rome's own self-proclaimed independence.[172]

---

[172] John 16:13-15; Galatians 4:6; Romans 8:9; Philippians 1:19: cf. John:15:26. For the background to these events in the Balkans, a debt is owed to the article on p. 20 of Part III of the *Daily Telegraph, 2000 Years of Christianity.*

The Church 71

The dispute rumbled inexorably on. Further mutual charges of heretical doctrine and practice were levelled. Arguments concerning the precise dating of Easter, the use of unleavened bread during the Eucharist, the tonsure style of the monastic orders and the celibacy of the clergy all served to heighten the tension.

By the mid-eleventh century, then, relationships between the two main strands of the church were at breaking point. Vitriolic correspondence between the two bull-nosed patriarchs, Pope Leo IX and Bishop Michael Cerularius, reveals the intractability and the polarised position of each. By 1053, mutual tolerance of the practice of Latin and Greek rituals in their respective spheres was effectively abandoned.

Hence the diplomatic mission led by Cardinal Humbert—he of our defining moment—to Constantinople to iron out endemic disputes and the more precise future of the disputed sees in southern Italy merely emphasised the intensity of feeling[173] and any negotiation was relegated to a dialogue of the deaf. Humbert's precipitous action on that July day was in reality a formal recognition of the inevitable parting of the ways. By this time, 'East and West could not understand each other because they could not understand each other'—a legacy that has its repercussions far beyond religious parameters down to the present century.[174]

---

[173] For more details on these disputes, see Deanesly, M., *A History of the Medieval Church 590-1500*, Methuen, 1947.

[174] A caveat must be inserted here. During the Crusades (see chapter 9), Baldwin of Flanders was installed as Latin emperor of Constantinople, in consequence of the complexities of motives and internal politics prevalent at the time. Recognised by Pope Innocent III, this action merely served to further embitter relationships between East and West, and after 1261, when a Greek emperor was reinstalled, the Greek character of the East was formally restored, its spirit never having been seriously threatened. See ch. 9.

Chapter 8

Emperor Henry IV penitent before Pope Gregory at Carossa
by Carlo Emanuelle

THE AID AND CONSOLATION OF APOSTOLIC MERCY

Few scenes can evoke a more striking image of the compelling pulling power of the Medieval Church than the drama played out during February 1077. At a castle perched within the slopes of Italy's northern Apennine mountain range, on the fringes of the Po Valley, some fifteen miles equidistant from the modern, well-appointed towns of Parma and Reggio, a Holy Roman emperor figured prominently, albeit in the most unlikely of guises. Henry IV (1056-1106) stood outside the second of the three well-fortified walls of this citadel at Canossa, ill-clad, barefoot, ankle-deep in snow, hungry, penitential. His mission to seek that all-important absolution upon which his political and eternal fortunes depended from the one man who could grant it: from the Pope, who was temporally holed up within the castle's secure inner sanctum, in starkly contrasting circumstances—the house guest of the influential Matilda, Countess of Tuscany, dining sumptuously on portions of the region's smoked ham, his salads enriched by the local balsamic vinegar and a sprinkling of Parmesan. This was Hildebrand, Pope Gregory VII (1073-85), who for three days tantalisingly kept the supplicant waiting,

The Church   73

the headmaster making the errant pupil stew (or freeze in this instance) while the latter's case was being considered. The suspense was palpable. How much of the drama was merely play-acting on the part of the pontiff knowing that, at that moment, he had the emperor grovelling and he was determined to make a meal of it. How much of it represented a genuine dilemma to him is not entirely clear. Documentation is sketchy: the whole incident clouded by passion. We know that Matilda herself and the influential Abbot Hugh of Cluny,[175] also present, advised conciliation and a requited response. At some point, Gregory came to a decision. In his own words, Gregory certainly gives the impression that his sense of the sacramental obligations won through. In response to the entreaties of his hostess in respect of the emperor's many tears, and 'the aid and consolation of apostolic mercy . . . he . . . moved all who were present there . . . to such compassion that . . . we loosed the bond of excommunication and received him back into communion'.

Any immediate advantage accruing to Gregory from his act of magnanimity was short-lived; he did not survive, as we shall see, the miserable set of circumstances, which resulted from his letting Henry off the hook. Yet the backdrop to our defining moment was a vital sign of a church prepared to reassert itself following a considerable period of squalid turmoil, faction and subservience to temporality in Rome itself. Not only were Gregory's dealings with the emperor a sign of insidious strength, but his internal reforms of the church were a pointer to the pinnacle of pontifical fortunes with the advent of Pope Innocent III (1198-1216). Gregory's stand and resolute pursuit of a rededicated church were to set a standard by which Western Christendom during the High Medieval Period was to grow in confidence, expressed in a proliferation of monastic observance, a monumental building enterprise and intellectually characterised by scholastic rigour.

The symbiotic idealism, as some regarded it, exhibited in the coronation of Charlemagne back in eight hundred had barely survived his own mortality. Though the imperial concept remained, his inheritance in tangible terms had been squandered by feuding descendants, while Western Christendom was being subject to predation from all sides. During a large part of the ninth and tenth centuries, Moslems, Magyars, Vikings and even Byzantines were snapping at its heels. In 846, the Saracens had terrorised Rome, desecrating everything in sight, including

---

[175] On the special relationship between Gregory and Hugh of Cluny, see Cowdrey, H. E. J.: *The Cluniacs and the Gregorian Reform*, Oxford, 1970, and quoted in Brooke, C: *Medieval Church and Society*, Sidgwick and Jackson, 1971.

the alleged tomb of Peter himself. A demoralised church, despite localised pockets of genuine piety, had been, on the whole, unable to offer much guidance, bearing witness to its perennially expedient association with the politics of temporal power. Already, the realms of Charlemagne had been partitioned between three of his descendants, by the so-called Treaty of Verdun in 843. Thus was created the seeds of Franco-German enmity such as would bedevil Europe for centuries: the rise of the lands of the Eastern Franks (Germany) and the Western Franks (France) with the Middle Franks (Burgundy) sandwiched between the two and over which the two former entities were to bicker. All of this activity clearly demonstrated that the centre of imperial political gravity was north of the Alps, leaving the Pope and his entourage exposed to the whims and fancies of the city factions in Rome. The position of the occupant of the papal dignity had plummeted to new depths. Lurid stories of the goings-on abound. Among the more bizarre is the incumbency of Pope Stephen IV (896-897) who, with a score to settle, disinterred the corpse of a predecessor, physically placed it on trial, in the dock of a Church Tribunal, and sentenced the cadaver to be thrown into the Tiber. Within a year, Stephen himself was deposed and strangled in his prison cell. Another less than edifying incident was the reported death of another pontiff as a result of a cerebral malfunction during an amorous interaction with another man's wife.

Nevertheless, despite the scandal, the church and papacy miraculously continued to function, with its status and structure more or less intact. Rulers throughout Western Christendom still deferred to it, in awe if not of the papal personality, then of the office. This was due, in part, to the work of Pope Nicholas I (858-867), who had invoked the (spurious) Pseudo-Isidorian Decretals to justify the independence of bishops generally from political interference and by implication to assert the centralising direction of authority from the bishop of Rome: papal supremacy in other words.

This trenchant declaration of authoritarianism from Rome and the proclamation of episcopal independence from the secular state were in part a response to an application of the growing feudal principle of princely patronage north of the Alps. This had led to an increasing tendency of secular rulers taking the initiative in spiritual affairs by cherry-picking their own bishops and abbots with a less than scrupulous regard for their spiritual piety. By such means, the princes had the potential to control more easily the hearts, minds and prayers of their subjects, while at the same time securing the loyalty of the new prelates as a quid pro quo. Such a policy was exploited ruthlessly by the Saxon leader, Otto I (936-73), who coincidentally had severely curtailed the

The Church 75

endemic Magyar incursions at the decisive battle of Lechfeld in 955. Having thus established his credentials as a German champion and its 'de facto' king, he set his sights even higher: the resurrection of the flagging Carolingian imperial ideal, marching on Lombardy and on to Rome itself. With superior forces and organisation, he stamped his own authority upon the city by unceremoniously dispensing with the services of those ill-disposed to his grand design. In 962, he was crowned emperor by Pope John XII (955-964), in return for services rendered. Under such circumstances, the concept, if not the physical extent, of an empire ostensibly Christian (and therefore holy) was fuelled by a new largely Germanic oriented impetus. Again, however, its reality rested upon an uneasy papal/imperial understanding upon which each side—spiritual and temporal—would vie with each other for pre-eminence and supremacy. For the church, and its spiritual standing, it was not, in fact, such a good deal. In the early stages, it turned out, perhaps inevitably, that it was to be the emperor who pulled the papal strings and called the shots: deposing and imposing the bishops of Rome at will. Otto's successor, Otto II (973-83) proclaimed himself Roman emperor—the incarnation of the *renovatio imperii Romanum*; under both Saxon and subsequent Salian auspices, succeeding emperors were to parade as the 'de facto', if not 'de jure' heads of the church in the West.

Things, however, were about to change. In 1056, the strong-minded, and relatively well-meaning emperor, Henry III (1039-56) had died, leaving a young minor, Henry IV (1056-1106), as his successor. This gave the papacy its chance to strike back. The initiative was seized by the Cluniac pope, Leo IX (1049-56), who publicly declared his own ex officio ultramontane authority: universal recognition of spiritual prerogatives and brooking no interference from temporal rulers over matters of spiritual import. The real dynamo behind such an unambivalent thrust was the Tuscan divine, Hildebrand. Hildebrand recognised that, at long last, the opportunity for a transnational Christian entity, at least in the West, overseen by a bishop of Rome with infallible and omnipotent aspirations, was within his grasp. In 1059, he successfully wrested control of the election of any succeeding pope from the aristocratic patronage of civilian Rome, to the College of Cardinals—a distinct body of the hierarchical church. He himself was subsequently elected as Pope Gregory VII in 1073, upon which he duly decreed that the designation 'pope' be the exclusive prerogative of the bishop of Rome. A strengthened and reformed church was his guiding spirit and in this he was to become embroiled with a, by now, mature Emperor Henry IV, and thus to the occasion of our defining moment.

As far as the church was concerned, Gregory's pontificate was a watershed in similar vein to that of his predecessor, Gregory I, four centuries earlier:[176] a pointer to the apogee of the fortunes of the papacy such as it was to enjoy in the twelfth century. Gregory was a man who was to take his role seriously and who would spare no effort in the reform and renewal of the church. To do this, he had to continue to wrest the substance of his authority away from secular interests in Rome and abroad into which his office until recently had fallen by default. This would inevitably result in a trial of strength with the emperor. Henry IV was equally determined to defend his own corner.

As pope, Gregory was determined to stamp out the abuses that had so tarnished the name of the church during its darkest years. With a view to preventing the priesthood from falling into the hands of a hereditary caste, with an independent will and power structure of its own, he clarified the position on clerical celibacy. It was to be total and it was to be binding. It had been a grey area before, although the implication had been that marital union and active sexuality were to be eschewed by the ordained ministry, certainly since the council of Nicaea had aired the issue in 325.[177] Yet while the former had, more or less, been observed, the widespread incidence of concubinage (Nicolaitism) suggests a palpable disregard for the latter. Gregory's decree at least clarified the situation while at the same time establishing an authoritative standard

---

[176] See chapter 5.

[177] Clerical celibacy, a contentious issue then, as now; at the Nicene Council, a proposal to compel all clergy to abandon cohabitation with their wives was defeated, although decretals emanating from Popes Siricius (386) and Innocent I (402-417) ordered celibacy for those already ordained. However, it has never been easy to reconcile total sexual abstinence with a priest's humanity to which well-documented case studies testify: from the problem of concubinage, particularly rife in the tenth century, which is what concerned Pope Gregory, through to the criticism of a licentious papacy of the fourteenth and fifteenth centuries and to the paedophilia scandals of the twentieth. The Catholic stand on celibate clergy, which was resolved within the Anglican Communion when it broke with Rome in the sixteenth century, and by most other Protestant denominations, continues to be a burning issue in various Catholic quarters, whereby fewer and fewer candidates are responding to the Catholic priestly vocation. This has left increasing numbers of parishes dependent more and more upon fewer (and older) priests. After Nicaea, in the Eastern (Orthodox) Church, priests and deacons could marry *before* ordination, but not afterwards, although bishops must remain celibate.

The Church

for the working priesthood. While this could be regarded as an internal church matter, other measures most assuredly were not. He launched a full-scale attack on the practice of simony (the wholesale buying and selling of ecclesiastical preferment for cash), linked to which was the key issue of lay investiture. It was this that was to bring matters to a head. Lay investiture was the process already alluded to whereby lay rulers appointed 'churchmen' to fulfil roles in the temporal state so as to utilise their literary skills, their learning and increasingly their contribution as bishops having temporal and spiritual jurisdiction as well as the military potential at their disposal within the context of the feudal system. Thus, the secular prince, as paymaster, had been calling the tune. For Gregory, simony was bad enough, but the actual investiture of church prelates by lay rulers was a bit much—an affront to the memory of St Peter to which he was personally devoted. Accordingly, the Pope in 1075 issued his strongest set of propositions yet. These were contained in the *Dictatus Papae*, which set out very clearly the direction from which he was coming and how he proposed to proceed. In this document, Gregory asserted the absolute supremacy of the bishop of Rome in terms of doctrine; a restatement of Augustine's position that the church is the exclusive vehicle by which personal salvation is to be secured and its inerrancy in spiritual matters. Significantly he proclaimed the unique right of the papacy to appoint bishops—no real notional problem with that, but also to depose emperors and to absolve their subjects from allegiance to any overlord with whom the church disagreed. None of this was exactly new, but the strident and lucid tone of its presentation undoubtedly was.

At a synod in Rome during 1075, the formal outlawing of lay investiture was decreed; a direct challenge to the emperor, who had already blatantly interfered in the appointment to the prestigious archbishopric of Milan[178] and who took umbrage when his protesting legates at the synod were unceremoniously excommunicated. During a synod the following year, Henry expressed his displeasure in the most forcible of terms. Claiming his own appointment to the illustrious imperial office to have been the result of God's direct initiative, he declared Gregory deposed and replaced him by a nominee of his own, Clement III. The synod responded by excommunicating Henry and his subjects placed under anathema. This was crunch time: who would buckle first?

---

[178] Prestigious, in so far as it had been the see of the legendary Ambrose (374-392) a doctor of the Catholic Church: see chapter 3 and later that of Borromeo (1560-84), the great Catholic reformation prelate: see chapter 14.

Henry's own political position was far from secure. Already under pressure from certain of his troublesome Saxon noblemen, a pan-German council, mindful of the terrible consequences of the Pope's anathema could inflict upon them, sought an urgent end to the crisis. An invitation was to be issued to Gregory to attend a meeting of the German magnates at Augsburg to negotiate having the sentence lifted by the 'real' pope and suitable concessions made in exchange. Henry was given one year by his fellow Germans to get the problem sorted; failing that they would depose him. A desperate Henry couldn't wait. Realising he had overstepped the mark, he took matters into his own hands, crossed the Alps, wife and child in tow, prepared to throw himself wherever and however at Gregory's mercy. The Pope and entourage, meanwhile had responded to the Germans' call for a diplomatic solution and were en route northward, near Reggio, when they learned of Henry's advance south. Initially alarmed and unsure of Henry's intentions, Gregory found refuge in the castle at Canossa—which is where we came in. As we have seen, Henry ate humble pie and Gregory graciously granted absolution; the papacy supreme! Yet mutual suspicion, not unnaturally, remained. The immediate crisis resolved and its pressure relieved, further mutual excommunications and depositions followed, until in 1084 Henry, his own patience exhausted, resorted once again to head for Rome, but this time with malicious intent. Subjecting Rome first to siege and then to pillage (again), Henry (again) deposed Gregory in favour of Clement. Holed up in his stronghold of Castel de San Angelo, Gregory witnessed from a distance, amidst the spoliation of his city, the formal coronation of Henry as emperor by the usurper Clement. Rescued from the ultimate humiliation by his friend Guiscard, duke of Calabria and a band of—all right—Saracen mercenaries, Gregory was never forgiven by the Roman citizenry for the misfortunes for which they felt him responsible. He was to die the following year, in exile in Salerno because, as he contended, 'I have loved justice and hated iniquity'. A sad end really to a man with a true sense of spiritual purpose, who for his era had a clear sense of his calling, but who lacked the diplomatic skills the complex times called for to give to his principles substance.

Nevertheless, Gregory's dream did not die with him. His action at Canossa inspired his successors to exploit the spiritual armoury that Gregory had used to great effect on that occasion of dramatic import. Pope Urban II (1088-99) was sufficiently inspired to issue canons to give strength to the stand taken by Gregory on the crucial issues of simony, clerical marriage and lay investiture, as well as proclaiming the First Crusade. Pope Calixtus II (1119-24) and Emperor Henry V (1106-25) managed to cobble together the Concordat of Worms (1122),

The Church 79

a compromise over the lay investiture squabble, whereby the latter consented to the papal right to *invest* church bishops and abbots with their spiritual prerogatives, provided the emperor or his delegate be present, whenever possible, at the crucial selection process and that church officials pledge appropriate allegiance to the respective temporal power.

Despite an interlude when the Hohenstaufen[179] Emperor Frederick I (Barbarossa) (1152-90), of crusade fame, attempted to reinstate imperial claims in Italy, the period of the so-called High Middle Ages, and arguably using Canossa as its symbolic starting point, witnessed the great flowering of the Catholic Church down to the close of the thirteenth century.

In terms of ideas, it was the classic age of dogma and scholasticism. A by-product of the Arabic incursions into Europe in the eighth century and of the crusades throughout the eleventh to the fourteenth centuries, was an increasing awareness not only of Arabic scholarship, but also a revival of the Greek contribution to philosophy and science. This led to the genuine attempt by churchmen of outstanding intellectual capacity to make sense of their inherited faith and its traditions, and upon which so much subsequent Catholic apologia has depended. One calls to mind the great influence of the Lombardian cleric, Anselm (1033-1109), and subsequently archbishop of Canterbury, whose popularisation of the cult of 'Mary, Ever Virgin' as the 'Mother of God' was a concept stridently proclaimed by Bernard of Clairvaux (1090-1153), reinforcing her role as a valid mediatrix between humanity and the Creator; an approach dear to the hearts of so many Catholics down to the present. It was Anselm who postulated the ontological premise that God's very existence is a necessity: a compelling 'a priori' metaphysical argument on the incontrovertible proof of the Supreme Being.[180] This thesis has had of course its detractors, but its sheer cutting force cannot be denied. There was the colourful lecturer, some would say maverick, Peter Abelard (1079-1142), in Paris, who was a pioneer of biblical criticism by seeking to make sense of apparently contradictory passages in scripture

---

[179] The German monarchy, and by extension, the office of Holy Roman emperor, was *elective*, not hereditary. It was to pass from the Carolingian 'dynasty' (800-918) through the Saxon dynasties (918-1024), the dynasty of the Salians (1024-1137), the Hohenstauffens (1138-1437) to the Habsburgs who dominated the position from 1438 until its demise in 1806.

[180] The argument runs thus that if God, who is by definition all powerful, all knowing, all loving—in short, all perfect—exists *only* in the mind, then He ceases to exhibit His total Being. Only in *reality* can perfection be obtained; therefore, He must exist.

in a treatise 'Sic et Non' ('yes and no'). A student of Albertus Magnus, the leading scholar in the West, Thomas Aquinas (1225-74), an Italian Dominican lecturer, and perhaps the sheer embodiment of Medieval Classicism at its height attempted to fuse the Aristotelian rationale of a universal first cause for existence (the 'prime unmoved mover') with the Christian God of faith and revelation, making thereby strong cosmological and intellectual claims for Christianity. By reintroducing Aristotle into Western thinking, Aquinas was making great claims for the human senses in one's effort to 'prove' God's existence in his celebrated 'five ways', including the moral imperative, which suggests that 'good' choices are ultimately derivative of the Supreme Author[181] of 'Goodness'; what is 'natural' as God ordained must be the guide to moral choice: the 'natural law theory'. Mention also should be made of Gratian (died c.1179), who by meticulous research into the papal archives engaged in building up a systematic compilation of historic decrees, treatises and pronouncements of the church in his 'decretum'—the genesis of canon law.[182] Duns Scotus (c.1264-1308), while at one with Aquinas in so far as divine revelation may be reconciled with reason, he was to take issue with him on the supremacy of the mind in our apprehension of the Godhead; Scotus placed greater emphasis upon the initiative of God's will and the emotive power of love. William of Occam (c.1300-49) went further, insisting that things are good because God wills them. Controversially, Occam advocated a 'constitutional papacy'; which was to have great influence upon the later Conciliar Movement and in respect of Henry VIII's break with Rome.

Theology and law were the inspiration for the first true universities in Europe at this time: Bologna founded around 1088 with its offshoot at Padua: Paris, dating from around 1150, and Oxford, 1167, with its breakaway foundation at Cambridge shortly afterwards. Each was symptomatic of a catholic, universal spirit as exhibited by a regenerated papacy and extending its dynamic into other disciplines. The ideas were fertilised by a transnational fluidity of scholars and the increasing popularity of the shrines of pilgrimage—to Compostela the alleged repository of the remains of James the Apostle; to Canterbury after the murder of Thomas a Beckett in 1170 and others.

It was the great age of the evolution of church building—from the stolid, sometimes ponderous barrel-vaulted Romanesque style such as to be seen at the Church of St Sernin in Toulouse to the refined Gothic

---

[181] Aquinas, T.: *Summa Theologica.*

[182] Canon law is the authoritative legislation of the Catholic Church on issues relating to discipline, faith and works.

The Church 81

elegance of the soaring dimensions of the thirteenth-century Cathedral at Amiens, typical with its slender columns, pointed arches, each supportive of its symmetrical rib-vaulted ceiling to the delicate lines of St Chapelle in Paris, its slim-stained, glass-like arrows, drawing the eye heavenwards: all height and light, in their creation to capture the numinous, the sheer multi-dimensioned expansiveness of God.

This was the era of the establishment of the great monastic institutions of Western Europe, as described elsewhere—the ruins of the great abbey churches, notably the Cistercian establishments in England at Rievaulx, and Fountains, North Yorkshire (c.1150) and the French Cluniac Church in Burgundy, dedicated by Pope Innocent in 1132. Each bears testimony not only to the piety of their founding fathers but also to the immense wealth and status with which such institutions became associated.

The true heir to the spirit of Gregory VII, however—the reincarnation of his noble objectives—was Pope Innocent III (1198-1216), who came closer than anyone before or since to establishing a theocratic society in Western Europe, based on Roman Catholic traditions and structures. As bishop of Rome, pope and pontiff, he saw himself as (just) a little lower than the angels,[183] but (certainly) a resident in the penthouse suite relative to other mortals and that included crowned princes. 'No king', Innocent declared, with scant concession to modesty, 'can reign rightly unless he devoutly serves Christ's vicar'. *The Oxford Dictionary of the Christian Church*[184] has Innocent seeing himself as Melchizidek—the priestly king, destined to institute the centralised Christian society.[185] Certainly he was prepared to put any temporal authority figure in his place with disarming imagery in his 1198 publication, *Sicut Universitatis Conditor.* Innocent declaimed that 'the moon derives her light from the sun, and is in truth inferior to the sun in both dignity (as are princes) from the pontifical authority'.

Thus, in 1209, Otto IV (1198-1218) was crowned emperor, having been summoned to Rome for the occasion. Here, Pope Innocent, seated at the high altar of St John Lateran, flanked by Italian and German bishops had demanded Otto's uncompromising obedience and obeisance as the price to be paid for the coronation.

---

[183]   Psalm 8:5.

[184]   Cross, F. L. (ed.): *The Oxford Dictionary of the Christian Church*, O.U.P., 1963.

[185]   The reference is to Genesis 14:18. Melchizidek was a mysterious figure, the 'king of Salem', who offered bread and wine to Abram following the latter's victory over certain other kings. Melchizidek's name has found its way into the Catholic mass, where his priestly offering has its analogy in the re-enactment by the clergy of Christ's own sacrifice.

82 The Aid and Consolation of Apostolic Mercy

Thus Innocent was not afraid to take on anyone. He was quite prepared to play the part of John the Baptist[186] by placing the French realm under interdict as punishment for King Philip Augustus's (1180-1223) adulterous relationship. Innocent fared somewhat better than his biblical mentor: he kept his head and Philip returned to his orthodox matrimonial duties. It was Innocent's celebrated spat with England's King John (1199-1216) that serves to further highlight the point. Although Innocent had consecrated Stephen Langton to the see of Canterbury back in 1207, John had refused to accept the nomination, had confiscated church lands and this had resulted in his own excommunication, as well as an imposed papal interdict over the kingdom. This was Canossa revisited, albeit without the dramatic histrionics. Like the German magnates of Henry IV's time, the English barons, and the church, feared the visitation of the vicarious wrath of God upon them: pressure on the king and he caves in. Restitution of king and realm follow at the price of the sovereign swearing allegiance to the Pope as his feudal overlord. The obeisance made at the tomb of Becket by John's father, Henry II (1154-89), in 1170 was within living memory; such a turnaround in the balance of the power exerted by a measured application of judicious spiritual blackmail!

Innocent was also concerned with regularising church doctrine and practice, and for this purpose called together the Fourth Lateran Council in 1215 comprising as it did a huge presence of bishops and lay rulers. The decisions taken here were, in Catholic minds, to hold good for centuries and which in many ways were to characterise the Catholic slant on Christianity. 'Only through the single organic unit of the church of Rome could salvation be attained', declared the council, confirming Gregory VII's *Dictatus Papae* of 1075, a dogma reinforced later by the Bull *Unam Sanctam* by Pope Boniface VIII (1294-1303) in 1302. As such, the fundamental importance of the seven sacraments were upheld at the council and drew upon the work of Peter Lombard (1100-60) who defined them as the 'outward signs of inward grace', having been 'instituted by Christ'. This last observation was always going to be a problem and was to become a major bone of contention with the Protestant reformers of the sixteenth century and beyond. Of the seven sacraments acknowledged at the council—baptism, confirmation, ordination, the Eucharist, marriage, penance and extreme unction—only two, really, have found universal scriptural acceptance: baptism and the Eucharist. Even with reference to these two, different interpretations have proved divisive. At the council, infant baptism was validated, while the priestly capacity to celebrate mass

---

[186] Mark 4:14-29.

The Church 83

by changing the 'substances' but not the 'accidents' of wine and bread into Christ's actual blood, and body—transubstantiation—was strictly upheld, initially by faith and subsequently by the Aristotelian precepts of Aquinas. Both premises were to be contested by reference to scripture and were to become significant issues over which intra-Christian acrimony was to ensue. Less controversially, a rigorous inspection of the ordained priesthood was to be instituted and (again) celibacy among the ordained was to be respected. Schools for the wealthy and the deserving poor were to be established and the practice of judicial ordeal outlawed. In order to secure tighter control of monastic practice, a measure to co-ordinate aims and procedure was established. Emboldened no doubt by his diplomatic success in both England and France, Innocent pressed through a resolution whereby church courts were to be respected by the laity and their decisions respected. On a far less endearing note, Jews were to be identified in public by their enforced wearing of appropriate insignia, while the ghettoisation of this increasingly marginalised community was to be encouraged.

While our dramatic defining moment at Canossa did not set in motion an immediate revival of church fortunes at a dark phase of its history, its perhaps exaggerated iconography served as inspiration for future champions of the church during which were to become the High Middle Ages. As such, therefore, it served as a model for Innocent III, and for the effective control exerted by him, even though he himself was only able to assume his powers, in reality, by virtue of political circumstances.[187] Later, Pope Boniface VIII (1294-1303) attempted to reinvigorate and enhance papal temporal and spiritual pretensions by proclaiming himself not simply as vicar of St Peter, but as the vicar of Christ Himself. Hence, the entire period between the eleventh and thirteenth centuries was, in the final analysis, bound up with power politics, diplomacy and warfare. The tension between the spiritual aspirations of the church and the temporal assertions of the secular rulers was sustained only with endemic unease. The grey area of the parameters between which each was to operate was always going to create dissension. Political realities on the ground so frequently determined who, at that moment, controlled the ship. By taking advantage of imperial weakness, coincidental to his own very determined outlook, Innocent was indeed in a position to preside over a Western Church that rejoiced in its confidence: its

---

[187] On the death of Emperor Henry VI (1190-97) in 1197, Innocent, shortly to be elected pope himself, was cast in the role as arbitrator between two rival claimants: hence the encouragement to press home the advantage on the issue of the papal 'imprimatur' upon the person elected.

burgeoning monastic dimension, its expression in terms of its building programme, its wealth and a clear doctrinal definition of what it stood for. In a superstitious age, which blurred the distinction between true Christian observance and pagan ritual, perhaps it is not surprising that the church commanded the hold that it did—out of all proportion to its worldly battalions or lack of them. In his attempts to reduce the impact of imperial influence over the church, one must deem Innocent successful, but by so doing, he was to enhance the standing of other national monarchies. Full advantage of this was to be taken by the French during the course of the ensuing century in which their monarchy in turn was to pocket the papacy. By insisting upon a rigid form of doctrinal dogma and incorporating church tradition, some of which was arguably spurious, into canon law, ammunition was being stored up for use by the later Protestant reformers and the ultimate breakdown in the unity of the Western Church. Gregory at Canossa had, however, rescued the church from total moral meltdown. It did provide the starting point and blueprint for its ultimate survival.

Chapter 9

Statue of Pope Urban II, Clermont-Ferrand

GOD WILLS IT

The schism between the Roman Church in the West and the Byzantine Church of the East during the course of the year 1054, from the vantage point of historical insight, represented the decisive breach. Yet in the minds of the contemporary big-time players, the coalescence of conditions and ambitions could yet rekindle ecumenical opportunities.

Our defining moment transports us in November 1095 to the Auvergne: that area of the sparsely populated, sprawling Massif Central in France, rejoicing in its fertile valleys, verdant pastures, mountains venerable and mysterious in their volcanic time-honoured spectacle, and to Clermont, its major city. Enveloped on three sides by hills, this concession to civilisation, supporting a bishop and two large monasteries, represented an ecclesiastical centre of considerable importance.

Addressing a formal church council comprising priests, knights and commoners assembled on the hillside just outside the protective stone walls of the metropolis, Pope Urban II (1088-99) unleashed a clarion call to action and to arms. Resplendently from his majestic dais, the pontiff was unambiguous in both tone and content: declining standards in church and monastic observance must be reversed, as decreed by his predecessor and mentor, the legendary Hildebrand, Pope Gregory VII

(1073-85). In an electrifying performance measured only by the response, and in the absence of a verifiable verbatim account, Urban then went on to the offensive. He appealed to knightly sentiment by exhorting the mobilisation of the chivalrous virtues of honour and Christian duty in a concerted campaign to be waged on his perception of international piracy, as he saw it. Nothing less than a 'war on terror' would do. Its objective, the humiliation and disarmament of the perceived perpetrators, the recently Islamicised Seljuk Turks,[188] the despoilers of the pilgrimage[189] routes to the Holy Land, the recent usurpers of the Holy City, Jerusalem, and the occupiers of the site of the Most Holy Sepulchre, it having been in relatively tolerant Moslem hands since the Byzantines had surrendered it in 636. In chilling words, 'that accursed race . . . utterly alienated from God', Urban urged the assembled company to appease its Christian conscience and in the name of the Frankish people 'to kill these Godless monsters and to exterminate this vile race from our lands'.

Thus 'la Cruzada' (marked with the cross)—the crusade—was officially launched: that symbol of a cynical, perverse religious fanaticism whose resonance has so frustrated the cause of Christ and human well-being both before and since.

At a stroke, Urban was seeking to reinforce papal (and sacred) authority over the imperial (and secular) pretensions, which had climaxed in such dramatic fashion during the investiture crisis involving Pope Gregory VII and Emperor Henry IV at Canossa in 1077.[190] Moreover, here was a golden opportunity to reassert Roman control over Byzantium, whose hapless Emperor Alexius I Comnenus (1081-1118)

---

[188] Originally a marauding people from the East, who had embraced Islam. Their guardianship over Jerusalem, however, was short-lived and passed to the Moslem Fatimid dynasty based in Egypt. Another branch of the Turkish people, the Ottomans, appeared on the fringes of Europe and whose influence on the continent was to be significant for centuries and who finally took Constantinople in 1453. See chapter 11.

[189] The idea of the pilgrimage to a Holy Site is common to many faiths. For Christians, it has been variously regarded as bestowing grace upon the pilgrim, spiritual and physical; or as a specific act of penance. Jerusalem, of course, having such intimate association with Christ, has been a prime place of pilgrimage and its accessibility of enduring sensitivity.

[190] The climax of the struggle for supremacy between pope and emperor: at Canossa, the emperor reportedly stood for three days in the snow, outside the Pope's temporary residence, before his excommunication could be rescinded. See chapter 8.

The Church 87

had conveniently appealed to Pope Urban in the name of Christendom for assistance in the defence of his Eastern realms in Asia Minor, lying exposed and vulnerable in the face of the 'marauding Islamic Turkish infidel'.

The implications of this invitation were not lost on Urban, whose vision of a reunited Latinised church danced seductively before his eyes if he played his cards right.[191] After all, the church in the West was already driving Saracens from Spain and Italy; Magyar and Viking invaders were being won for Christianity. His tail was up. The more he thought about it, the more expansive the vista before him: here was an opportunity to harness positively the pent-up energies of younger sons of the nobility otherwise frustrated by feudal constraints on their ever-decreasing share of the land, to re-engage with Byzantium from a position of strength and to secure lucrative trading arrangements for Mediterranean coastal cities such as Venice, Genoa and Pisa. The ultimate reward, of course, would be a restored Christianised Jerusalem, the Holy City, romanised, the symbol of millennial aspirations and the church of the Holy Sepulchre appropriately reconsecrated.[192]

The tone and content of the promises made by the Pope on that November day in Clermont was dynamite. The assembled bishops, duly edified, dispersed to their sees galvanised by a melange of Pentecostal vibrance, political spin and World Cup hype, their task to enlist the support of the populace in the crusading cause.

To the poor, on offer was the opportunity to secure the chance of escape from serfdom and dire poverty; to the pious, the opportunity of salvation through an act of penance and indulgence and to the nobility and merchant classes, a share in the prospective material gains. 'God wills it' was the unanimous acclamation of those assembled on that Clermont hillside in response to Urban's appeal. Herein lies their justification for the launch of the First Crusade.

The First Crusade (there were to be several over the ensuing centuries) launched in 1096 was itself a somewhat disparate affair, albeit essentially Frankish, and as it turned out the most successful one. On the one hand, it represented a roll of honour of the great and the

---

[191] See chapter 7.

[192] The political argument for the initiation of the crusades is strongly argued in Asbridge, T.: *The First Crusade*, Simon and Schuster, 2004. However, Cowdrey, H. E. J., in *The Crudades: The Essential Readings*, Madden T. (ed.), emphasises Urban's recovery of Jerusalem and the Holy Land project as the prime focus of his appeal.

good: there was Adhemar de Monteil, the eyes and ears of the Pope, who accompanied Raymond, (count of Toulouse), Robert, count of Flanders and the duke of Normandy, kinsmen to King William Rufus of England (1087-1100), Godfrey of Bouillon with his brother Baldwin and Bohemund of Apulia—each having at his disposal substantial forces. At the other end of the spectrum was the 'People's Crusade', recruited and motivated by the mysterious barefoot horseman, Peter the Hermit (c.1050-1115)—a diverse collection of folk largely of peasant stock, mindful perhaps of Christ's injunction to discipleship that they may leave houses, fields or family[193] in return for a hundred-fold payback—to be given eternal life—thus induced by the prospect of adventure, freedom and a 'collective act of penance'.

The first group to arrive in Constantinople was this undisciplined accretion of self-professed high-minded humanity. Having already demonstrated its crusading credentials by massacring Jews along its route through Europe,[194] it hardly served to inspire Emperor Alexius with a great deal of confidence. We are led to believe, in fact, that he wasted little time in facilitating the passage of this band of New Age travellers across the straits to seek out its Glastonbury. The 'People's Crusade', moreover, fell far short of its high expectations, by meeting a vainglorious nemesis at the hands of the Turks barely weeks out of Constantinople.[195]

It was the force under Godfrey of Bouillon and Raymond, which was to reap the anticipated reward. Nicea was captured in 1097, whence the crusaders traversed Asia Minor and finally fought their way into Palestine itself. The Armenian city of Edessa was to acknowledge Crusader tutelage under Baldwin and in 1098 Antioch succumbed to the cross. In the same year, following an impressive siege, Godfrey took Jerusalem by storm, celebrating his feat by organising a wholesale massacre of its Islamic

---

[193] Luke 14:26, 33.

[194] Hindley, G., in *A Brief History of the Crusades*, Constable and Robinson Ltd, 2004, goes so far as to suggest that in response to Urban's appeal, the crusade should 'start at home, so to speak, with war on local Jewish communities', while Albert of Aix, the contemporary chronicler, tells of the crusaders as quoted by Read, P. P. in *The Templars*, Phoenix Press, 1999, ' . . . having broken the locks and knocked in the doors . . . seized and killed seven hundred . . . and the young children, whatever their sex, were put to the sword'.

[195] Peter the Hermit, in fact, escaped death on this occasion and joined Bouillon's main army, entering Jerusalem with him in triumph. Peter ultimately returned to Europe as an Augustinian prior.

The Church   89

defenders. Any pretence by this time that the crusaders were in the service of Byzantium was patently disavowed. Godfrey was proclaimed Latin governor of Jerusalem, modestly declining the crown of gold in deference to the recognition of 'his Saviour's Crown of Thorns' in 1100.[196] His tenure, however, was short-lived—a matter of months in reality—for he died within weeks of Pope Urban II, his official sponsor.

The Latin kingdom of Jerusalem was officially proclaimed, with Baldwin, seconded from Edessa, prepared to accept the crown so coyly abjured by his brother.

The Holy Sepulchre and the Holy Places were once again open to unfettered Christian access, paving the way for the soon-to-be-created knights of chivalry, the hospitallers, Templars and Teutons[197] to present themselves purportedly as defenders of the new order. By 1130, the Roman Church was able to flaunt its triumphs throughout Asia Minor and Palestine; Byzantium had been sidelined, its plans hijacked; Catholicism was supreme in pockets of the Holy Land, but it was not to last.

Far from their lands of origin, the position of the Frankish crusading occupiers of the Holy Land was always going to be at best tenuous. News that Edessa had been recaptured by a Moslem force in 1144 inspired Bernard of Clairvaux[198]—sanctimonious, zealous, mystical and possibly Masonic—to respond to the Pope's call for action by proclaiming at Vezelay the Second Crusade in 1147 to retake the lost city. Rivalry between its two principal leaders, Louis VII of France (1137-80) and Conrad III of the German lands (1138-52), ensured its conspicuous failure in 1149.

---

[196] According to Baigent, M., Leigh, R. and Lincoln, H. in *The Holy Blood and the Holy Grail*, Arrow, 1996, Godfrey may well have seen himself as a descendant of a very significant bloodline indeed and the reclaiming of Jerusalem of far-reaching symbolic consequence.

[197] Originally organised to provide help, sustenance and protection for pilgrims in the Holy Land. Over time, their functions mutated. The Templars became very wealthy in their own right, being suppressed by Pope Clement V in 1312 for allegedly abusing their quasi-monastic and knightly status. The hospitallers (knights of St John) still exist, having enjoyed mixed political and economic fortunes down the centuries. The Teutonic Knights, founded later, ultimately became influential, politically and economically in Northern Germany; they are still extant, working their charity principally in schools and hospitals.

[198] The allegedly sinister motives behind Bernard's proclamation are dealt with into fascinating studies by Knight, C. and Lomas, R., *The Second Messiah*, Century, 1997.

By far, the most spectacular catastrophe from the Christian perspective, however, was the recapture of Jerusalem in 1187 by the legendary Saladin, sultan of Egypt (1169-93) and scourge of the crusaders. A considerable band of territory in the Middle East was now under his authority: for the hospitallers (knights of St John) and the Templars, a blow to power and pride, although significantly not to their material wealth.

This humiliation revealed the resilience of Islam, not only to survive but also to bounce back—a recurrent theme. Whatever be the case, the divisions within Christianity itself, the exposed nature of the Latin kingdom, and the lack of a cohesive leadership laid bare the vulnerability of the church in the Middle East.

The Third Crusade (1188-92) revealed these weaknesses all too vividly. On paper, its leadership was impressive: the Holy Roman emperor, Frederick I (Barbarossa) (1152-90), Philip II of France (1180-1223) and Richard I (Lionheart) of England (1189-99). Initially successful, the crusading forces gave Saladin a bloody nose at Arsuf in 1191, recapturing the coastal strip around Acre, which henceforth served as the nerve centre of the remaining Frankish possessions in the Levant.

Nonetheless, Jerusalem remained defiantly in Islamic hands. Frederick had, in any case, drowned en route; Philip quickly hauled tail back to Europe to take advantage there of Richard's preoccupation in Palestine, leaving him to make the best terms he could with Saladin, while England was effectively abandoned to the mercy of his treacherous brother and successor, John (1199-1216).

The next ten years were to reveal the depths to which the entire squalid crusading enterprise had sunk. The Fourth Crusade, proclaimed in 1202, ostensibly aimed at emasculating the Islamic powerhouse concentrated in Egypt, must be seen more realistically as a tool of Venetian mercenary opportunism. Beholden to Venice for ships, the crusading armies dropped anchor at Constantinople in 1204; taking advantage of one of the city's endemic constitutional crises, they took the city by storm, looted its fabled wealth, installing a Latin emperor and Roman patriarch. Not Jerusalem, perhaps but here was a part fulfilment of Urban II's dream, an act conspicuously lacking in Christian charity. Valuable land was parcelled out to the Venetian and Frankish nobility, while the Greek Orthodox remnant salvaged what it could, setting up shop across the Bosphorus at Nicea in Asia Minor.

This Latin kingdom of Constantinople was to prove both ineffectual and ephemeral, for in 1261, an enfeebled client emperor surrendered to Greek forces and another ill-fated crusading experiment bit the

The Church 91

dust. Such an episode hardly inspired an ecumenical spirit let alone a reinvigoration of the church in the Holy Land.

It didn't seem as if it could get worse, but it did! The so-called Children's Crusade of 1212, hailed by the ironically named Pope Innocent III as a brand of heroism and overlaid with romantic licence, would do more credit to King Herod[199] than to the Church of Christ. While not officially endorsing the enterprise, his professed reticence carried little conviction.

Bands of children were evidently recruited from much of Western Europe, with the objective of 'recapturing Jerusalem', armed only with that innocence, which belongs to a child and the deluded vision of leaders barely, if at all, older than themselves, with tragic results matched only by their futility. Contemporary chronicles record that scores and scores of children who seriously believed that the waves would part for them to cross the sea died even before leaving their homeland; many more succumbed as easy pickings for gangs of robbers who waylaid them en route, while others ended up in the hands of 'Christian' slave traders and were sold to Arab merchants: the closest these victims of 'the Pied Piper'[200] came to tackling the infidel in Jerusalem.

From hereinon, the crusading spirit, such as it was, waxed and waned. Several further expeditions were indeed mounted throughout the thirteenth century although one hesitates to call them crusades—especially when the Holy Roman emperor and king of the hybrid state of Sicily,[201] Frederick II (1198-1250), actually negotiated the return to Christian rule of Jerusalem, Bethlehem and Nazareth, with himself as king in 1229. Paradoxically, he was excommuniated by the Pope at the time, so he could scarcely be seen as acting in the name of the church! Albeit, the Holy Places reverted to Moslem control in 1244.

Other crusading sorties led by King (St) Louis of France (1226-70) were launched in North Africa, where he died of plague at Tunis in 1270, but by the end of the thirteenth century, it was clear that Urban II's vision was effectively over. The final crusader stronghold at Acre finally fell in

---

[199] See Matthew 2:16-18: The massacre of the Holy Innocents by Herod. Apparently, it was felt that where corrupted adults had failed to retake Jerusalem, children untainted by sin would succeed.

[200] The legend of the *Pied Piper of Hamelin* is said to have been inspired by the Children's Crusade.

[201] Sicily, where for some years a Christian state existed, embracing Orthodox, Catholics and even Arabic traditions.

1291 and Moslem dominance of the Middle East and the Holy Places was to remain until the advent of Allenby and the British in 1917.

Yet crusading practice died hard. The church was already beginning to exert the pressure upon heretics nearer home: rigorous attacks upon the Moors in Spain, intensified hostility towards Jewry and the genesis of robust inquisitional tactics first employed by the Dominicans against the heretical Albigensian sects[202] in Southern France at the start of the thirteenth century. Relationships between the Eastern and Western churches, wracked by recrimination and a mutual sense of betrayal, deteriorated still further. The material—and one suspects spiritual—interests of most European people had been compromised, if not sacrificed, on the crusading altar, their lifeblood in England sucked dry by the Saladin Tithe of Richard I: he who would 'sell the city of London (to raise funds for the crusade) if I can find a buyer' just about sums it up. Small wonder that the initial popular enthusiasm for the wars didn't last, as the scourge of imported leprosy appeared as a significant visible consequence.

The best that can be said of the crusades, if we discount the romantic accounts of the pious, is that the adventurers brought back with them an enhanced knowledge of the world—a more sophisticated understanding of the science of mathematics and astronomy, some lucrative trading

---

[202] The Albigensians—one of a number of extreme, ascetic, egalitarian puritanical Christian sects. Dualists, they regarded all matter as evil and only the spiritual dimension as good. As such, therefore, Christ's human form was a phantom experience and never tasted death in a corporeal sense. The purpose of enlightened believers was to seek release for their imprisoned spirit from their inherently tainted body until achieving ultimate perfection in union with God through prayer, meditation and right living. Reincarnation was a feature of the process. They took their name from the town of Albi in the Tarn Department of France. Often associated with the Cult of Magdalene, these 'Cathars', as they are generically known, have attracted considerable interest among those seeking to suggest a plausible alternative to the conventional interpretation of the Gospel and which would explain the ferocity with which the Roman Church attempted to exterminate them: through the armed agency of the French nobility and the relentless Dominican inquisition. It might also account for the curious activities of the priest of Rennes-le-Chateau in the Languedoc region of France at the turn of the twentieth century, the Abbé Saunière, whose motives have been explored by such writers as, Baigent, M., Leigh, R. and Lincoln, H. in *The Holy Blood and the Holy Grail*, Arrow Books, 1996, and Picknett, L., and Prince, C. in *The Templar Revelation*, Corgi Books, 1998.

The Church 93

opportunities for the mercantile class in Italy—enticing novel fruits such as apricots, dates, limes and melons; fabrics in the guise of muslin, satin and velvet; gemstones, dyes, perfume and tapisserie. All this, and a wealth of Greek, Islamic and Jewish scholarship was to fuel the advance of Europe and the church into the Modern Age. In the view of Hugh Trevor-Roper,[203] these benefits were destined to lead to a further wave of European expansion on a far more pervasive and intimidating level and thus to the intensification of racial and religious conflict. The crusades, he maintains, were a cynical political and economic ploy by which 'marked with the cross' became 'God wills it'. Divine approval was apparently sealed on questionable motives, which has so bedevilled inter-communal intercourse worldwide. None of the great religions can, in all honesty, escape blame.

Today, one hundred or so ruined castles dot the Palestinian landscape as grim reminders of the attempts by the crusaders to defend their Latin kingdom and testify to the ultimate folly of their 'armed pilgrimage': testimony, moreover, to the heady, idealistic spirit proclaimed as our defining moment at Clermont in 1095. The vibes are still being felt around the conference tables at Camp David, the conurbation of Lower Manhattan, the Taliban remnant at Jalalabad, the starved hospitals of Baghdad, the reoccupation of Fallujah, in the streets of Bradford and Marseilles, within the soul of the suicide bomber of Janin and the daily suffering of Gaza and of Jerusalem itself.

---

[203] Trevor-Roger, H.: *The Rise of Christian Europe*, The History Book Club, 1967.

Chapter 10

The Palace of the Popes, Avignon

ROME AWAY FROM ROME

The pilgrimage to the tomb of Santiago de Compostela[204] in north-western Spain has, since the twelfth century, been viewed by the faithful and others as an experience—dutiful, penitential, aesthetic or a mixture of all three. Nowadays supported by a sophisticated network of the traditional routes from all corners of Western Christendom, along its many hundreds of miles, it has scenery as varied as the spiritual experiences and expectations of those engaged in the enterprise. On the major French routes, large and important cities remain as key watering holes and rallying points for pilgrims prior to their assault on the Pyrenean stage and into Iberia—Le Puy, Clermont, Lyon, Tours, Poitiers, Bordeaux. Then there are the smaller settlements, by today's standards, overshadowed in importance by the relative proximity of more recent conurbations, which likewise served the weary pilgrim, strategically located perhaps at a gap in a range of hills or at a river

---

[204] Compostela is the town in which the remains of James the Apostle are reputedly buried. It is one of the premier resorts of Christian pilgrims from all over the world. It is the symbol of the Spanish thrust to drive the Moslems from Spain in the fifteenth century.

The Church

crossing point. At such a trans-fluvial rendezvous lies the delightful little town of St Jean d'Angely, defining itself astride the sun-kissed valley of the Boutonne, in the Charente region of Western France. While what the modern traveller sees of the old town today—the Clock Tower and Pillory Fountain—are of fifteenth—and sixteenth-century provenance, its large Romanesque church overseeing a maze of narrow streets acknowledge a human presence of earlier epochs. Out of this hub of a once very vibrant community arises a twin-towered abbey of considerable Romanesque characteristics itself, now restored after its destruction by Huguenot forces in 1562 but which, in its original incarnation, was to be the venue of our defining moment in 1305.

It was here, within the monastic confines, that Philip ('the Fair') (1285-1314), the fourth of that name in the Capetian line of French kings, engaged in a pre-arranged rendezvous with the Gascon Archbishop of Bordeaux, Bertrand de Got. Despite what must have been the generous hospitality of a well-endowed abbey, the meeting, lubricated courtesy of the distillation process characteristic of the nearby town of Cognac, could not have been easy and held in an atmosphere of intensity, intimacy and seclusion. There were two reasons for this. One, the two men were barely on speaking terms: members of the archbishop's family had been worsted, with terminal consequences, in violent confrontations with Philip's authority. Second, at stake was the very future complexion of the papacy itself. To add to the archbishop's natural inclination to caution, it was a barely unsubstantiated rumour that the previous pontifical incumbent Benedict XI (1303-5) had met his demise at the instigation of Philip himself. The College of Cardinals'[205] meeting in Rome to elect a successor had, for ten months previously, failed to come up with a mutually amenable candidate, until a name emerged who was repugnant to both the dominant French and the Italian factions on the conclave and who in consequence might be acceptable! Thus, Bertrand de Got was to be approached by Philip in the knowledge that his unabashed ambition would override any reservations he might entertain. The king was more than willing to have a go in the art of persuading this nominee to accept, given the less than edifying opportunities open to him should he succeed. Hence, the private interview at St Jean d'Angely

---

[205] Nowadays, the status of cardinal is recognised as second only in rank to that of the Pope. The role of cardinals over the centuries has been varied, but they are valued by the Pope as influential advisers. Their unique responsibility is to meet in conclave to elect a new pope, an exclusive right established at the Third Lateran Council in 1179, thereby ratifying Hildebrand's actions in 1059.

was arranged—so private in fact that the full extent of its detail has never been fully revealed. Suffice it to say that king and archbishop milked their respective bargaining powers to the limit. Both sides appeared to get what they wanted. A deal was struck at the crucial point in the negotiation, which constitutes our defining moment: Bertrand accepted the offer and Philip returned to Paris well satisfied that subject to formal ratification by the cardinals, he had a papacy commensurate with his avaricious agenda.

The upshot of this defining moment, as far as the church was concerned, was an uprooting of its traditional, hallowed centre of gravity in Rome to the relative tranquility of its fiefdom north of the Alps on the banks of the Rhone. For nearly seventy years, the heartbeat of the Western Church was to emanate from its so-called 'Babylonish Captivity'[206] in Avignon, described acidly by Petrarch, mouthpiece of its Roman detractors, as that 'sink of vice and corruption'. Here, Pope Clement V (1305-14) as Bertrand became known and his six successors of this captivity ordered the affairs of the church. Here they were relieved of the frenetic political and social instability of Rome in favour of the initially more easy-going laxity derivative of the Provençal slopes gracing the Rhone Valley.

Part of the agreement that Clement had made with Philip was that he should reside within striking distance of the French king. This in itself marked a shift in papal orientation from its theoretically natural alignment with the Holy Roman emperor. It was a recognition of the incipient papal realisation of the reality of sovereign power being coterminous with national and natural frontiers, and with the French kingdom in particular. Having been closely associated with the legendary, yet ill-fated dynamism associated with the crusades, the medieval French realm had embraced so much of the Medieval Christian ideal: the monasticism of the Cluniacs, the Carthusians and Cistercians,[207] for example. These foundations provided the cells from which daughter

---

[206] This imagery stems from the captivity and exile of the Old Testament people of Judah, as a result of their deportation to Babylon by King Nebuchadnazzar in 586 BC (see 2 Kings 24:14-16, 25:11). The book of Daniel alludes to the period of captivity itself and the books of Ezra and Nehemiah relate to the Jewish return to Jerusalem, from 538 BC onwards. Here it must not be confused with Martin Luther's use of the term, later on, in one of his tracts, which links the so-called bondage of the church to its spurious Roman Catholic traditions, citing New Testament allusions: the 'Whore of Babylon' (Revelation 17:1, 16 and 18).

[207] Monastic orders founded in France. See chapter 4.

The Church 97

abbeys were planted throughout Christendom and upon which the French secular establishment was open to any opportunity to cash in on the blessings its patronage might afford. King Louis IX (1226-70), of the French Capetian dynasty, raised to sainthood so shortly after his physical demise, had attempted to reincarnate the Old Testament ideal of a monarchical melange of the secular, military and spiritual: priest and king rolled into one. His requisition of the 'authentic' crown of thorns with which Christ Himself had been adorned tended to reinforce Louis's lofty opinion of himself and the construction of the quintessentially Gothic of Ste Chapelle within the Palais de Justice in Paris to house it is his enduring monument. Its delicate array of pin-striped stained glass opulence pointing heavenwards to illuminate the Almighty with the piety of its founder.

While Louis's exploits might well have brought prestige to the French monarchy, their pecuniary legacy was less than sanguine. When, therefore, Philip the Fair, his grandson, succeeded as king in 1285, he was anxious to fund a throne and an inheritance such as would perpetuate the lifestyle and dignity worthy of a successor to his revered ancestor, St Louis. How better to fund this, in the short term, than paradoxically target the resources of its most obvious and vulnerable institution, the church, and its immensely wealthy order of the Templars?[208] In this quest, he was to initiate a long-running and far-reaching dispute with Boniface VIII, pope between 1294 and 1303. Here he was up against a clever, scheming intellect whose unbridled ambition to secure dynastic (and therefore secular) advantage from his possession of the Papal States derived from his recognition that his possession of the patrimony of Peter was not based upon the hereditary principle. One needed to secure family fortune by making the most of the tenure of the highest office, while one could—by foul means, if fair efforts failed.

Hence, Boniface, despite his preference for repose at his country retreat at Anagni where he could indulge his alleged sexual cravings both ways and play off the leading Roman families the Orsini and Colonna against each other, was keen to ensure the church was financially secure; or at least, to tap its resources to promote his family's secular interests in Italy. Inevitably the French king and the pontiff came to blows. At root, of course, was the endemic arm-wrestling between the spiritual ruler and the secular leader over the issue of precedence. The symptom

---

[208] A Christian military order founded in 1118 ostensibly to protect Jerusalem from the Moslems after its capture during the First Crusade (1099). They subsequently amassed great wealth, status and power; hence Philip's designs upon them. See ch.4.

of this tension surfaced when Boniface issued the bull[209] 'Clericis Laicos' in 1296, forbidding the secular rulers to levy taxation on the clergy without the consent of the bishop of Rome. Philip, particularly aggrieved, retaliated by halting the trade in gold and precious metals into Northern Italy, thus starving the papacy of a major source of income. This was particularly bad timing for Boniface who was engaged in an intensified and undignified wrangle within the murky and mucky waters of Roman politics, the upshot of which was the enforced deprivation of extensive possessions of the city's powerful Colonna family and its consequent defection into the welcoming embrace of the French court. The simmering cauldron boiled over in 1301 when Philip demanded the appearance of the papal legate in France, for trial. A furious Boniface then summoned up all the spiritual armoury at his disposal, by rushing through two further bulls—*Ausculto Fili* (1301) and *Unam Sanctam* (1302). The burden of these pronouncements was to re-emphasise the doctrine of papal supremacy over secular authorities, and indeed over all creatures, citing numerous references by the early Church Fathers to support this claim. It was made very plain that human salvation was dependent upon unalloyed subjection to the Roman pontiff. Philip ignored a summons to attend a disciplinary hearing in Rome and brushed off papal threats of excommunication and a papal offer of the French throne to the emperor. No longer, it seems the pretensions of the church could strike terror into the hearts of those who had battalions at their disposal. The growth of national sentiment in the hands of determined worldly princes was more than ready to challenge the primacy previously accorded to the likes of Popes Gregory VII (1073-85) and Innocent III (1198-1216) and whom Boniface sought to emulate. The issue was put beyond doubt when in 1303 a band of mercenary soldiers in Philip's name, led by William de Nogaret and Sciarra Colonna burning for revenge, burst into the Pope's apartments at Anagni subjecting him to such an ordeal as to hasten the enfeebled octogenarian's demise a few weeks later. Peter's scathing epitaph on a pope at the gates of Paradise, as allegorised by Dante, sums up the contemporary poet's contempt for the man who ' . . . has made a sewer from my sepulchre full of blood and pus . . . '[210]

Such a humiliation cast the church back on the defensive, thrown once more onto the mercies of Rome where the unruly politicians made life difficult for Benedict IX (1303-04), Boniface's successor, who

---

[209] A written order issued by the Pope.

[210] Dante Alighieri: *Commedia, Paradiso* (27).

The Church 99

hung on in there for barely two years before falling victim to Philip's caprice.[211]

It was fortuitous for Philip that the wrangling between the Italian and French cardinals, then, led to himself being cast in the role of arbitrator, which gave rise to the defining moment—his meeting with Bertrand at St Jean d'Angely. As we have seen, the results were momentous: a French king, and not even the emperor, holding the church's future in his hands. Bertrand, known to be ever ready to sell his grandmother for a shilling, paid the price for accepting the prize: a licence for the French king to tax the clergy and a categorical recognition of the king's right to do so; a suspected complicity to dissolve the order of the Templars, the disposal of its assets into secular coffers and Bertrand's relocation to Avignon where Philip could keep an eye on him—a hostage to fortune. Thus Clement V's unholy alliance with his patron was to move 'Rome away from Rome'. In his own mind, perhaps, conscious that a predecessor, the saintly Celestine V (1294), had functioned from Naples—albeit for a brief moment in time.

Henceforth, Clement never ventured beyond the South of France. Philip IV now had the Pope and the bulk of the cardinals in his pocket. The flower of the Templars' leadership was duly excised from history with clinical precision on a day of the long knives, 13 October 1307, and its order officially suppressed by the Pope in 1313 many of its considerable assets passing to the French crown as arranged. Their Grand Master, Jacques de Molay, was publicly roasted to death amidst the flames and within sight and earshot of Notre-Dame de Paris, showering dire imprecations upon his tormentors to the last. Within months, both Philip and Clement were dead.

Another sixty-four years were to elapse, and the passage of a further six pontiffs, before the papal court was to return to Rome. In the dissolute atmosphere of Avignon, surprisingly little changed in terms of church structure, or indeed obedience, apart from taking the opportunity to create a more efficient machinery of administration. For the vast bulk of Europe's population living beyond a few days' journey beyond its focal point, the mystical stature of St Peter's successor still held; it made very little material difference whether the apex of spiritual authority resided in Rome, Avignon or Moscow for that matter.

Yet the siren call of Rome could neither be silenced nor be ignored. The initial calm and comforts of Avignon gave way to a sense of unease as the fourteenth century wore on. Bands of mercenaries, unpaid and

---

[211] He is believed to have been poisoned.

on leave during respites in the Hundred Years' War[212] were a constant threat to the city and Pope Clement VI (1342-52) felt constrained to erect the massive fortifications around it, which still characterise Avignon today. Gibbon's inimitable imagery likens the move out of Rome to a person who fells a tree in order to gather the fruit, thereby 'for momentary repose (sacrifices) the long and secure possession of the most important blessings'.[213] During the Babylonian exile, the city of Rome and the Papal States in Italy grew ever more factious, lawless and materially decadent without the presence of their leader. At the behest of the Emperor Charles IV (1346-78), Pope Urban V (1362-70) agreed to relocate to Rome, but the French connection was as yet too strong to effect a permanent transfer; the blessings of the Pope on French soil were needed in the renewed fighting in the Hundred Years' War. Yet while Dante[214] despaired of the church's lack of grace and the humiliation of the empire, Petrarch[215] and the mystical Catherine of Siena[216] implored its prodigal son to return home to whose cri de cœur Pope Gregory XI (1370-78) eventually surrendered in 1377, making the Vatican itself, for the first time, the Pope's official residence; St John Lateran was in ruins—unfit for the papal dignity.

Gregory's death the following year resulted in the election of the first Italian pope for seventy years. If this was to be a return to business as usual, then its protagonists were to become sadly disabused. Urban VI (1378-89) was to prove overbearing, autocratic, insensitive and militaristic: quite possibly a mental case and very probably callous, cruel and downright murderous, a man who deserted Rome for five years in pursuit of real estate in Southern Italy. Certainly his performance from the outset did nothing to mollify the French cardinals still smarting from

---

[212] The period of punctuated warfare between England and France lasting from 1338 to 1453; at root, it centred around the claim of the English kings to the throne of France.

[213] Gibbon, E., *Decline and Fall of the Roman Empire*, Low, D. M. (ed.), Pelican Books, 1960, p. 858.

[214] Italian poet, 1265-1321 whose *Commedia* is considered a masterpiece of spiritual imagery. He consistently advocated the culmination of the ideal European community based upon the joint authority of emperor and pope.

[215] Italian poet, early Renaissance writer, 1304-74, famous for the evolution of the sonnet form, and a strong advocate of papal return to Rome.

[216] Italian mystic associated with the Dominican order. She practised works of mercy and is remembered for her inspirational letters and prayers. She was later canonised.

The Church   101

the bulk of the Curia's vacation of Avignon. In 1378, they unilaterally declared an annulment of Urban's election. The city of Rome became, briefly, an unseemly battleground between the rival factions; a 'pitiful state of affairs', as Froissart describes it, wherein 'every day people who were in no way involved suffered severely'.[217] With Rome itself so hostile to the new nominee, the French cardinals retreated to Avignon with the 'anti-pope', whom they proclaimed as Clement VII[218] in tow. Thus began one of the greatest scandals and embarrassments in the entire saga of the Western Church: the undignified spectacle of two rival claimants and pretenders to the chair of St Peter spitting blood and splitting fealty. The French, not surprisingly, pledged allegiance to Avignon, along with Austria, Aragon and Scotland; the English, equally unsurprisingly, in company with the Burgundian lands and Castile, firm in their adherence to Rome, with clerics and orders divided across the board. Not only was this to be a crisis of complex jurisdictional and organisational dimensions, but also it threw into relief the question concerning the derivation of true spiritual authority and the consequent veracity and legitimacy of the apostolic succession through whose veins the validity of the sacraments flows. It also raised the hypothesis as to whether there could, or indeed should, be a distinction between clerical office and the personal qualities of an incumbent, as justification for a performance of sacerdotal duties in the name of Christ. In short, was one individual alone, given his human concupiscence, capable of, or indeed worthy to execute the authority of Christ on earth, or should a more representative body oversee the affairs of the church? With opinion growing in the minds of the cardinals themselves, given the farce being played out before them, and for which they in part were responsible, called a council at Pisa in 1409. In an attempt to minimise the desecration of Christ's memory, French and Italian cardinals having responded to the prompting by respective theologians from the Sorbonne convoked this gathering of the secular and spiritual great and the good in an attempt to repair the damage. Not surprisingly, the two rival popes, by this time, Benedict XIII at Avignon and Gregory XII in Rome, failed to show up. Neither of course did they regard the convention as authoritative or legitimate. Their stubborn refusal to stare reality in the face brought upon them a vain invitation to resign their respective posts in favour of the council's

---

[217]   *Froissart's Chronicles*, Jollifre, J. (ed.), Harvill Press, London, 1962.

[218]   'Anti-popes', such as the Clement VII, Benedict XIII and John XXIII mentioned in this chapter, have never been recognised by ensuing Catholic authorities and in fact subsequent office holders have assumed their title and designation.

nominated replacement, Alexander V (1409-10). An unprepossessing and nightmarish scenario then ensued, wherein not two, but *three* nominal popes busily engaged, not in the acts of Christian charity, but in the process of mutually firing bulls of anathema and excommunication. Clearly the problem could not remain if the church were to retain any structural credibility at all. It was the Emperor Sigismund (1410-32) who took it upon himself to seize the initiative and to reassert his authority by leaning on Alexander's successor, John XXIII (1410-17), to convene a general church council.

The Council of Constance that deliberated between 1414 and 1418 is regarded by many as one of the most significant, yet controversial, meetings in the history of the church. The meeting, kick-started by the emperor, was steered through much of its treacherous course by a French cardinal and driven by the theological dynamism of Jean Gerson of the Sorbonne. With the precedent of scripture to guide him,[219] he restated the principle that underlay the Council of Pisa that abuse of the papal office could only be checked by subjecting the incumbent to certain constitutional constraints and his submission to the decisions of the council. It was proposed that all three would-be popes, each of whom in his own way had contributed to the existing scandal, should resign his office to make way for a truly ecumenical successor. John XXIII, seeing the contrary direction from which the wind was blowing and mindful of the likelihood that his own moral shortcomings would be open to scrutiny, accordingly fled the scene in the tenuous belief that without his papal authority, the council would be deprived of legitimacy. Sigismund, however, was not going to let go that easily and kept it going to enable the articles of Constance to be passed, in 1415, whereby the council was officially declared a general council of the church, having its authority directly from God and therefore not dependent upon papal imprimatur. John was soon captured and unceremoniously returned to Constance as a prisoner, where he was formally deposed for abusing the papal office on the grounds of piracy, rape, murder, sodomy and incest—excessive charges even by the questionable standards of the late medieval papacy. Gregory XII now agreed to abdicate in more or less honourable fashion, although it took until 1417 to enforce a deposition order on the 'pope' in Avignon, Benedict XIII. This he did with less

---

[219] The Council of Jerusalem as described by Luke in Acts 15 is considered the first such council of the church. Although Peter plays an important role in the proceedings, it seems as though James was the chief executive at the time. The decisions arrived at appear to have been authoritative as far as their injunction upon Jewish Christians at the time were concerned.

The Church 103

than good grace, retiring to his native Spain where he was to act out his fantasies by excommunicating—twice a day—the sovereign he perceived to have betrayed his interests.

The way was at last clear for a conclave to elect a new pontiff. Odo Colonna, scion of the Roman nobility, was proclaimed as Pope Martin V (1417-31), the now virtually undisputed head of the Catholic Church, and the man most practically placed to deal locally with Rome's endemic predators. Having resolved this fractious issue, the council now had a golden opportunity to examine those other questionable canonical and functional practices which had crept into the church over the years and which, by any objective appraisal, would be regarded as inconsistent with the will of its founder—abuses such as nepotism, simony, pluralism and avarice. Sadly, so preoccupied had the council been over the healing of its divisions, so intense had been the diplomatic and political posturing to secure agreement on electing a single head that sheer exhaustion and relief precluded any more than tinkering around the edges of reform. Indeed, any whiff of theological dissent within or outside its ranks was perhaps understandably considered potentially schismatic. Despite the emperor's guarantee of safe conduct, Jan Huss,[220] the Bohemian reformer, responded to a summons to Constance and for his trouble was burnt for heresy; the disinterment of the bones of John Wycliffe[221] was ordered for which, at least, no betrayal of trust was occasioned. An attempt to mend fences with Byzantium at the council foundered on the rock of the *filioque* clause, which had bedevilled relationships for centuries. The legacy of Constance is not to be found in church reform, but in the restoration of a single, and for the time being only, voice of Western Christendom; that, and the endemic hankering by some for a conciliar, rather than an authoritarian, approach to decision-making.

The significance, then, of our defining moment for the church, is far reaching. It represents the confident assertion of the muscle the emerging national monarchies of late Medieval Europe were to exhibit over the papacy. The threat, of course, had been implicit from the start,

---

[220] Priest and rector of Prague University, Huss (c.1370-1415), was critical of the moral decadence of the contemporary church and foreshadowed Luther's attachment to scripture as the true source of God's word.

[221] Rector of Lutterworth, Wycliffe (c.1324-84), attacked the immoral conduct of the church, particularly the worldly power and evil lives of the clergy; he denied the doctrine of transubstantiation and his dedication to scriptural authority is marked by the first complete translation of the Bible into English, associated with his name. Huss was very much influenced by him.

but the old imperial/papal tension that had been tested and by and large held for five hundred years was now inexorably veering in favour of the secular state. Subservience to French interests during the resultant Avignon period signifies a loss of prestige to the imperial arm of the axis as well, and while the Emperor Sigismund redeemed the position somewhat at the Council of Constance, the concept of the Holy Roman Empire was to wither slowly on the vine from this point. Internally, the role of the Pope in regard to decision-making was weakened at a crucial time. That two general councils, whether recognised as such or not, took it upon *themselves* to resolve the consequences of the exile from Rome, gave renewed impetus to those pushing for government by church council—the Conciliar Movement: he who pays the piper calls the tune. It certainly featured later on at the Council of Basel/Ferrara/Florence (1431-49) when the conundrum of a rival 'anti-pope' again surfaced and it figured very much in the thinking of Martin Luther one hundred years later. The schism, as we have seen, exposed the weakness of the doctrinal basis of the historic church: the axiomatic concept of apostolic succession and the validity of the sacraments when two or more rival branches vied for power and the question as to whether or not the personal qualities—the moral or spiritual standing of the individual administering or presiding over those sacraments—should be a constraint as regards their efficacy or even legitimacy. It is therefore not coincidental that the 'heresies' of Wycliffe and Huss, who tended to appeal to a scriptural basis as the source of Christian doctrine and truth, rather than to a church whose degenerate exhibition seemed so much at variance with it, were active and widely accepted during this period: an ominous pointer to a full-blown reformation a century on. Constance had the opportunity to tackle the abuses, but it failed to grasp the nettle. The temporary move to Avignon, however, only served to highlight the powerful magnetism that the city of Rome possessed as the fountainhead of the church. Here, after all, were the supposed relics of Peter and the substantial grounds for according primacy to its bishop in the first place. The city had so often found it difficult to live with its ecclesiastical presence but missed it dreadfully when it was elsewhere. Gone was the status, and with it the pilgrimages, not to mention the financial advantage accruing to the heart of a Catholic Colossus. The ancient sites crumbled, the money dried up and the vacuum only served to encourage forces outside to take advantage. Some, throughout Europe, saw the visitation of the Black Death (1348-49), which so ravaged and decimated the continent as a sign of God's displeasure at the sacrilege of the church's desertion of the Petrine City. If the head is deprived of its life-giving oxygen, what hope exists for its members? Put another way, a church dislocated from the heart of St Peter was a contradiction in terms. The church did return. Maybe the Lord's words to Simon Peter to turn back to him that the 'brothers' might be strengthened struck a chord somewhere.[222]

Schism, secularism, scandal, cynicism all pervaded the atmosphere of the later medieval papacy in the wake of that fateful meeting between Philip IV and Bertrand de Got at St Jean d'Angely in 1305. It sowed the seeds of an unprecedented disaffection that was to presage its institutional fragmentation.

---

[222] Luke 22:31-32.

Chapter 11

Scene from the battle defending Constantinople, Paris 1499

RATHER THE TURKISH FEZ THAN A CARDINAL'S HAT

Istanbul today: something of an outpost, now, of the modern secular state of Turkey, yet the one major city that can boast of having its two feet on different continents. Here, Europe and Asia can join hands across the Bosphorus: cosmopolitan, in the casbah, one is likely to rub shoulders with Islamic clerics, Greek Orthodox monks, local vendors, Western and Japanese tourists as well as the westernised Turkish sophisticate, and in the background, the plaintiff cry of the muezzin from a nearby minaret summoning the Moslem faithful to prayer, quaintly incongruous perhaps in this busting metropolis. Somewhat grubby and run down in parts, here, in its previous incarnation, stood the bastion and symbol of Christianity in the east. This was the heart of Greek Byzantium and later the repository of the glories of ancient Rome to which its emperor and his successors had repaired in the fourth century AD.[223] This had been the apex of the Christian ideal—its holy relics jealously protected in bejewelled reliquaries, its stunning architecture somehow

---

[223] See chapter 2.

The Church 107

complementing the piety of Orthodox religious observance, and emperor and patriarch presiding over a new Jerusalem to whom subjects of its far-flung possessions had paid tribute. All this excited the imagination of people outside its domain. This was Constantinople. On 29 May 1453, the known world reverberated to the news that this symbolic eminence, this standard bearer of Levantine Christendom for over one thousand years, had fallen.

On the afternoon of 28 May, its emperor, Constantine XI Palaeologus (1448-53), had urged the defenders of the city to mount a desperate stand, indeed to make the final sacrifice, in the face of the Islamic forces laying siege to it. Hammering away at the outer walls, in the process of softening up the target, Sultan Mohammed II's huge cannon capable of firing a missile in excess of 1,000 lbs led a determined force of around 100,000 comprising Turkish conscripts, Christian renegades, Moslem fanatics, assorted mercenaries and the sultan's elite guard of Janissaries.[224] Spurred on, if not by the purely physical anticipation of either material gain or the dignity of martyrdom, then by the consequent assurance of a posthumous Valhalla experience amidst the cooling streams meandering through perfumed gardens in the tender loving care of dark-eyed virgins (presumably ephemeral), the besieging forces had all to play for.

Inside, the emperor summoned all charged with his city's defence—a mere ten thousand at most and armed with inferior catapults and cannon—to what was to prove the very last Christian service to be held in the Cathedral of St Sophia—that seemingly eternal monument to Constantine's vision and Justinian's enterprise: under its huge dome, the largest in all Christendom, symbolising the encompassing embrace of a world subject to God,[225] the service was in effect the requiem for a passing era. St Sophia, protector of the Orthodox faith, the spiritual heart of a city whose one-time wealth had been 'like that of (which) is not to be found in the whole world',[226] witnessed its most sombre and sublime moment. Here, on this day in May, the composite service, embracing elements of both Orthodox and Latin tradition in order to accommodate those defenders from the West, was held—an enactment of spiritual defiance in the face of the infidel. Then, it was back to the practical business of manning their posts.

---

[224] Janissaries were a corps of Turkish soldiers—young men, the sons of captured Christian prisoners of war. They were brought up under strict discipline according to the tenets of Islam, remaining an effective fighting force until abolished following a mutiny in 1825.

[225] Symbolic of the firmament as expressed in Genesis 1:6-7.

[226] Benjamin of Tudela, a contemporary observer.

Few events symbolise *so* accurately the failure of Christianity to present a common unity in the face of a common foe than the fall of Constantinople. Yet almost to the end, few anywhere were prepared to accept that demise was ever conceivable. Despite the progressive reverses and decline over the centuries, many were confident that the city—the decadent glories of the imperial palace, the forum of Constantine, the hippodrome, St Sophia itself and the Golden Horn, anchorage to ships laden with goodies from halfway round the world—would stand tall protected by walls of triple thickness. Failing that, as the historian Phranza[227] recounts, surely the repository of that most revered collection of holy relics—the robe of the Virgin Mary, the linen cloth worn by the infant Jesus, the lance that pierced his side on the cross, the stone from His tomb—would ensure deliverance. According to Gibbon, a long-standing prophecy had led the citizens to anticipate that in the event of the Turks' entry into the city, 'an angel would descend from heaven with sword in hand' at the square of St Sophia and the heathen driven from their shores.[228]

Yet the human and ballistic resources of the sultan were to prove too much. Having already superhumanly hauled his galleys and brigantines by land over the scrubby high ground from the Bosphorus into the harbour of the Golden Horn, the battering ram and the aforesaid 'mechanical engines for casting stones and darts'[229] had taken their toll, but the line had been held. Then, on the morning of the twenty-ninth comes our defining moment. Much of the city's armed force was in fact manned by Westerners—those from Italy who had become residents in the Galata quarter engaged in the community's commercial life. One Giustiniani, a Genoese, and a trusted lieutenant of the emperor, was given command of a Latin squad at a crucial section of the outer walls. Apparently suffering from a superficial wound, he withdrew from his post, seeking treatment. Rebuked by the indefatigable emperor, he refused all entreaty to return immediately to his position. Betraying his mercenary considerations, Giustiniani reportedly declared he would retire 'by the same road which God has given to the Turks'.[230] Prising open one of the breeches of the inner wall at its weakest point, he was followed by many of his Latin supporters to abandon the sinking ship, through the pockmarked outer wall, and beyond into the history books, a stereotypical deserter.

---

[227] Phranza, a contemporary chronicler of the times.

[228] Quoted in Gibbon, E.: *Decline and Fall of the Roman Empire*, Low, D. M. (ed.), Pelican, 1966, p. 845.

[229] Low, D. M. (ed.), ibid p. 536.

[230] Quoted in Low, D. M. (ed.), ibid p. 844.

Through the breech thus made poured the jubilant Turks and they were inside the city. After a siege of fifty-three days, with Emperor Constantine XI Palaeologus himself dying in the heat of battle, the infidel fighters were in a position to reap their reward.

Giustiniani's alleged cowardice or betrayal has been challenged. His advocates have suggested that his exit from the city was in fact a heroic strategy to attack the Turkish forces on their own ground. Be that as it may, it is beyond doubt that his action—our defining moment—demoralised his troops. In sensing their deflation, the Turks scaled the walls precipitating the fall of the city and even more tellingly exposed the underlying and endemic tensions between the Latin and Greek arms of the Christian faith. Appeals for assistance by the emperor to Western Christendom had been met with, at best, a tardy material response—too little, too late—while in any case the average Byzantine, on past experience, feared any interaction or interference from a potentially dubious Roman provenance—'rather a Turkish Fez than a Cardinal's hat'[231]—hardly surprising to many of them that the city should be let down by a Genoese!

For one thousand years, then, Constantinople had exuded a kind of mystique over the rest of the known world. Astride the great trade routes, east and west, north and south, its one-time wealth had been legendary; its deviant religious observances increasingly alien to the Roman papacy never reconciled to the schism of 1054.[232] There had been the endemic residual hope that a reunited structure would evolve on Rome's terms of course; there had been bickering, as we have seen, over jurisdictions in Sicily and parts of Central Europe and then there would be rich commercial pickings for the West if advantage could be taken from the loosening imperial grip of the sprawling polity, which at its height extended from Armenia—the world's oldest Christian state to the Balkans, from the Crimea to the Levant. The Fourth Crusade, in 1204, had witnessed the shameless looting of the city urged by the trading centres of Northern Italy, resulting in the establishment of the temporary ill-starred Latin kingdom of Byzantium down to 1261, whereafter an uneasy truce prevailed between the two.

Constantinople's ultimate demise, however, was to emanate ultimately from the East. Already the Seljuk Turks had nibbled away at the extremities in Asia Minor. Al Aslan's victory at the Battle of Manzikert in 1071 sealed the fate of Armenia in favour of the Seljuks and seriously alerted far-distant Rome to the incipient threat to the survival

---

[231] Fisher, H. A. L.: *A History of Europe*, Fontana, 1979, p. 424. See chapter 9.
[232] See chapter 7.

of Christianity in the Holy Land; Turkish warlords systematically hacked away at the rest of Asia Minor. The crusaders had followed hard on its heels. By the beginning of the fourteenth century, the Seljuk branch of the Turkish tribes had given way to the Ottoman Emirate whose grand designs recognised few bounds. By 1329, Nicea in Western Asia Minor had fallen, and ominously, in 1356, Ottoman forces had crossed the Dardanelles into Europe, establishing at Adrianople in Western Thrace a new menacing base for future expansionism. In 1389, the backbone of Serb resistance to the unwelcome intruders was broken at Kossovo and much of the Greek peninsula was in Ottoman hands by the close of the century. All that remained of the Byzantium Empire was Constantinople itself, already depleted by the Black Death, its environs and some Greek settlements in Morea and its island appendages. Only Tamerlaine's pressure on the Ottomans at Ankara had saved Constantinople as early as 1402.

By this time, the West had indeed become seriously alarmed. Various attempts at reconciling the two churches in the thirteenth and fourteenth centuries had faltered on the altar of Byzantium's suspicion of Western motives. The Turkish threat to Belgrade in 1439 had prompted the signature of a declaration of principles aimed at reunification, but it proceeded no further, save for a Western-inspired crusade led by King Ladislav of Poland and Cardinal Cesarini in a final attempt to relieve the pressure on Constantinople, in 1444. This half-hearted effort had ultimately foundered in Kossovo by 1448. Byzantium was now abandoned to its fate and so to our defining moment.

Thus, with the Ottoman flag hoisted over the despoiled imperial palace, and St Sophia converted with indecent haste into a mosque, Constantine's ideal bit the dust, but its repercussions continue to resound. For a start, the Orthodox tradition of the Byzantine Church survived. The new Turkish masters were remarkably indulgent towards the Christian remnant who remained. The monasteries of Mount Athos and islands in the Aegean tenaciously sustained their old way of life. In the Greek peninsula itself, a sullen population bedded down to three and a half centuries of Ottoman rule, never absorbed, never reconciled, and since their successful bid for independence in 1821, never forgotten; the modern tragedy that is Cyprus, and Gladstone's insistence that the Ottomans must be ejected bag and baggage from Europe, is its residue.[233] None the less ominous was the infiltration of Ottoman culture and the

---

[233] Disraeli's handling of the Eastern question in the 1870s was much criticised by Gladstone, who accused the prime minister of propping up a corrupt and sometimes oppressive Ottoman regime in the Balkans in order to

The Church 111

Islamic faith in the process of Balkanisation among pre-existing Serb, Albanian, Montenegran and Croat communities existing side by side in uneasy coexistence until the eruption of the ethnic cleansing crisis of the 1990s.

If anything, it was in Russia, where continuity of the old imperial ideal was picked up. Having been 'Christianised' by Byzantine missions, the lands of the grand duke of Muscovy, Ivan III (1462-1505), were well prepared for the call. Secure from immediate Islamic threat, he was in a good position to assume Constantinople's mantle, marrying Sophia, the niece of the last emperor. His successor, Ivan the Terrible (1537-84), assumed the title of Czar (Caesar), adopting the imperial double-headed eagle as the arms of Moscow. The dualistic posture of an autocratic semi-divine emperor presiding over 'Holy Russia' served to reinforce his secular authority in the tradition of Constantine. It further bolstered the chances of the survival of the Orthodox rite, while at the same time accentuating the mutual suspicion harboured between the Eastern and Western worlds, politically and ideologically through the Cold War and beyond.

The effect of Constantinople's fall upon Rome was profound; not only shock horror at the fate of Christendom in the East but also in many quarters a sense of guilt in professing minimal assistance in its time of need. Pope Nicholas V (1447-55), by now taking fright at the prospect of a clear run through the Balkans by the infidel renewed attempts to mount a coalition in the West to recover the lost city. Memories of previous ill-fated ventures into the region precluded a positive response from the secular rulers upon whose goodwill such an enterprise was dependent. That, plus the spectre of a pontificate indulging itself in the hedonistically cultural, humanistic pleasures of the renaissance, descending in the process to selfish, secular and dynastic preoccupations, which characterise the holders of the office in the second half of the fifteenth century, scarcely endeared many to the prospect of yet another spiritual crusade.

The influence of the fall of Constantinople over that remarkable movement known as the European Renaissance has been much disputed. It is most certainly true that most of the ingredients of that cultural revolution, which was to pave the way for the reformation, were in place well before that cataclysmic event. The rise of the great trading urban centres of Northern Italy enhanced by the crusades—Genoa, Florence, Lucca, Pisa, Siena—during the twelfth and thirteenth centuries gave

---

confine Russia. At the congress of Berlin, 1878, Cyprus, itself bitterly divided between Greek and Turkish communities, was ceded to Britain.

rise to the need for unprecedented literary and banking skills, and the evolution of a wealthy leisured class, whose money was to contribute to the artistic flowering that typifies renaissance Italy. The demise of the feudal regimes in the region in favour of a capitalistic orientation of the city communes had already spawned the outpouring of the emotional cadences of Petrarch (1304-74), and the vernacular allegory of Dante's *Divine Comedy* (1265-1366) and the *Decameron* tales by Boccaccio (1313-75). Perhaps in deference to a more spiritual age which appeared to be passing, Giotto (1266-1336) had been experimenting artistically with real-life forms to be found in his priceless frescoes at the Church of St Francis at Assisi, while his design for the campanile was to constitute a perfect foil for Brunelleschi's (1377-1476) Dome over Cambio's existing Cathedral of Santa Maria de Fiore in Florence, which represents the work of pioneering genius. The master sculptor and painter Donatello (1386-1466) had displayed his artistic talent in the sculpture of John the Baptist in the Cathedral at Siena. At the time, the writer Palmieri rejoiced in the principle that permitted him 'to be born in this new age' so full of hope and promise. Herein he was wont to contrast, as he saw it, the dawn of a new approach to the human condition—a new way of looking at things—with the feudally sterile heavenly piety of the Middle Ages such as that had separated his time from the fall of classical Rome to the Barbarians in the fifth century.

Thus, a new outlook on life had already begun to energise the Italian communes in the north of the peninsula—practical and humanistic, pouring tacit scorn upon the medieval scholasticism with its preoccupation with the reconciliation of reason and metaphysics.[234] No longer was man to be valued as a pale reflection of the Godhead and of significance for that alone; now humankind was pertinent for itself and the contribution it could make by the development of God-given talent. Such a spirit pervaded the work of Lorenzo Valla who was prepared to apply the process of literary criticism to sacred and respected documents, submitting them to a test of their veracity by means of rational scrutiny, to defend the truth rather than accept a received tradition simply because

---

[234] Scholasticism was the major theological impulse of the Medieval theologians, aiming to rationalise and to better understand revealed truths. Major exponents of this process were Anselm, Abelard and of course Aquinas, who drew heavily upon the work of Aristotle and his concept of God as the 'prime, unmoved mover'.

The church said so. It was he who, in 1440, exposed the fraudulence of the *Donation of Constantine* document by such methods.[235]

As, one by one, the Byzantine cities fell to the Ottomans throughout the fourteenth and fifteenth centuries, it was natural that their displaced scholars, armed with as many of their precious manuscripts as they could transport, found refuge in Northern Italy to salvage what they could of their invaluable heritage. Here many were, at first, tentatively welcomed into the circles of the growing urbane burghers, already undergoing economic and social change. Bringing with them the works of Greek and Roman classicism—Sophocles, Livy, Tacitus, Cicero, Seneca—the eyes of the Italian elite were opened to what was all around them—decaying architectural evidence of past glories—and the means to lend sophistication to the art of business and government, and to add an elan to their increasingly comfortable lifestyle. Here, they were to be made aware that in Italy, of all places, was the stuff of which classical Rome had been made. The Rome of antiquity had not been built by God, but by human endeavour, and neither in one day nor for that matter in six either. Even before Constantinople's demise, there had already existed the stimulus to rediscover what had made that greatest of ancient empires tick. What the fall of Constantinople did, however, was to sharpen the focus of the new learning and to drive it with a greater intensity. As more and more scholars found refuge in Italy, so they encountered a populous eager to learn and to bury themselves in the precious documents now available to them. For many, it was of enhanced importance to conserve all that was best in ancient civilisation and to marshal it in the perceived interests of Christendom. Hence, Pope Nicholas V, already captivated by the rediscovered archives and a man dedicated to establishing the Vatican Library, would have been willing to have a go at the Turk if contemporary secular support had been forthcoming. So it is not surprising that the renaissance trend moved into a yet higher gear after 1453 and Western Christendom, subconsciously perhaps, now needed to put itself on show. It fell to the patricians of the Italian communes—Borgias, Sforza, Medicis, Farneses, the holders of the papal office itself to vie with each other in their patronage of the most brilliant minds, artists and sculptors of their day in order to surround themselves with this humanistic spirit. There is irony here, for in its attempts to recreate and rediscover the glories of pre-Christian Rome, the papacy was playing a dangerous game by embracing the pagan origins of Rome while still trying to come to terms with Christianity's losses in the East. The tensions between the

---

[235] Lorenzo Valla (1406-57) was an outspoken critic of scholasticism and a pioneer of modern historical criticism. See chapters 2, 8.

secular and spiritual roles of the pontiff were going to be difficult to sustain. Office holders such as Nicholas V, Julius II, Leo X, Clement VII were each, in his own way, to be captivated by the new humano-centric dynamic, energetically patronising at 'public expense' the pop stars of the High Renaissance: Michelangelo's (1475-1564) adornment of the Sistine Chapel and his design for the great dome of St Peter's, Leonardo's (1452-1519) *Virgin of the Rocks,* Titian's (1488-1576) *Portrait of Paul III and his nephews,* Raphael's (1483-1520) *School of Athens* and the risqué artistry as exemplified in Boticelli's (c.1445-1510) *Primavera.* Herein is expressed, in art form, the expression of humankind's boundless potential. The artist's treatment of the human body (light, shade, form, expression), the use of perspective and the naturalistic treatment of the local surroundings (buildings, trees, landscape) ooze confidence in human capacity; in truth, a different world from that represented by the anonymous artisans of the Middle Ages with their depictions of flat, two-dimensional po-faced functionaries deferring to authority figures of a sacred, secular or clerical nature.

Inevitably this new approach to mankind's place in the world drifted into a reappraisal of the role of the church and the assumptions upon which it had based its claims. Tentative biblical and textual criticism being an expression of the spreading of renaissance ideas into Northern Europe was the armoury of the tentative Christian humanists in Europe North of the Alps—notably Reuchlin (1455-1522) and Erasmus (1467-1536). Each using newly discovered manuscripts in Hebrew and Greek, respectively, they threw doubt upon some of the medieval foundations upon which the church had been built. Jerome's Latin Vulgate—the 'official' Bible of the church—was found to contain weaknesses in translation in the light of more reliable source material and questions were raised as to the efficacy or veracity, which had crept into church doctrine and practice over time. In his attempts to recapture the world of the early church and to re-infuse its spirit into contemporary conduct, Erasmus and his friend Thomas More, in particular, were highly critical of the degeneracy, which he saw was corrupting the church to which, in principle, he was passionately attached.

While Erasmus was applying critical analysis to the theological basis of the church, Machiavelli (1469-1527) was satirising the process of government in *The Prince* and Leonardo was pushing ahead with his own investigations into the workings of the natural world. This self-acknowledged 'disciple of experiment' was prepared to take no received knowledge on trust. His anatomical studies, his forays into the theories of aerodynamics, his intricate study of plant life and his interest in the sub-aqua world: nothing escaped his curiosity in his thirst to delve

The Church 115

into the whys and wherefores of existence. It was this experimental method that led to Copernicus (1473-1543) to publish in 1540 his belief in the round earth and the sun's centrality, to its confirmation by Kepler (1571-1630) and Galileo (1564-1642) and for the church then to condemn the findings as contradictory to its cherished postulation of an earth-centric universe.[236] By its initial enthusiasm for the humanistic dynamism unleashed during the fourteenth and fifteenth centuries, the papacy itself had colluded, as far as the church was concerned, in a creation worthy of Victor Frankenstein,[237] laying itself open to attack from within and from without. Henceforth, the church was to be seen to play a rearguard action if not in an attempt to close Pandora's box, at least to limit the effects, but it has never totally shaken off the image of a conservative monolith, being induced reluctantly into facing up to theological and scientific advance. However, the church did manage to emulate Pandora by preserving the promise of hope and to that we must briefly turn.

Islam's depredations on Europe's landward trade with the Far East—China and India—coincided with the renaissance quest for knowledge. This included renewed interest in Ptolemy's theory[238] of the round world. In their attempts to put this theory to the test, Portugal's Prince Henry ('The Navigator') (1394-1490) and others made substantial advances in maritime development—the use of the mariner's compass, the Astrolabe, and improved sailing ships—the Caravel in particular—and to the age of reconnaissance. Somehow Islam must be outflanked and a passage to the East must be found by sea. Bartholomew Diaz (c.1455-1500) finally rounded the Cape of Good Hope in 1486 and Vasco da Gama (1460-1524) arrived in India in 1498. This, and the misconstrued transatlantic voyages of Columbus (1451-1506) between 1492 and 1506, opened hitherto undreamed-of opportunities for Christian enterprise in lands beyond the confines of Europe and the Near East into the virgin territories of Africa, the Americas and the Orient.

Our defining moment that of the ill-fated action of Giustiniani such as that facilitated the passage of the sultan into Constantinople was of momentous import. For many, it marks the end of the Old World and the beginning of the New, for it leads us into an acute stage of the

---

[236] See chapter 15.

[237] From Mary Shelley's *Frankenstein*, a romantic novel first published in 1818.

[238] Ptolemy (c.85-c.168), an Egyptian astronomer and geographer, had postulated a round earth, albeit at the centre of the universe, during the second century AD.

renaissance. It represents the hammering of the final nail into the coffin of Constantine's ideal polity. It exposed the divisions and weaknesses of a Christianity consequent upon the circumstances of the schism of 1054 and the disparity between the Eastern and Western doctrinal variants in terms of both cause and effect. It reinforced the dilemma for future generations on not only how it was to cope internally with these divisions but also how it was to accommodate a militant Islamic dynamo that was not going to go away: how to reconcile the concomitant social and political divisions between East and West. The Latin Church as we have seen tended to grasp the material effects that the 'new' learning from Byzantium was presenting itself without appreciating the spiritual fallout. This was to lead to what many now see as the inevitability of the Protestant Reformation, the opening up of new mission fields worldwide; in the longer term, to a church vulnerable to accusations of a masquerading, dogmatic, self-indulgent chimera being dragged, kicking and screaming, into a world with which its hidebound structure was bound to struggle.

Chapter 12

Luther before the Diet of Worms, 1521 by Anton von Werner

HERE I STAND

For the relatively non-discerning, a pleasantly sweet, full-flavoured, moderately priced liebfraumilch makes an agreeable accompaniment to a palatable meal. This soft white, in its distinctive reddish brown bottle from the Rhineland, nurtured by the lush verdant meadows bisected by the river from which the region derives its name has its origins, in the folklore of viniculture, centred on a small vineyard that surrounds the Church of Our Lady (the Liebfrauenkirche) and from which the appellation derives. Here, in the city of Worms, on the left bank of the Rhine, there developed a significant centre of trade, an important distribution nexus for the wine industry: home to the oldest synagogue in Europe and graced by one of the finest examples of a thirteenth-century Romanesque cathedral. This town, now modest in terms of both size and importance within the context of post-war industrial Germany, was, during the Middle Ages, a thriving crossroads of religion, culture and business. An episcopal see, an imperial free city,[239] Worms had already played its part, in 1122, by acting as host to the signatories to

---

[239] An imperial free city was a city owing direct allegiance to the Holy Roman emperor, and thus independent of the state ruler.

the papal-imperial concordat that healed the potentially fatal rift such as that had threatened the medieval equanimity between pontiff and emperor.[240] Ironically it was here, in 1521, the scene of our defining moment that not only this tension was tested to its limits but also the entire structure of a Universal Church in the West began to unravel. It was here, personified by the pre-arranged encounter between a fairy tale prince presiding over former glories and a humble Augustinian monk pinning his hopes on the assurance of the Holy Scriptures, that, in Roland Bainton's words, 'the past and the future were (destined) to meet'.[241]

Martin Luther arrived in the city during April 1521, attired in his monastic habit, wearied not only by days of travel in a two-wheeled Saxon cart bedded by straw throughout his journey from Wittenberg, but burdened by years of a digestive malady probably exacerbated by mental torture and emotional stress.

Summoned thither to disown his widely publicised and published 'heretical' ideas on the doctrine and structure of the church, Luther was to stand in judgement before the Assembled Diet[242] of the German regions of the Holy Roman Empire. This was a gathering of the great and the good—dukes, margraves, landgraves, electors, prince archbishops, nominally subject to the authority of the mightiest prince in Europe, Charles V—king of Spain, Naples and the Americas, archduke of Austria and the hereditary Central European Habsburg lands, duke of Burgundy—and in 1519, the elected Holy Roman emperor (1519-56).[243] It was in the judgement hall of the Bischofshof that in the minds of

---

[240]   The so-called *Investiture Controversy*. See chapter 8.

[241]   Bainton, R.: *Here I Stand*, Lion Books, 1983.

[242]   The German diet or Reichstag was the closest equivalent to a German parliament, comprising the local hereditary rulers of the quasi-autonomous states as well as ecclesiastical figures who performed secular functions in addition. Germany, at the time, was a disparate entity comprising some three hundred or so self- governing regions. It was not until 1871 that it became a united nation. Effectively, by 1500, most of the executive powers had in fact passed to the local prince.

[243]   The office of Holy Roman emperor was not hereditary, but elective. There were seven elector/princes of seven German states, whose function was to fill the vacancy when it arose. Although they technically had a free choice, by long-standing tradition, the position had been held by the senior member of the Habsburg dynasty. What made it significant at this time was the election and lobbying for the new imperial dignity in 1519 on the death of Emperor Maximilian (1493-1519).

The Church   119

his supporters, Luther was to be cast in the role of Christ before Pilate; the Word versus Rome; eternity taking on fifteen hundred years of Roman pretension and seven hundred years of Medieval Carolingian presuppositions; a confrontation with Caesar, Charlemagne's young successor—a paper tiger as it was to turn out—whose majestic inheritance 'like earth's proud empires (was doomed to) pass away'.[244]

The daunting prospect facing Luther, as he faced this august assemblage, would have intimidated the most leonine of hearts. Yet this frail, sickly, short stocky figure was shored up by the promises of scripture—the truth upon which his own position rested in the face of a plethora of worldly self-seekers, assembled in the name of the German lands, at the behest of the church in Rome: recant or possibly die were the alternatives facing him.

On the previous day, before a committee of the Diet, Luther's tracts and pamphlets had been laid out in front of him. To the substantive question as to whether they were in fact his work, Luther responded unequivocally that indeed they were and that there were yet more. Then, demanded the papal inquisitor Eck, 'Do you recant them?' A momentary flicker of hesitation registered on the lone monk's countenance. He needed a night to sleep on it to consider his response. The new day signalled a plenary session of the Diet with the emperor presiding and standing room only: the setting for our defining moment. It was perhaps the theatrical moment for which Luther had been calculating and realising the worst fears of the papal legate, Aleander, who had feared the danger of creating an opportunity for the defence to take charge and centre stage. In place of a straightforward reply, the Diet was subjected to a withering apologia for Luther's position from the man himself. Concluding his statement, Luther's words have long re-echoed in the annals of Protestant iconography:

> Unless I am convinced by Scripture and plain reason, I do not accept the authority of popes and councils, for they have contradicted each other. My conscience is to the Word of God. I cannot and will not recant anything, for to go against conscience is neither right nor safe. (Here I Stand. I can do no other). So help me God. Amen.

The words, the mood, the occasion, each in juxtaposition sealed the fate of the Universal Catholic Church in the West. In his stark loneliness

---

[244] From a hymn by Ellerton, J.: *The day Thou gavest*, no. 648 in *Hymns and Psalms*, Methodist Publishing House, 1983.

and humility, emboldened as he saw it only by the Spirit of Christ and finding expression in the sheer bald temerity of tone, he shook to their very foundations, the very premises upon which the church in the West had based its authority.

Charles V, by now abandoning all sense of formality and any attempts to follow the script, responded in perhaps the only way the princely protector of Rome could as follows:

'A single friar who goes counter to all Christianity for one thousand years must be wrong', and on that basis, he secured the passage of the 'Edict of Worms' declaring Luther to be an Outlaw throughout Germany, officially excommunicated from the church; save for a guaranteed journey home, Luther was left to sink or swim.

From humble beginnings of mining, peasant parentage, Luther had been born at Eisleben in the eastern Germanic lands in 1483. Turning to religion at an early age, he took his monastic vows according to the Augustinian rite at Erfurt before being offered a professorship in theology at the University of Wittenberg, where an interest in the classics and humanist theology, quintessentially expressed by Desiderius Erasmus (1465-1536), pan-European scholar and intellect, combined to mould his thinking: get back to the raw Gospel and put medieval Catholic Scholasticism in its place. Nevertheless, moods of dark depression clouded his vision of an otherwise brilliant future. He could not shake off the dread despair of the fires of hell, given the Augustinian interpretation of original sin, in which he had been schooled. If the wages of sin is death,[245] then how could he escape the eternal punishment? The traditional panacea as taught by the Roman Church seemed straightforward enough. Baldly stated, chalk up sufficient brownie points in heaven's community chest by numerous acts of kindness, sacrifice and piety, then one ought to fast-track through the purgatorial[246] waiting room and the pearly gates with a strong wind at one's back. Where one did backslide in this life—to err and to sin—there were the priestly sacraments of confession and penance to fall back on: confess the sin and repay the debt through acts of contrition, penitence and reparation, as the price of ecclesiastical absolution. There was also the excess of merit from the 'saints' upon which the penitent who fell short could draw: more on this later. Luther, nurtured by a solid intellectual dose of the judgemental and vengeful predisposition of God, had gone further,

---

[245] Romans 6:23.

[246] The Catholic doctrine of purgatory whereby at death the soul remains for an unspecified time in an unpleasant state, while being cleansed of sins as yet 'unpurged', prior to the hoped for reward in heaven.

The Church 121

much further, in his own strength than most, in order to circumvent his Maker's wrath. Yet the more he tried, the more emotionally alienated he felt himself from God and increasingly disaffected by the premise that 'good works' facilitated salvation. It was increasingly apparent to him that the gulf between his own efforts and God's standards was not only vast, but unbridgeable; his own feeble attempts to make it right with the Almighty were as a drop in the ocean in terms of the impact they made. Try even harder and for him the depression intensified. Mentally anguished and physically wrecked, Luther sought spiritual advice from his monastic superior, Staupitz, who advised him, cryptically, to 'get to know God'.

An increasingly focused revisitation of the scriptures was repaid by his lighting upon a verse in Paul's letter to the Romans: 'the just shall live by faith'.[247] The phrase hit Luther straight between the eyes. Of course! As the burden began to lift from his shoulders, Luther had turned his own theological preconceptions on their head and understood God differently, as Staupitz had implied that he should. Now God was perceived as recognising human weakness and by His grace and mercy provides believers with the means of bridging that gap. Christ's atonement on the cross has done for humankind what we, in all our puerile attempts to do 'all ourselves', will always fail to accomplish. 'By grace, you are saved by faith'.[248]

In point of fact, Luther was by no means the first to have recognised this fundamental doctrine, and Wycliffe[249] and Huss[250] had already suffered at the hands of the church for proclaiming it. What made Luther's findings so momentous was the coalescence of a seemingly unrelated set of factors concentrated in the German states of his day, which together precipitated the irrevocable spilt in Western Christendom.

---

[247] Romans 1:17.

[248] Ephesians 2:8-9.

[249] John Wycliffe (c.1324-84). An English cleric and scholar who denounced certain doctrines of the church as well as the corrupt practices of the clergy. Reputedly making the first complete translation of the Bible into English, he was denied promotion by the state although his life was spared and his followers, the Lollards, played a part in the English Peasants Revolt (1380-81).

[250] Jan Huss (c.1370-1415) was a Czech ecclesiastic who preached Wycliffe's reformed doctrines. Summoned by the Emperor Sigismund to account for himself under the promise of safe conduct to the Council of Constance, he was treacherously betrayed and burnt as a heretic, hence Luther's tenuous position.

Around the same time, a Dominican friar, Johann Tetzel, was, in the name of the church, exploiting the doctrine of indulgences in Germany in a manner which would do justice to the techniques of a latter day double-glazing salesman. An indulgence was originally a papally authorised certificate by which a penitent could access surplus merit, which the saints of the past had left over, following their own successful translation from purgatory into heaven. At first, a genuine act of penance—service in the crusades or a pilgrimage to a holy shrine—was demanded. However, by the beginning of the sixteenth century, Tetzel and others had reduced the theory into a rapacious, money-grabbing exercise to reduce an archbishop's debts[251] and, as many believed, for home improvements at the Vatican,[252] whereby for a fiscal consideration alone, the penitent or his loved ones would be hustled through the trials of purgatory:

> As soon as the coin in the coffer rings, the soul from purgatory springs.

Not that Luther was, by any means, the first to expose such cynical exploitation of the medieval masses, Chaucer, for example, an acute observer of ecclesiastical foibles in fourteenth-century England, has the pardoner provoke 'mine host' to retort:

> Thou woldest make me kiss thyn old breech
> And swere it were a relik of a seint[253]

In the light of the scripture that had released Luther from his own perceived condition of hopelessness, not only was Tetzel peddling theological blasphemy and abuse, but also he was ripping off a German peasantry already crippled by rising prices and higher rents: a national scandal, perpetrated in the selfish interests of a distant, foreign papacy whose commissioning of Bramante (1444-1514), Bernini (1598-1680),

---

[251] The archbishop of Mainz, also one of the seven electors, had accumulated enormous debts to secure his own election to the office.

[252] Pope Julius II (1503-13) had approved the complete rebuilding of St Peter's in Rome: reconstruction of the Basilica and of course the recommissioning of Michelangelo to adorn the Sistine Chapel. Pope Leo X (1513-22) needed more money to complete the task, employing Raphael, Leonardo and Michelangelo to adorn it.

[253] Chaucer, G. (c.1340-1400): *The Pardoneres Tale* from *The Canterbury Tales* (lines 620-621).

Raphael and Michelangelo to transform St Peters and the Vatican with sublime renaissance artistry and technology seemed alien and remote. Luther, incensed by what he saw as a thinly veiled money-making racket, in his role as university professor, nailed his famous *Ninety-Five Theses*, or arguments, levelled against the entire concept of indulgences on the door of the Castle Church of Wittenberg on the eve of the Feast of All Saints, 31 October 1517—an action akin to posting one's ideas on the internet and inviting (from fellow academics) a civilised response. That was all apart from despatching a copy to the archbishop of Mainz whose secular pragmatism had brought the issue into clear focus. Events however overtook him. Proprietors of the newly invented printing presses, ever eager to cash in on the latest exposé of the high and mighty, got hold of the theses and began to flood the German market, for a people already smarting under ecclesiastical financial obligations and an increasingly unstable social order as the imperial political cohesion was straining under the growing tendency towards local princely particularism. Add to this the growing number of artists willing and able to exploit the situation by producing crude but effective woodcuts for learned and illiterate consumption, and one has the ingredients for an explosive cocktail. Initially, Rome was slow to respond: 'a mere monkish squabble', declared Pope Leo X (1513-22)—typical of a Medici pontiff's reaction who found the whole affair something of an irritation, best swept under the carpet. After all, events in faraway Wittenberg shouldn't be allowed to detract from his unashamed assertion that God had entrusted him with the papacy for his own enjoyment—a newly refurbished pad at the Vatican and the patronage at his disposal by which he could further enrich his own extensive family.

The years 1517-21 were crucial. Luther's ideas spread like wildfire across the German states. Rather than act in tandem to dampen the burning faggots of dissension, the two Catholic potentates, Leo X and successive emperors Maximilian and Charles V, were more often than not engaged in locked horns and mutually inflicted pain. As indicated, the Pope's reaction was a case of too little, too late and in any event too much for this mediocre scion of an essentially secular Florentine dynasty. During these four years, Luther was shielded by the extramural diversions occupying the attention of the leaders of Catholicism. There was the external threat to Christendom at large from the advancing forces of the Ottoman Turks: rivalry between the Valois kings of France and the Habsburgs for supremacy in Italy, snapping at the heals of the extensive papal territories on the peninsula. Then there had been the rift occasioned by the campaign and subsequent election of Charles V as Holy Roman emperor in 1519.

Thus Luther's position moved inexorably from a respected member of the university's senior common room to the iconic champion of German liberties—the long-sought 'Holy Man', the epitome of German piety and national sensitivities.

Under the protection of his own patron, the electoral prince of saxony, Frederick the Wise (1463-1525), during those crucial first years, Luther was subjected to a fraternal visitation by papal legate, Cajetan in 1518, and engaged in a very public disputation at Leipzig with the Dominican Jan Eck the following year in which Luther's credentials as a heretic were laid bare. By 1520, it had all turned very nasty with Luther's vitriolic attack not only upon aspects of church doctrine, but also on the very institution of the Roman Church itself.

It had been, then, Luther's denigration of the indulgence theory, which had launched his journey towards stardom. First, he had asserted that indulgences had no scriptural authority: we are saved not by works (or payment), but by faith, and if the papacy stubbornly taught contrary to scripture, then the papacy must be wrong! If the papacy persisted in this fundamental error, then, on Luther's terms, it could not claim to be the authentic valid voice of Christ or His church. 'Scripture alone' for truth and 'faith alone' for salvation were Luther's take on the foundations of the Christian Gospel and the basis, therefore, upon which the whole fabric of the Roman Catholic Church was now called into question. If 'faith alone', why then the necessity for the mediation of a priestly caste? After all, was it not stated in one of the New Testament letters ascribed to Peter himself that *all* believers are projected into a priestly role?[254] If so what was the need for any Christian to acknowledge the church's self-proclaimed arcane route to God when Christ himself claimed that, uniquely, 'no-one comes to the Father but by me'?[255] Luther's logical momentum was relentless. Was not Christ's sacrifice a once-and-for-all atonement for the sin of humankind?[256] How can this be reconciled with the routine re-enactment of this sacrifice by the clergy, which claimed that the elements of bread and wine transubstantiated into Christ's Body and Blood on the elevation of the host during the mass? Indeed, declared Luther ultimately, only two of the seven sacraments of the church—baptism and the Holy Communion[257]—had any scriptural

---

[254]   1 Peter 2:9.

[255]   John 14:6.

[256]   Romans 6:10; 2 Corinthians 5:14.

[257]   The sacraments are, officially, the channels by which God confers his grace or authority to human beings. The Catholic version recognised that these could only be conferred by means of a priest that salvation is unattainable

validity at all. The 'relics'—thorns of the 'true crown worn by Jesus' at his crucifixion, slivers of wood from the 'original cross', strands of hair from long, dead saints, and the invocation and veneration of the Virgin Mary—to which the faithful had resorted for special favour, in return for the appropriate 'consideration', were rubbished by Luther as spurious, and symptomatic of a church reliant on magic and superstition for sustenance. All this he identified with church tradition increasingly preoccupied with its self-preservation and utilised by the devil himself to lead the erstwhile righteous into a state of perdition. As the debate hotted up, Luther's attacks became more and more personal—the Pope now the very anti-Christ, the fount of a structure rotten to its very core, citing instances of priesthood and religious orders as being ignorant, idle, pluralistic, nepotic, simonic, worldly and inherently immoral, satirised as such by the Catholic humanist Erasmus[258] a few years earlier.

The tension and bitterness all boiled over in 1520 when Luther consolidated his ideas in the form of his three famous publications: *The Liberty of the Christian Man* extolled the virtue of unlimited access to and interpretation of the scriptures, as the means of the believer's *direct* hotline to Christ unhampered by priestly mediation. In his *Appeal to the German Nobility*, Luther urged all German state rulers to seize control of the church's assets in their territories and impose his reformed doctrines. In his *On the Babylonish Captivity of the Church*, he castigated the Roman Church as the great 'whore' as represented in the Book of Revelation.[259]

Papal patience snapped. By now, Luther had burnt his boats and the church burnt his books. Only the intercession of Frederick the Wise, Luther's own prince and patron, saved him from following them to the flames as a direct consequence of the publication of his excommunication in January 1521. Jan Huss had suffered no less for adopting a similar stance as we have seen.

---

without acknowledging them and that there were in fact seven, the others being confirmation, marriage, penance, ordination and extreme unction. The Protestant line has consistently maintained that the sacraments are beneficial but not *essential* to the sinner's salvation—'an outward and visible sign of an inward and spiritual grace'.

[258] Desiderius Erasmus, a European scholar of great renown and a Christian humanist who had been highly critical of the Catholic Church, but who remained faithful to it. Initially sympathetic to Luther, he became an implacable enemy.

[259] Revelation 17:1, 16; 18, passim.

Summoned instead, before the German Diet—our defining moment—Luther, then, stood his ground as described above, armed only with his scriptural assurance, in consequence of which the assembled company decreed his status as an outlaw as befitted the unrepentant heretic. The chivalrous emperor, despite the representation of Aleander, the papal legate, was a man of his word and guaranteed Luther safe passage home. Captured for his own protection by 'friendly' agents en route,[260] and spending the ensuing nine months in the Wartburg Castle, Luther used the opportunity to translate Bible sections into German and composed hymns for congregational use. Meanwhile, in Wittenberg itself, freed from Catholic control and Luther's own restraining influence, radical preaching by Carlstadt and some self-styled 'prophets' from Zwickau precipitated an orgy of mass destruction of papal symbolism—relics, statues, carvings all fell victim to this wanton rampage. Only Luther's timely return to the city, safeguarded by Electoral Prince Frederick, saved the city from complete religious meltdown. The same could not be said for other areas though. However, as if on cue, German city after German city throughout the 1520s declared for reform, the burgers sensing not only religious freedom, but also the social and economic advantages of so doing. The moribund orders of the so-called imperial knights[261] of Germany, led by the philosopher Ulrich von Hutten, rose in the name of what was to become known as the reformation. For the imperial knights themselves this was, in fact, to prove a last despairing and fatal throw of the dice to reinvigorate their ailing fortunes. Much the most serious consequence however was the so-called Peasants Revolt of 1524-25. Reading more into Luther's libertarian tracts than the reformer ever intended, peasants throughout the German lands took up arms to overturn the entire social order—church *and* secular—lock, stock and barrel. Luther's condemnation of their actions in his treatise entitled *Against the Thieving and Murderous Hordes of Peasants* is sufficient to summarise his unambiguous message to their leader Thomas Muntzer (c.1488-1525) and his like. This apparent betrayal of the simple masses on the face of it cost Luther dearly as he condoned the harsh repression of the revolt.

Nevertheless, it endeared him to many of the wavering princes who saw him as a supporter of an *ordered* society based on their governance, while simultaneously standing up to the monolithic, centrist church. The 'peasants rising' was ruthlessly crushed when, in 1529, the

---

[260] Probably at the behest of Frederick the Wise.

[261] The aristocratic remnants of a land owning caste owing allegiance not to their local prince, but directly to the emperor himself.

The Church   127

much-harassed Charles V having been given breathing space from multitudinous distractions elsewhere, called a further German Diet in the city of Speier, expressly to enforce Catholicism throughout the empire. Several of the assembled princes registered their protest in no uncertain terms: thus was coined the 'Protestant' tag on those opposing the established Catholic order. Henceforth the German lands large and small were to be split along religious lines according to the respective persuasion of the three hundred or so princes entrusted to their care. The failure to resolve the doctrinal disputes, which had, by 1530, rent Western Christendom asunder, was to have repercussions far beyond the death of Martin Luther in 1546, that of his much respected spokesman Phillip Melanchton (1497-1560) and indeed of the abdication of the well meaning, overburdened and disillusioned Charles V ten years later, whose attempts at reuniting Western Christendom were buried at the peace of Augsburg in 1555.[262]

In essence, Martin Luther, by first exposing and then challenging Catholic weaknesses, and the various premises upon which its strength had been based, opened the way for far more radical and far-reaching religious movements. In Germany itself, the failed Peasants Revolt spawned the rise of the radical Anabaptist movement in the 1520s and 1530s. The Anabaptist societies were indeed diffuse—all of them recognised adult (believer's) baptism alone; most accepted the inner, personal, workings of the Holy Spirit as the predominant source of religious authority and many either passively despised, ignored or actively resisted any claim the state might have over them. All such pockets of the Anabaptist persuasion occasioned the joint opprobrium of both Lutheran and Catholic authorities, who exacted a harsh, even cruel price, from the failure of these scattered groups to combine in common cause. Nevertheless, they were to leave their marks upon the puritan, congregational and baptist societies of ensuing centuries.

It was, however, in Switzerland that enigmatic, mountainous and autonomous domain in the heart of Europe, which was to become the centre for the dispersion of a brand of Protestantism distinctive from that of Lutheranism, which had been confined largely to Germany, Scandinavia and by extension to the Americas. Initially, it appeared likely that the Swiss canton of Zurich would work hand in hand with Lutheranism to promote a cohesive Protestant front. Its religious

---

[262] This treaty signed by the emperor officially recognised the principle, in Germany, of *cuius regio, eius religio*—the religion of each state (Lutheran or Catholic) will be determined by the religion of its prince.

leader, Zwingli (1484-1531), had established a reformed church there, based very much on Lutheran principles. He nevertheless consistently maintained that his theological views were arrived at independently of Luther's work, which did little to mutually endear the two reformers. An attempt was made at Marburg in 1529 to harness the efforts of the two men in common cause, but failed in part due to personality differences, but substantially over doctrinal interpretation. This centred around the theory of the Holy Communion.[263] Luther's idea that Christ's presence is *real* (but not mutated) within the elements of the bread and wine (consubstantiation—'This is my Body'[264]) was far too convoluted for Zwingli—nothing more than a fudged compromise with Rome's emphasis on the metamorphosis of the elements (transubstantiation). 'No', argued Zwingli, the purpose of the Eucharist is to call to mind Christ's all-important sacrifice—with considerably more significance attached to His injunction to 'Do this in Remembrance of Me'.[265] Such a fundamental difference had the effect of isolating Zwingli and his overall influence on the course of the reformation was relatively small. To Luther belonged the drama, the politics, the elan 'coming out' as he did a year or two earlier, while outliving Zwingli whose premature death left his own movement stranded. Indeed, the Swiss Reform dynamic was ultimately subsumed by the work of the Frenchman John Calvin (1509-64), who by force of an unrelenting logic, coupled with a highly developed sense of moral rectitude, came close to creating a theocratic community embracing the city of Geneva. It was here to which zealous seekers for a reformed faith were to repair after 1540 and from whence dedicated converts to Calvinist thought expressed in his *Institute of the Christian Religion* were to disperse and penetrate those regions of Europe where Lutheranism had limited appeal. Preaching the doctrine of an unchanging, stern and judgemental God, the power of whose being governed the process from the moment of an individual's conception to one's ultimate destiny in heaven or hell, Calvinism's omniscient, omnipresent, all-powerful Creator tempered only by Christ's atonement was logically satisfying. This was to find fertile soil in such areas as France (the Huguenots), the Netherlands, Poland, Bohemia, parts of Germany and the Presbyterian variety expounded by John Knox (c.1510-72) in Scotland.

---

[263] The generic term for what Catholics refer as the mass and Protestants as, variously, the Eucharist or simply the Lord's supper commemorating the passion of Christ.

[264] Matthew 26:26-28; Mark 14:22-23; Luke 22:19-20; 1 Corinthians 11:24-25.

[265] Luke 22:19; 1 Corinthians 11:24.

The Church 129

Thus, by the close of the sixteenth century, much of Western Europe had rejected Rome and Protestant national churches had been set up. Significant Protestant minorities prevailed elsewhere, notably in France, while in England a distinctive brand of Christian expression was embodied within the Anglican establishment.

What Luther had done was to expose the weaknesses of the Roman Church, prise open Pandora's box through which was to pour a plethora of religious reform, promoted by people riding a tidal wave of opportunism, sincerity or a mixture of both. The Catholic Church girded its loins and fought back. However, few can deny the implications of our defining moment in the Bischofshof—the melodramatic monk taking on the tried and tested crown and indeed heir of the Carolingian ideal: the catalyst for a further four hundred years of frequently bitter inter-Christian acrimony, infighting and suspicion. In the words of Luther's biographer, 'some would see at this point the beginning of modern times',[266] no less, to some, than the germ of Western Democracy. Around the table of an increasingly less abstemious Protestant household today, a glass of Rhenish Liebfraumilch may well be raised in affirmation, 'I'll drink to that!' A simultaneous gathering in the heart of Rioja Spain might well have cause to feel less charitable.

---

[266] Bainton, R.: op. cit. At the German Diet of Augsburg in 1530, the failure of a compromise over doctrine resulted in the Augsburg Confession of Faith of the Lutheran Church, the basic tenets of which resulted in the fundamental teaching of that branch of the church. At what turned out to be one final attempt to heal the differences between Lutherans and Catholics, a meeting was held at Regensburg in 1541 between moderate representatives of both persuasions; despite some progress on some issues, the hierarchies of both rejected the compromises reached with sad consequences for the short term of Germany and some would say for the long-term health of the church.

Chapter 13

The Coronation of Henry VIII and Catherine of Aragon (engraving.)

THE KING'S GREAT MATTER

The Shropshire town of Ludlow today affords its inhabitants and visitors alike the opportunity to experience the vibrancy of an industrious small urban centre while accommodating a sensitivity to its gently evolving colourful past: a location where ancient, medieval and modern appear to coexist in delicate harmony. 'The perfect historic town', according to Sir John Betjeman, its success is in recognition of an easy-going ambience that eschews the brash, garish commercialism so typical of communities in a hurry to get nowhere in particular. This little gem of a place, with its ascetically pleasing juxtaposition of the Tudor timber-framed hostelry and Georgian stone facade along Broad Street, bounded by the Guildhall at one end and Broad Gate at the other, is nowadays very much on the tourist beat.

On a commanding elevation above the town, competing quite successfully for pre-eminence with the 135-foot tall Gothic tower of the Parish Church of St Laurence and overlooking the river Tarn snaking its way through the valley onward via the Severn towards the Bristol Channel, stand the ruins of the twelfth-century Norman castle—one of a chain of fortifications designed in more turbulent times to police the border between England and Wales. Our defining moment in the fortunes of

The Church 131

the church invites us to step inside the confines of its red-stoned walls, back to Easter Sunday, 27 March 1502. Within its unusual circular chapel, the prayers of the faithful acknowledging the joyful reality of a Risen Saviour would have been tempered by the sombre and foreboding intercessions for its most important resident, the young Prince of Wales. This fifteen-year-old was, that day, confined to bed within the royal sanctum. Having been despatched to Ludlow in the service of his royal obligations towards the Council of the Marches,[267] he had been taken very seriously ill indeed. He was evidently in grievous distress; that is, if the testimony of the herald charged with the duty of announcing his inevitable demise is to be believed: The young Prince Arthur, barely half a year married to a girl a few months older than himself, suffered in his last hours from the 'most pitiful disease that with so sore and great violence had battled and driven, in the singular parts of him inward, (so) that cruel and fervent enemy of nature, did utterly vanquish and overcome the pure and friendful blood'.[268]

When death came as a welcome relief to the sorely stricken prince, his Spanish wife, now a widow at the age of sixteen, was left to contemplate a future which, given the exigencies of the time, would not be hers to determine. The castle, which had once been 'home' to the two tragic princes in the tower,[269] must have induced a dire sense of foreboding to the bereft Catherine of Aragon (1485-1536). As one door in her short life closed, the key to the next would be tied up in the tangled web of European diplomacy.

This defining moment—this sombre account of the passing of the Prince of Wales—was, despite its unprepossessing circumstances, to prove the catalyst for the conception and evolution of that amorphous, inscrutable Christian organism known worldwide as the Anglican Communion, or in Britain as the Church of England and to its break with Rome. Of course nobody at Ludlow at the time, or anyone else, could envisage this, but all the features of human experience—love, lust, jealousy, religious sentiment, power politics, the dynamics of commerce,

---

[267] The Council of the Marshes was an outpost of the king's council to deal with matters relating to Wales and the border counties. Its specific functions varied over the years; in Arthur's time, it featured in ecclesiastical concerns and issues relating to inheritance. The council was abolished in 1689.

[268] Quoted in Starkey, D.: *The Six Wives of Henry VIII*, The Sunday Telegraph Supplement, 2:9:1.

[269] The child king, Edward V (1483), and his younger brother, the duke of York, allegedly murdered in the Tower of London on the orders of their uncle, Richard III (1483-85).

The King's Great Matter

dynastic concerns—reverberated from this untimely end to a marriage in the culmination of which so much time and energy had been invested.

This marriage had not been exactly fired by the passion of a prince of hearts winning the fair hand of his princess. Crudely stated, it was a contract honoured in the light of an Anglo-Spanish Treaty of 1499[270] to marry off the first son of England's king, Henry VII (1485-1509), to the youngest daughter of Ferdinand and Isabella, king and queen of Spain (1479-1516). It had been a diplomatic and dynastic coup. It is scarcely surprising, therefore, that, despite having apparently boasted on his wedding night that he had been in the midst of Spain, it is evident that the union was of minimal emotional import as far as Arthur was concerned. For Catherine, there seems to have been a marginally greater sense of marital attachment, who somewhat paradoxically, yet with overwhelming long-term significance, never publicly deviated from her denial that her marriage to Arthur had ever been consummated.

To Ferdinand, the early demise of his new son-in-law was an issue of distinct frustration, anxious as he was to use England as an ally against the French in respect of his own forward policy in Italy. To Henry VII, his paternal grief was compounded by the potential recall of a considerable dowry, which had accompanied Catherine to England. A solution was at hand—the king's younger son, the ten-year-old Henry was not yet spoken for and clearly available as an appropriate suitor for Catherine. Problem eventually solved having endured several diplomatic hiccups along the way: signed, sealed and delivered, the deal was struck, committing the two as yet innocent pawns to the marital state on the attainment of Henry's maturity—a condition fulfilled in 1509 when he succeeded to the throne. 'Seldom', writes Prof. Bindoff on Henry VII's cynical role in this affair, 'has greed (ultimately) been more grievously punished'.[271]

There had been one ecclesiastical hurdle to clear for the conclusion of this matter. Scripturally, the Book of Leviticus specifically discourages, if not forbids, the remarriage of an erstwhile wife to her husband's brother.[272] A successful appeal to the Pope, however, could result in his granting of a dispensation in regard to this injunction in the name of the Roman Church and to whose authority England still submitted. Pope

---

[270] The Treaty of Medina del Campo.

[271] Bindoff, S. T.: *Tudor England*, Pelican Books, 1963. Henry VII was not totally averse to seeking alternative prospective brides for his younger son, but it seems probable that the match with Catherine appeared the one with the brightest prospects. It was certainly the one that prevailed.

[272] Leviticus 20:21. See MacCulloch, D. (ed.), *The Reign of Henry VIII: Politics, Policy and Piety*, 1995, p. 139.

The Church

Julius II (1503-13), never one to miss the opportunity to grant a favour when sensing diplomatic advantage to be had, was happy to oblige; a mere sideshow, this, as far as Julius was concerned, when weighed alongside the rebuilding of St Peter's, the acquisition of the finest art treasures and wars of his own in Italy to prosecute.

Throughout the early years of Henry VIII's reign, the king was indeed most anxious to prove his ardent Roman Catholic credentials. He had every reason to avoid the religious turbulence brewing in Germany after 1517, as Luther's rebellious stance took hold. Henry had even written a strident polemic countering Luther's position on the seven sacraments in 1521[273] and for which the monarchy was awarded the papal accolade of defender of the faith. After all, his father-in-law Ferdinand, himself staunchly Catholic, was a potential, albeit unreliable, ally in regard to Henry's own designs upon France; the Burgundian inheritance of Catherine's nephew Charles included the vital commercial centre of Antwerp upon which England's profitable wool trade depended. It was this Charles who was to succeed Ferdinand as king of Spain in 1516. It was the same who was to inherit the Habsburg dominions in Central Europe on the death of another kinsman, Maximilian, in 1519 and who in the same year would be elected as Charles V, Holy Roman emperor, a devout son of the Catholic Church. Here was a continental potentate whose sensitivities Henry recognised he could not ignore. As it turned out, how right he was. Furthermore, Henry was as anxious as his father had been to secure the seal of approval for a Tudor dynasty still feeling its way and there was Cardinal Wolsey (c.1470-1530) from 1515 onwards: papal legate, abbot of St Albans, archbishop of York, Lord Chancellor and much else besides as the embodiment of that wish.

However, to the dilettante king, indulging himself in the whimsies and diversions as befitted an accomplished renaissance prince, one preoccupation outweighed other considerations: the burden of 'The King's Great Matter'. It centred around the one area in which his otherwise acceptable wife was, in his eyes, palpably failing him. Her six or seven pregnancies resulted in just one survivor—a girl, Mary born in 1516—a very dubious prospect for an enduring Tudor succession. With his swashbuckling charm, oozing testosterone, as Simon Schama's explicit imagery would have it,[274] and with at least one illegitimate son to his credit, Henry was not averse to amorous adventures outside the marital closet, but only a son born within wedlock actually counted and as the decade of the 1520s inexorably petered out, so did the king's

---

[273] 'Assertio Septem Sacramentorum'.

[274] Schama, S.: *A History of Britain*, Pt. 1, BBC Publications, 2000.

patience. Hence, with a roving eye and an insatiable desire to do his duty as both man and king, Henry was captivated and then manipulated by the sprightly courtier Anne Boleyn (c.1504-36) into floating the idea of annulling his marriage to Catherine so that Anne herself would supplant her as 'all his', as wife and queen consort.

Armed with selective Protestant ideals gleaned from her years spent on the continent, Anne encouraged Henry to resort to scriptural premise in order to support his increasing desire to ditch Catherine in her favour after 1525.

It was certainly clear to Henry that, Anne aside, his marriage to Catherine was cursed—no surviving son, and by this time, no prospect of one either. So what *did* the Bible say about it? A closer look at the Leviticus passage, which could have aborted the proposal of marriage to Catherine in the first place, was a good place to start and there was the ammunition he needed. Not only is it 'an unclean thing should a man take his brother's wife', but 'they shall remain childless'.[275] Despite the fact that Henry did, in fact, have a daughter by Catherine, the slight inconsistency was not enough to deny Henry the self-conviction that he had sinned in the sight of God by marrying his (deceased) brother's wife, and as many scholars pointed out to him, the original Hebrew text did specify the lack of a son rather than a generic child as encountered in Jerome's Vulgate, hence the union was blighted as a result. It was on this basis that Henry petitioned the incumbent pope, Clement VII (1523-34), for an annulment of his marriage to Catherine on the grounds that Pope Julius II had had no legitimate authority to grant the initial dispensation in the first place. Inconveniently for Henry, there is a seemingly contradictory verse in the Pentateuch upon which nothing less than the very existence of the man perceived by the monarch as a quintessential role model and preceptor, the revered Jewish King David had depended: 'If a (married) man dies without a son . . . his brother shall take (his widow) and marry her . . .'[276]

It was how to interpret these two scriptures, which was to exercise the great contemporary minds, and upon which the happiness of the king, his mistress, and for that matter his wife, depended.

---

[275] Leviticus 20:21.

[276] Deuteronomy 25:5-6 et passim. King David's great-grandmother, Ruth, had married Boaz, who was to become his great-grandfather, and who was, in fact, a very close kinsman to Ruth's first husband, Mahlon, whose widow she was (see Ruth 4:7-22). Henry saw in David the epitome of monarchical theocracy to which he himself aspired.

The Church   135

It was to prove a bridge too far for the ill-fated Wolsey in his attempt to secure from the Pope the sanction upon which the king's hopes were pinned. Wolsey who had turned so much to gold in his twenty or so years at court ultimately failed the king in the one thing that really counted.

Given the theological complexities involved, Henry VIII's convoluted foreign policy in 1526-27 and the Pope's subservience to Charles V after the Sack of Rome in 1527, the timing of Wolsey's petition could scarcely be less propitious. Wolsey's attempts to elicit a confession of a consummate marriage to Arthur from Catherine before papal legate Campeggio at Black Friars in 1528 miscarried when the discarded queen rose to the occasion in words, which caught the imagination of the people and as embellished for dramatic effect by Shakespeare as follows:

> . . . if in the course
> And process of this time, you can report,
> And prove it too, against mine honour aught,
> My bond to wedlock or my love and duty,
> Against your sacred person, in God's name,
> Turn me away . . . [277]

Catherine's impressive performance and the unswerving assertion of her monosexuality on this occasion sealed Wolsey's fate and left the king momentarily in check. Henry, however, was not going down without making even more of a fight of it and neither for that matter was Anne. The wily young woman had presented Henry with a copy of Tyndale's[278] *The Obedience of a Christian Man,* which in essence argued for the Erastian philosophy that in his own state the church was under the authority of its prince, not a distant pope, whose office rested upon spurious interpretation.

---

[277] Shakespeare, W.: *King Henry VIII,* II. iii.

[278] William Tyndale, a Protestant sympathiser and scholar, who argued strongly for the availability of the scriptures in English. Ironically, his printed translations of the New Testament in particular were effectively banned by Henry VIII and Tyndale was murdered in Antwerp in 1535. However, his translations were to be very influential in the production of Henry's sponsored 'Great Bible' of 1539 and ordered to be read in English Churches. Anne's role in these complex machinations has been subjected to a fascinating revisionist interpretation by Bernard, GW, in his "Anne Boleyn: Fatal Attractions", Yale U.P. 2010.

These sentiments were not entirely new, for they had been expressed during the Middle Ages by the respected academic, Marsilius of Padua.[279] Reference to scripture certainly flagged up the possibility of this as a valid argument. The saintly Old Testament King Josiah of Judah had certainly set about expunging 'the carved idols and cast images'[280] throughout his dominions and 'made *everyone* pledge themselves' to the strictures of the law of Moses having himself proclaimed God's law to all his people.[281] Here indeed was a role model for Henry—Josiah and indeed David before him had put the religious authorities in their place. If further justification were needed, then surely the crowning scriptural gobbet must come from the pen of Paul: 'Let every soul be subject to the higher powers, for there is no power but of God: the powers that be are ordained of God, and they that resist shall receive to themselves damnation'.[282]

It was dawning on Henry that the papal office to which he had been so attached in his earlier days was but a usurper and a charlatan. Ultimate power in both secular and spiritual spheres were uniquely his within the confines of his state. As an emperor, no less, he was responsible to no one but God in his state's internal affairs. Having by 1529 secured the support of some theological academics,[283] notably Thomas Cromwell (c.1485-1540) and in particular Thomas Cranmer (1489-1556), Henry was coming to the conclusion that if the Pope couldn't, or wouldn't help him, then he would have to help himself. This isn't quite as straightforward as it seems, for he would need to convince his people, already sympathetic to Catherine's plight, that drastic measures needed to be taken in order to secure a resolution to his great matter. There had certainly been no cohesive expression of a desire for such a radical change in religious direction from the populace at large.

---

[279] Marsilus of Padua (c.1275-1342) was the author of *Defensor Pacis* and an academic of repute at the University of Paris in which he argues that the state is the guarantor of society and to which the church must be subordinated: hardly a palatable doctrine for the Roman hierarchy of the Middle Ages.

[280] 2 Chronicles 34:3.

[281] 2 Chronicles 34:32, 2 Kings 23:1-3; Cranmer was later to impress these precepts upon the young Edward VI (1547-53) with strident reinforcement.

[282] Romans 13:1-2.

[283] Cranmer in particular had been detailed by the king to sound out academics throughout Europe in order to bolster his claims for an annulment. Cranmer reported a measure of success and on this basis, Henry proceeded with greater confidence.

The Church

In the early 1530s, therefore, Henry embarked upon what amounted to a euphemistically termed public relations exercise in order to provide himself and Anne with a secure base for his policy of brinkmanship with Rome. The clergy had to be won over, as this they were by 1532 when, intimidated by the threat of Praemunire[284] hanging over their individual and collective heads, the prelates in convocation signed their submission to the king's thesis in principle that he was all powerful in church matters. Fortuitously for Henry, the aged conservative archbishop of Canterbury, Warham (c.1450-1532), finally departed the mortal coil in 1532 to be replaced by Cranmer in the following year. The new man had supported, on theological grounds, many of the king's claims: widely travelled, a Cambridge scholar, imbued with Protestant leanings (Cranmer had, in fact, secretly married a Lutheran girl in Germany) and was, for good measure, a friend of the Boleyn family. Anne herself was declared pregnant early in 1533 and Cranmer performed a secret marriage ceremony betwixt her and Henry to celebrate the fact. Yet with still no formal annulment of his marriage to Catherine, the king was technically a bigamist and as such Anne's unborn child potentially illegitimate.

Parliament, the other arm of Henry's pincer movement against Rome, meanwhile, was preparing the ground for a final assault. Increasingly under the watchful gaze of the MP for Taunton, Mr Secretary Cromwell, whose Protestant inclinations were useful armoury in his desire to secure for the king what he wanted, parliament vented its anger against real and imagined vices of the activities of the Roman Church in England—its worldliness, immorality and extortion. By 1532, parliament had been induced to suspend the payments of annates[285] to Rome.

---

[284] Praemunire: a legal term imposing penalties of restricted freedom and deprivation of property on those who incurred the king's displeasure, regarded marginally less serious than Treason. Specifically it was designed, as per the statutes of 1353, 1365 and 1395, to protect the prerogatives of the English crown in the face of papal encroachment. These statutes were invoked to propel Wolsey's downfall and by means of which Henry threatened the acquiescent clergy in 1531. Prosecution was conducted by parliament, not in the regular courts of law.

[285] Annates: the material symbol of Rome's authority in England. They were payments made to the Pope constituting an annual contribution from the senior prelates of the land, calculated in accordance with their revenue. Obviously, their suspension by Henry—initially only threatened—was a direct challenge to the papacy.

In the middle of 1533, Cranmer pronounced Henry's marriage to Catherine null and void on the theological grounds that Julius II had had no legitimate power to allow it from the start and to Cranmer's satisfaction that, despite her protestations, Catherine's marriage to Arthur had indeed been consummated. Parliament was persuaded to play ball with this 'fait accompli' by passing the Appeals Act, which legally blocked any appeal that Catherine, or any subsequent appellant, might wish to make to Rome. In retaliation, Pope Paul III (1534-49) ultimately excommunicated Henry. The way was now open for the brash, feisty Anne to be crowned queen consort, as she duly was in June 1533: a pyrrhic victory for her, as it turned out.

It now remained for the Reformation Parliament to give legislative effect to the country's separation from Rome. Three acts were passed in 1534: The Act of Succession declared Mary illegitimate and Anne's prospective children the legal heirs to the throne.[286] Thus Elizabeth, her one child, was heiress presumptive, but sons were hoped for. Any failure on the part of the great and the good to acknowledge the fact, as indeed Bishop Fisher of Rochester (c.1469-1535) and Sir Thomas More (1478-1535), Lord Chancellor, were to discover, ran the risk of capital penalties. It was the Act of Supremacy that gave the king the lawful title as head of the Church of England and the Treason Act that stated that any denial of the fact amounted to treachery. Henry and parliament were playing the patriotic card. The severance with Rome was legislatively sanctioned.

Cromwell, as vice-regent in spirituals and vicar-general of the realm, after 1535, and Henry's hatchet man, proceeded to press on with the complementary and consolidating measures in order to set a seal on the new order of things. Queen Anne lasted just three more years, a disposable asset given that no male heirs proceeded from the queen consort's womb: beheaded in 1536. The monasteries, so much a feature and fabric of English life, were dissolved between 1536 and 1539 with Cromwell's ruthless efficiency: their roofs denuded of lead, bells recast as munitions, stone plundered for reuse as building materials for royal patronage and land similarly given away or sold off, bringing much needed revenue to the crown that Henry systematically squandered on futile wars (and the pensions credited to many of the compliant dispossessed monastic brothers): the biggest washout in history according to J. J. Scarisbrick;[287]

---

[286] This act was later repealed; Edward, Mary and Elizabeth succeeded appropriately.

[287] As stated by Scarisbrick, J. J., in a lecture to the Hastings branch of the Historical Association in 1965 and whose standard biography *Henry VIII*, Yale University Press, 1997, must be regarded as a definitive study of the

The Church 139

Cromwell paid for his loyalty by following Anne Boleyn to the block in 1540 for mismanaging a marital arrangement with Henry's fourth wife, Anne of Cleves (1516-57). Cranmer outstripped them all, but he ended up a victim of Queen Mary's revenge—burnt at the stake in Oxford 1556.

Henry's final years were far from happy: to show for it, two daughters Mary and Elizabeth, from polarised maternal backgrounds; a sole surviving son at last (by the one woman he may have truly loved, Jane Seymour). Sadly she died within a fortnight of giving birth, retribution indeed. Three wives later, Henry himself succumbed, in 1547, an ulcerated, cantankerous, obese hulk, old beyond his years, with a nine-year-old boy to succeed him.

Thus, in such inauspicious circumstances, the Church of England was born. As Henry conceived it, the only significant changes to be made were the break with Rome and the winding up of monastic observance, whose abbey churches now alone stand integral at such former Benedictine foundations as Canterbury, Winchester and Durham: residual memorials to the all-pervasive power and influence that was theirs. Henry probably desired little or no modification to traditional church doctrine and practice, although a by-product of the break with Rome led to an incidental nudge towards Protestantism.[288] Cranmer's natural caution meant that more radical proposals for a movement in a Protestant direction, if they were to happen at all, had to wait until the accession of the child Edward VI (1547-53), whose tutors, Ascham and Cheke, were decidedly of that persuasion.

Henry had somewhat cynically authorised the reading of the Bible in English in churches when the appropriate passages proclaiming the king's

---

issues. The monasteries, having been 'audited' by Cromwell's 'visitations' in the 1530s received the predicted and desired generic thumbs down whether deserved or not. In some cases, such as the scandalous instance of Abbot Caslock of Faversham Abbey, actually collaborated with Cromwell for financial gain, (Tefler, W. D. D., *Faversham Abbey and its Last Abbot, John Caslock*), Faversham Society, 1965, while the loss of others undoubtedly impoverished the community of spiritual, economic and material substance.

[288] Rex, R.: *Henry VIII and his Church*, in 'History Review', December 1997, reiterates the point that the dissolution of the monasteries was prompted by a desire by the king to eradicate any vestige of papal influence in his realm as well as reinforcing his authority over the priesthood at large. An English Bible, Rex maintains, was primarily intended to reinforce the ideas of the king's supremacy in spiritual matters—a further by-product of his severance with Rome.

supremacy would be pronounced and had secured the appointment of Protestant-leaning bishops. Having abolished the cult of Thomas à Becket (c.1120-70) at Canterbury in 1538, Henry was further stamping monarchical authority over the priesthood. Consequently under Edward's Protector Somerset (1547-49) and Lord President Northumberland (1549-53),[289] England's establishment shifted in a decidedly Protestant orientation, with the erudite young king playing a far greater lead in the process than that had once been thought to be the case.[290] Catholic vestments were dispensed with, statues and relics destroyed, obliterated in an orgy of desecration, such as would do justice to the Taliban or in some cases discreetly hidden to await a return to a revival of Catholic fortunes; altars were removed from the chancel into the nave of the church, where they were to serve as communion tables emphasising the increased importance attached to the laity in the sacrament. Perhaps, however, the most enduring monument to Cranmer's activities at this time was the publication of his two English Prayer Books: one in 1549 and a more radical version in 1552. Herein, judged by any standards, he elevated the majesty of the English language to such sublime heights as to move paradise, heaven verbalised.

That all this reforming activity occurred during Edward's brief reign (1547-53) was due in no small part not only to the lifting of Henry's dead weight from the scene, but also to the winds of radical reform blowing in from the continent.

These influences were to encourage those who for their own reasons sought to give English reform a decidedly Protestant flavour. Edward's early demise in 1553 paved the way for the accession of Catherine of Aragon's Catholic daughter, Mary. Northumberland's attempts to secure the succession of the Protestant Lady Jane Grey (1534-54) failed and the country's acceptance of Mary suggested that religious conservatism was still alive among the populace at large. Relics, statues, paintings and vestments were spontaneously taken out of their closets and restored to prominence in many churches,[291] and by 1554, the Pope was restored to nominal authority in the kingdom. The Romanist Cardinal Reginald

---

[289] Somerset and Northumberland: successively the most powerful ministers of state during the reign of the adolescent king, Edward VI.

[290] MacCulloch, D.: *Tudor Church Militant*, Allen Lane, 2000, and Alford, S., *Kingship and Politics in the Reign of Edward VI*, CUP, 2002, as cited by Matusiak, J., in his article 'A Lamb in Lion's Garb' (*The Journal of Historical Studies*, March 2004), certainly credit Edward with far more initiative than older scholars such as Elton, G., previously suggested.

[291] Duffy, E.: *The Stripping of the Altars*.

Pole (1500-58) replaced Cranmer as archbishop of Canterbury. The excesses associated with Mary's reign (1553-58)—the very public burning of recalcitrant Protestants—and the 'Spanish Marriage' of Queen Mary tended to convince many in England that, in her attempts to Romanise the realm once again, they were in a safer pair of hands when a 'foreign pope' was out of their hair. It was over to Queen Elizabeth (1558-1603) to bite the bullet and to establish a Church of England, broadly based, capable of embracing a modicum of Catholic tradition and Protestant innovation. The Act of Settlement and a revised version of Cranmer's Prayer Book of 1559 accommodated many, but satisfied not everyone as the ensuing century was to witness. Nevertheless, Richard Hooker's masterly rationale, 'Of the Laws of Ecclesiastical Polity',[292] remains a classic apologia for the validity of the Church of England. He denies that the Bible is the *sole* source of Christian truth, yet neither is the church to be hidebound by its 'sacred' traditions. The church, he argues, is an evolving organism and its form of government must change over time and with circumstances. Bishop John Jewel, a near contemporary of Hooker's, in his *Apologia Ecclesiae Anglicanae* had convinced many in the establishment that the Church of England was possessed of all the qualities synthesised in the Holy Scriptures and the spirit of the first six hundred years of the Christian Church, having been purged of Romish accretions and unyielding in the face of certain Protestant excesses.[293] Herein lays Christ's seal of approval upon it.

Historians have long agonised over the underlying causes of what we know today as the Henrician Reformation. The modern consensus, however, seems to be this: There was apparently little innate desire for change, let alone a break from Rome, from the people at large. Although the pre-Reformation Roman Church in England did have its detractors and critics, such as John Colet, dean of St Paul's,[294] but for most, both in terms of doctrine and discipline, the church provided a source of

---

[292] Richard Hooker (1554-1600) was an Oxford academic, who is regarded as the philosophical apologist for the establishment of the Anglican Church.

[293] John Jewel (1522-71) was bishop of Salisbury, and an Oxford don, who believed that authority in the church was legitimately held by the monarch, acting in and through parliament, working in its capacity as a church council.

[294] John Colet (1457-1519) had preached a sermon highly critical of the lax standards of the English clergy in 1511, at convocation (the assembly of prelates). This was similar in vein to an exhortation a year previously by William Melon, chancellor of York Minster, for the clergy to buck their ideas up. However, these were isolated expressions of complaint.

comfort to the vast majority, who had really known nothing different, and the church was not generally seen at the time as the rampant, grasping rapacious gannet that had fuelled the Lutheran movement in Germany. Among the English monastic inmates, many, it's accepted, were indeed living down to Chaucer's well-heeled, well-fed, well-tailored, fun-loving Canterbury-bound monk[295] and some of them doubtless less than reputable had, nevertheless, provided succour, employment and economic viability for those outside their ranks. The well-to-do, the aristocracy, on the whole, continued to endow monasteries and chantries to fast-track their application for a purgatorial exit visa on behalf of themselves or their family. The monarchy itself could hardly complain of excessive or burdensome demands from the see of Rome. Over the years, the English Church had already evolved into a discreet Anglican identity with the king an active participant in all major decisions including the appointment of bishops. In reality, the bishop of Rome was seen as a distant, peripheral symbol, rather than as a hands-on executive. Admittedly, there had been those, pre-Henry, who had sought a more progressive and dynamic faith. John Wycliffe[296] had campaigned for this in the fourteenth century and his large following had made some impact. Yet by the beginning of the sixteenth century, there had been no serious cohesive campaign to challenge the legitimacy of the Roman Church in England. Indeed, the reaction to Henry's repudiation of Rome resulted in some co-ordinated protest in the form of the 1536 Pilgrimage of Grace.[297] The anti-Roman iconoclastic fervour associated with Edward's reign led to a serious reactionary uprising in 1549. It would appear, therefore, that the English Reformation was at root, a dynastically driven device by the monarch to secure his realm. Yet for all that, the old church crumbled with relative ease. For a start, the intelligentsia at least had been unwittingly softened up by the humanist expressions of Colet, More and Erasmus, facilitating the spread of Lutheran, Calvinist and Zwinglian influences inevitably inching their way across the channel, all the more ready to aid and abet anyone willing and able to demonise the Pope and all his works. Ironically, it was the Catholic Queen Mary whose

---

[295] Chaucer, G. (c.1340-1400): 'The Prologue' from *The Canterbury Tales*.

[296] Wycliffe (c.1329-84) was a medieval English academic who believed in the supremacy of grace in salvation terms, over the role of the organised church that he felt was too sin-laden to be an effective conduit to God.

[297] The Pilgrimage of Grace: a petitioning march from the North and East under the leadership of Robert Aske, seeking a restoration of Roman principles of the church. Initially placated, and then double-crossed by Henry, Aske was subsequently executed.

The Church 143

insensitive measures designed to turn back the clock by attempting to bulldoze the country's return to the Roman fold, who probably did more to secure the Church of England in the hearts of most English people than the legislative activity of either Henry or Edward. Her unpopular marriage to Philip of Spain, the association of 'foreign' popery with the high-profile burnings[298] and the loss of Calais fuelled a primitive form of patriotic ardour—reinforced by the Elizabethan defeat of the Armada some thirty years later. The return of the Protestant exiles—some eight hundred of them—on Mary's death in 1558 was accompanied by a determination to rid the country of popery.

Thus, on Elizabeth's succession, as we have seen, many strands of religious opinion were banging on her door in the hope she would see things 'their way'! A strong puritan and independent streak was emerging in some quarters, demanding far more extensive radical religious reform. More would certainly be heard from them. Then there were those who still hankered for the old certainties of Rome; those imbued with the charged batteries inspired by the Catholic Reform Movement at the Council of Trent (1545-63) had not given up. Hence, Elizabeth's 1559 'Act of Settlement' accommodated many, but assuredly not all. Toleration for those who in conscience couldn't subscribe to the Thirty-nine Articles of the Church of England, as formulated in 1571, was still a long way off. The idea that England was now an imperial, Erastian state, its monarchy supreme in spiritual as well as secular matters was, by Elizabeth's death in 1603, an accepted formula, if not a totally unchallenged one. The Church of England, thus established, was ironically destined to provide the spiritual umbrella serving the parochial needs of the country for the foreseeable future, despite the hiatus of disestablishment during Oliver Cromwell's Puritan Protectorate (1649-60) in the wake of the English Civil War (1642-49). The established Church of England was to make its comeback with a vengeance with the restoration of the monarchy in 1660.

Our defining moment at Ludlow is a very poignant one—at centre stage are two young innocents, merely 'players' on Shakespeare's 'world stage'.[299] It represents a very human tragedy whose tentacles reached out into the entire fabric of the land: the butterfly effect, one supposes. For the Body of Christ, it was to represent not just the birth of a new organic expression, but the acceleration of the break-up of the old.

---

[298] Graphically detailed in Foxe, J.: *History of the English Martyrs*, Spire Books, 1973 (*Foxe's Book of Martyrs*).

[299] Shakespeare, W.: *As You Like It*, II. vii.

Chapter 14

Sack of Rome, engraving by Martin Van Heemskerck

HOW ANGRY IS HEAVEN

One would assume that the challenge to its authority by the Protestant reformers—Luther in particular—would have been sufficient to provoke an instant reaction from the Roman Church so as to preserve its own dignity and its universal status. At the very least, it might have provided the opportunity to indulge immediately in some timely navel gazing. Yet again, the church, with fifteen hundred years of almost unbroken tradition behind it, and with previous upstarts like Huss,[300] Wycliffe[301] and Savonarola[302] having been successfully seen off, what prospects

---

[300] Jan Huss: a Bohemian reformer (c.1370-1415), who had gained a following in the Czech Lands; critical of some Catholic teaching, he died at the stake in Constance, while defending his beliefs at the council there. See chapter 12, and Footnote p. 81.

[301] John Wycliffe: English reformer (c.1324-84), leader of the lollards, attacked monastic abuses and certain Catholic doctrines, as well as calling for the scriptures in English. His views were condemned at the Council of Constance, 1415. See chapter 12, and Footnote p. 80.

[302] Giralamo Savonarola: Italian preacher and reformer (1452-98), called for a radical reversal of the moral decline, which he felt characterised Renaissance

would a minor querulous Augustinian monk have if he were to try to rattle its complacency? Such an irritant could be dealt with, given all the resources at the disposal of the church, in its time-honoured fashion, without the need for radical self-assessment. What is clear is that even if its ultimate response was not too little, it was most certainly too late.

It is, nevertheless, self-evident that throughout the course of the sixteenth century, an internally inspired reform programme was promoted, such as that was destined to ensure the future continuity of the Catholic Church. When, precisely, and why have been hotly debated by historians.[303] We have seen that Christian humanists, such as Erasmus (stubbornly from within), and reformers like Luther (ultimately from without) had each identified a string of abuses emanating from the renaissance inspired papal hierarchy and the blurring of principles between its temporal and spiritual responsibilities. The indisputable fact remains that despite the many unprepossessing signals from the very pinnacle of its structure, the Spirit of Christ had not been entirely eradicated. The scandal of a divided papacy had been resolved at the Council of Constance (1414-18); in Spain under Ferdinand and Isabella (1479-1516), Xavier Cisneros had reinvigorated church discipline and monastic observance; a papally inspired Lateran Council (1512-17) had recommended measures, which would have reassessed the priorities of the church, while at the local level, initiatives had been undertaken to offer a caring, spiritual and meaningful presence among the needy—the Brothers (and Sisters) of the Common Life[304] and the Oratories of Divine Love,[305] for example—loosely bound Catholic communities—members

---

Florence, and for the deposition of Pope Alexander VI (1492-1503). He was executed as a schismatic and heretic there.

[303] Older historians such as Elton and Dickens tend to use the term Counter-Reformation, implying that reform of the Catholic Church was motivated by the Protestant challenge. Revisionists such as Everette, Jedin, Delumeau and Bossy tend to see it as largely self-motivated and see the movement as a continuing strand of spirituality lurking within the soul of the church.

[304] Loosely organised communities founded by de Groote in the fourteenth century, comprising clergy and laity, in the Netherlands, and spreading to Germany. They promoted education and preached a high moral code.

[305] Similar unstructured fraternities to the Brethren of the Common Life, but based largely in Italy; the best known was the Oratory meeting in Rome, founded in 1517, through which such prominent reformers as Carafa and Contarini emerged.

146 How Angry Is Heaven

of which took the pastoral side of their faith very seriously indeed. The work of Bishop Giberti of Verona is often cited in this regard.

While the papacies of Leo X (1513-22) and Clement VII (1523-34) were hamstrung by the complexities of an office with political, dynastic and temporal expectations to satisfy, Lutheranism was unwittingly sowing mayhem in Germany throughout the 1520s.

It was the political dilemma facing Pope Clement that provides us with the background for our defining moment. The Papal States, that coterminous block of territory ruled by the Pope as a secular prince in Central Italy, were seen as increasingly vulnerable, flanked as they were by Habsburg lands immediately to the south and encroaching menacingly to the north. To Clement, his biggest threat spiritually as well as politically was seen, therefore, as none other than Charles V, head of the House of Habsburg, Holy Roman emperor and coincidentally king of Spain, duke of Burgundy, as well as hereditary ruler of the Austrian lands in Central Europe. Clement, throwing caution to the winds by turning his back on his theoretical protector, signed up an ill-fated alliance, the League of Cognac, comprising himself, Francis I of France (1494-1547), the duke of Milan and the Venetian Republic in 1526. The objective was to weaken, if not dislodge, the Habsburg grip in Northern Italy. Such derring-do on Clement's part was destined to turn decidedly pear-shaped when his folly was 'compounded by his overestimate of the papacy's strengths, and of Francis I's dependability, along with a fatal underestimation of Charles'.[306]

What happened, as a consequence, in May 1527 was an outcome of cataclysmic and apocalyptic proportions. As such, it qualifies for a defining moment in the history of the church. Not only did the League of Cognac fail to eject the Habsburgs from one square inch of Italian soil, but also Charles V's huge army there had degenerated into an undisciplined assortment of German and Spanish foot soldiers who were ominously unpaid and increasingly hungry. This was a fatal combination of coincidences as far as Rome was concerned and it was upon whose well-endowed head that the full fury of this wild bunch descended. No building, no person was spared from this mutinous crew: nothing and nobody was sacrosanct, nuns were violated from soldier to soldier and the Pope himself captured. Charles, to be fair, was mortified at the chain of events he had unintentionally unleashed, yet he was momentarily

---

[306] Po-Chia, Hsia: *The World of Catholic Renewal*, references contained in Mullett, M. A.: *The Catholic Reformation*, Routledge, 1999. For Emperor Charles V, see also chapters 12 and 13.

The Church 147

powerless to limit the scale of the devastation. As for the hapless Clement, already up to his ears in a certain divorce controversy involving Henry VIII and Charles's aunt, Catherine of Aragon, and contemplating in his prison cell in Castel Sant'Angelo the haemorrhaging of the Catholic fold in Europe, he was the impotent observer of a church in a tailspin. Upon his release months later, he realistically recognised he was henceforth to 'live and die a Habsburg'.

If the papacy, the Curia and hierarchy were, at best, lukewarm to the cause of reform before, their complacency was comprehensively shattered by this Sack of Rome in May. Those few reform-minded cardinals whose voices had been crying in the wilderness were now vindicated. 'The Emperor's Army', acknowledged Cardinal Giles of Viterbo, 'tearing to pieces the barbaric filth ... (the) untrained, disorganised ... immoral ... usurers and pimps', who masqueraded as the priesthood, an action duly sanctioned by God's imprimatur, yet more: 'how angry is Heaven (that God) even carries it out himself'.[307] Pope Adrian VI—well-intentioned, short reign (1522-23)—had stated with measured prescience that the sickness of the church had spread 'from the head to the members' and that true healing and regeneration could only emanate 'from Rome'.[308] This fact was not lost on the Emperor Charles V, who saw the meeting of a general church council as a possible means to healing the rift in Germany.

Yet Clement VII—he in the eye of the hurricane and cast in the prevailing mould of the Renaissance papacy—was not the man best suited to effect the necessary changes in direction. Vague promises were the best he could come up with. Lacking the political leverage to stake out a policy of his own or with a convincing and clearly articulated plan of reform such as that would impress the entrenched interests within the Curia, Clement's death in 1534 paved the way for the election of the enigmatic Alexander Farnese as Pope Paul III. In the overall context of the fortunes of the Church of Rome, this choice must stand as one of its more inspired choices and this man as one of its pivotal figures. Throughout his fifteen-year tenure of office, this complex individual paved the way for an officially sponsored Catholic renewal process, facilitating the internal reforming zeal that without doubt arrested its otherwise terminal decline. Paul III (1534-49) was the bridge between the old—and new-style papacies. Notwithstanding

---

[307] Giles of Viterbo (c.1529): *Schechina e Libellus* quoted in Jones, M. D. W.: *The Counter Reformation*, CUP., 2000.

[308] Pope Adrian VI to the Diet of Augsburg quoted in Jones, M. D. W, op. cit.

148   How Angry Is Heaven

the shameless exploitation of his office to further the interests of his family, Paul was sufficiently realistic, after the 1527 debacle in Rome, to appreciate that something must be done. This sixty-six-year-old, possessed of the vitality and inscrutability of a teenager, perceived that if anything were to happen at all, he had first of all to cut through the web of politics, corruption and vested interests such as that had constrained previous incumbents in their frustratingly half-hearted attempts at reform.

He wasted little time in establishing a Papal Commission chaired by the highly respected Cardinal Contarini[309] to propose the best way forward. The commission's report in 1537 pulled no punches. It launched a scathing attack on the failure of the church to fulfil its moral and spiritual obligations: popes, cardinals, bishops, the lot, were portrayed as money-grubbing spivs, robbing the ordinary people of their souls and the church of its sacred duty. Once leaked, the document presented the Protestants with a smug affirmation that Luther had been right all along. No amount of gloss or spin could translate these accusations into comfortable reading for an inherently conservative pope. Realistically, the only chance of effecting the clean-up operation would be the meeting of minds from a wide a cross section of Europe's catholic prelates; that is, the summoning of a general church council. Even this had to wait until Charles V and Francis I, Continental Europe's leading secular players, patched up their differences and stopped bickering.[310] Without at least their mutual condescension, such a council would be toothless. When the council did finally convene, in 1545, at Trent,[311] in Northern Italy, it was to prove one of the most momentous conventions in Roman Church history. It was destined to drag on through three main sessions, spasmodically over the ensuing eighteen years. Given the tenuous political background, the sheer uncertainties of travel, coupled with the shambolic arrangements for accommodating the delegates, and the

---

[309] Contarini (1483-1542) was the Catholic representative to the abortive conference at Regensburg in 1541, in dialogue with the Lutheran Melanchton, to find common ground between Catholics and Protestants. See chapter 12.

[310] Peace was in fact brokered at Crépy in 1544 with Francis I a somewhat sullen and battered acquiescent.

[311] Ultimately chosen as a somewhat poor compromise: sufficiently 'Italian' to satisfy the Pope, nominally part of the Holy Roman Empire to placate Charles V and sufficiently close to France for Francis I—equally uncomfortably cold for everybody in winter.

The Church   149

very imprecise procedural protocol in the council itself, prelates from across Western Europe managed, by 1563, to hammer out an agreed final document, which was to stand the Church of Rome in relatively good stead for the next 450 years. If anything could still lend credence to the old term *Counter-Reformation* to describe Catholic renewal in the sixteenth century, according to Randell,[312] it was the Council of Trent that provided it.

The council tackled the problems under two main heads: First, it looked at the question of *belief*, i.e. what did the Roman Church stand for? It tackled the Protestant 'heresies' head-on. Authority and truth were determined to be a duality based on both scripture *and* the spiritually inspired pronouncements of the church down the centuries. As such, the seven sacraments were to retain their validity and within which the doctrine of transubstantiation reaffirmed. The dogma of purgatory was guaranteed a place in Catholic theology, as indeed were the associated efficacy of a 'good works' theory of salvation and the *principle* of indulgences—that which had sparked Luther's attack in the first place. Despite its manifest imperfections, Jerome's Latin Vulgate version of the Bible was to remain the kosher scriptural diet, while veneration of the Virgin Mary, the saints and relics was to be an integral part of Catholic observance. The divine functions of priests, bishops and the Pope were left intact. All of this, of course, was designed to put clear blue water between what the Roman Church stood for and the Protestant position. Significantly, the principle of papal supremacy was tacitly affirmed. Thus, the Council of Trent effectively closed the door on any possible accommodation with Protestants, Lutheran or otherwise, by such uncompromising statements of dogma and, as such, fossilised their respective positions until well on into the twentieth century.

Far less contentious was the council's pronouncements on church *discipline*. In terms of tackling what Cardinal Pole[313] described as the 'ambition . . . avarice and . . . cupidity' which so characterised the Holy See, the Tridentine reformers went for them root and branches: Bishops were henceforth to be residents in their sees, the more conscientiously to supervise all monastic activity and to monitor the

---

[312] Randell, K.: *The Catholic and Counter Reformations*, Hodder and Stoughton, 2000.

[313] Cardinal Reginald Pole (1500-58): English Catholic reformer, much respected, and archbishop of Canterbury (1557-58) under Mary I (1553-58), during England's temporary reversion to the Roman fold. See also chapter 13.

training, propriety and suitability of the priests in their care; adequate provision for the establishment of seminaries was to be made to facilitate a much higher calibre of clergy. The nepotism, pluralism and absenteeism in the priesthood generally, which had so adversely characterised so much of the Roman Church at the beginning of the sixteenth century, were to be discontinued. The excessive abuses associated with the selling of indulgences and the granting of exemptions were to be curtailed.

Its work accomplished: Pope Pius IV (1559-65) ordered the Tridentine decrees into effect in 1564 reversing the scandalous example set by popes Alexander VI (1492-1503) and Julius II (1503-13). Naturally, such far-reaching measures could not be implemented overnight as soon as the wax was dry: it would take many years and would require the active co-operation of the future papal incumbents, the religious orders, bishops, priests, laity and not least the secular rulers of the Catholic states of Europe.

It was indeed fortunate for the Catholic Church that, since our defining moment, coincidentally or otherwise, men of reforming zeal were rising to prominence. Most noteworthy among these was Ignatius Loyola (c.1491-1556) whose 'Society of Jesus' (or Jesuits) was formally commissioned by Paul III in 1540. In many respects, it was this order, above all others, with its emphasis upon discipline, morality, education, missionary work and conservatism in regard to doctrine, which provided the Catholic Reform Movement with its ground troops. Loyola's manual of *Spiritual Exercises* was the handbook of personal piety and indirectly as a means of practical evangelism. It was largely the work of the Jesuits who restored to the Catholic fold many, particularly in Central Europe, for whom the initial zeal for Protestantism was becoming blunted by time and who more or less successfully held the line in Belgium and Southern Germany inspired by the legendary Peter Canisius (1521-97). It was the Jesuits who pioneered the Christian missions beyond Europe—notably the saintly Francis Xavier (1506-52) and Matteo Ricci (1552-1610) in the Orient: following hard on the heels of the conquistadores in South America, Loyola insisted that members of his order insidiously enter the door of the 'heathen' or 'heretic', provided that all involved exit by the door of the Jesuit. Win 'their' confidence and go for the jugular, subtlety with a sting in its tail.

In fact, the sting was never far from the reformers' armoury. The authoritarian Carafa—Pope Paul IV (1555-59), himself no great fan of the Council of Trent, unlike his predecessor Julius III (1550-55), preferred the more direct and combative approach, prosecuting by

The Church 151

means of the Papal Inquisition ('the Holy Office')[314] with particular vigour in Italy. His introduction of the 'Index of Prohibited Books' in 1557 had the effect of distancing Rome from Protestantism still further.

Overall, though, a new breed of Catholic grandee was emerging. It appears that the sacking of Rome did hasten the advent of a new spirit within the church by raising the profile of reformists from within. People of the calibre of Giberti (1495-1543), Contarini, Carafa, Loyola, the Jesuit missionaries, Borromeo (1538-84), the saintly bishop of Milan, the mystics Theresa of Avila (1515-82); John of the Cross (1542-91), Philip Neri (1515-95) in Rome; pontiffs of the quality of Pius V (1566-72), Gregory XIII (1572-85) and Sixtus V (1585-90), as well as the willingness of secular rulers such as Philip II of Spain (1556-98)[315] to co-operate albeit conditionally in the reforming dynamic, all ensured the revival of the fortunes and standing of the Roman Church: the ultimate fulfilment of the work of the Tridentine reformers.

Of course there were many casualties on the way: the ubiquitous Charles V abdicated and surrendered his titles in 1556, retiring to a paradoxically obscure monastery in Yuste, Spain, with his collection of clocks in melancholy contemplation as to what might have been. The death of Francis I in 1547 was to precede a cycle of cynical religious warfare, which was to engulf France until 1589, while the infamous Thirty Years' War (1618-48), with its religious overtones, was to lay waste to much of Germany.

Nevertheless, by 1600, the Catholic Church had clawed its way back from the edge of the abyss. It had restored its moral sense of purpose and the primacy of the papacy's spiritual functions over its former political preoccupations. True, its tardiness in responding at the level of 'head and members' to the charges levelled against it at the turn of the sixteenth century had enabled a variety of Protestant schismatics to justify their actions and so push the Church of Rome into such a corner

---

[314] Carafa had, in fact, instituted the Papal Inquisition with the blessing of his predecessor Paul III, in 1542, largely to counter the alarming incidence of defections to Protestantism in Italy.

[315] Philip II, while supporting in principle the Tridentine Decrees, insisted that each reform must have his explicit approval such as the appointment of bishops, while the French Crown resisted many of the Pope's claims to implement changes directly in the French Church. Even in the parts of Germany where loyalty to Catholicism was sustained, the implementation of the Tridentine decrees was inconsistent.

that it would not emerge as anything more than one 'denomination' among many. Its pretension to spiritual monopoly and universality in the West was over. Yet survive it did, with a living, organic potency as a testimony to those who recognised in our defining moment—the Sack of Rome, 1527—as indeed 'an act of God'.

Chapter 15

Galileo before the Holy Office,
by J-N Robert-Flewy, nineteenth century

BUT IT DOES MOVE

The challenge to the Roman Church by the reformers of the sixteenth century had shattered the medieval consensus relating to the theological building blocks, which had evolved over the centuries in the Western Church and upon which it had relied: the recognition of the papal office, the validity of the apostolic priesthood and the interpretation of the sacramental ordinances. The fundamental quarrel had been about how fallen humanity gains access to God and the means by which salvation can be assured. The ecclesiastical, as well as the political, social and economic fallout was far reaching as we have seen. Yet the medievalist thinkers of the likes of Augustine, Anselm and Aquinas continued to command respect in both reformed and Catholic circles in so far as their cosmological understanding was concerned. That is, the basic idea that the relationship between God and (planet) earth operated in accordance with the literal teaching in Genesis:[316] as something rather special and distinct within the context of the universe at large. This assumption prevailed, but not for much longer.

---

[316] Genesis 1:1-2, 4(a); Genesis 2:4(b)-3:24.

Today, any would-be international visitor to the renaissance cradleland will, in all likelihood, jet in to the modernistic airport at Pisa, lying at the Western extremity of the Arno Valley, and named not after its out of kilter tower, but after its most famous son, Galileo Galilei (1564-1642). Our defining moment in fact takes us again to Rome: to the closing drama of this man's celebrated trial, upbraided in front of the Holy Office of the Inquisition[317] assembled in the capacious Basilica of the Dominican Convent of Santa Maria Sopra Minerva on 22 June 1633.

Having already been subjected for several days to the intense pressure applied at their headquarters next door by the inquisitors, Galileo was now clad top to toe in a white, coarse, loosely draped robe as befitted a penitent, his beard unkempt. Here he knelt before his seated accusers. These were a dozen or so sanctimonious cardinals, resplendent in their finely spun scarlet apparel with Commissary Firenzuola acting as chief prosecutor, awaiting the defendant to disavow his scientific theories unequivocally: a public humiliation before a packed assemblage relishing the spectacle and all in the interests of the alleged health of the Mother Church. Given the pressure, Galileo duly made appropriate obeisance for his 'vehement heresy' of proclaiming the Copernican postulate of heliocentricity: that theory which placed the *sun* at the centre of the solar system, and not the *earth*, such as the church had held uncompromisingly. Galileo appended his signature acknowledging his 'error'. Here, was a man seventy years old, armed with empirical certainty, yet lacking perhaps that spiritual integrity that had held Luther together one hundred years before at Worms, who had flown in the face of a church resurgent in its counter-revolutionary militancy. Whether or not on being led away from the inquisitional building to begin his penitential sentence, he actually muttered, with biting irony, ' . . . but it does move', is really academic. That's what he believed and few were in any doubt that his signature on a piece of parchment dismissing his postulate that the earth revolved around the sun was just a paper exercise in appeasement. 'Peace in our time . . . 'The church had got its man, but not his ideas. The power of the printing press had seen to that.

---

[317] The Holy Office of the Inquisition, or Inquisition for short, had been established by Pope Paul III in 1542 as the highest ecclesiastical court in matters of heresy. There had been inquisitions before, notably in Spain, but under the control and direction of the secular rulers. Its sentences were often draconian. For the unrepentant heretic burning by the secular authorities was a likely outcome. See chapters 13 and 14.

The trial of Galileo and the dawn of the so-called Scientific Revolution represents to Herbert Butterfield[318] the 'most important event in European History since the rise of Christianity'. At stake was the entire human perception of the individual human being's relationship to the earth, the universe and to God. As stated, the Medieval Church had claimed a monopoly over the authoritative interpretation of all branches of knowledge. During the Middle Ages, Catholic scholars had cleverly synthesised much of the classical (and pagan) work of the Alexandrian, Ptolemy (c. AD 90-168) in the realm of cosmology and the physical laws of motion as propounded by Aristotle (384-322 BC) in order to lend credence to its own theory relative to God's relationship to the universe. In straight terms, the church had invoked the Aristotelian/Ptolemaic conclusion that there exists a material and substantial difference between planet earth and the celestial elements 'above'. According to this theory, the earth, unique amidst the swirling cosmos, in its central, immobile, imperfect state, exists in direct contrast to the universe, which screams aloud with its perfect constant motion, whose purpose is to dance attendance upon humanity firmly planted on terra firma. That was what the Aristotelian prime unmoved mover, the God of Aquinas, had ordained and, in the eyes of the church, to deny otherwise constituted heresy.

In 1543, the Polish Thinker Nicholas Copernicus (1473-1543) had reluctantly published his *De Revolutionibus Orbium Coelistium* on the basis of mathematical formulae and their concomitant logical certainties. If proved, he recognised that the Aristotelian/Ptolemaic cosmological hypothesis would be demolished and bring down the condemnation of the church on his head. What Copernicus had done was to dismiss, theoretically, the ethnocentric (earth-centred) universe in favour of a heliocentric (sun-centred) planetary system: a universal natural circular motion prevalent throughout with the sun as the earth's source of life. He recognised that it is in the nature of things for a *small* body (earth, for example) to be subject to a *large* body, like the sun. He contended, then, that there could be no basic qualitative difference between planet earth and other galactic bodies, and that the human form be but an outcome of natural forces. He got away with it largely because even he had recognised that this was a theory, as Osiander[319] in his preface to the work was keen to emphasise. He recognised that

---

[318] Butterfield, H.: *The Origins of Modern Science*, London, 1947.

[319] Andreas Osiander (1498-1552) was, interestingly, a Protestant professor at Koningsberg, who nevertheless disagreed with Luther on several fundamental issues.

156 But It Does Move

confirmation had to await the empirical investigation and observation in order to verify or disprove his findings and he died, anyway, shortly after publication.

Paradoxically, when the abstract of this work had been published in 1531, Pope Clement VII, reflecting his Medici pedigree, had described its findings as 'interesting', while it had been left, characteristically, to Martin Luther to point out that, scripturally, Joshua had commanded the *sun* to stand still, not the earth.[320] In any case, Copernicus was operative at Heilsberg and Freuenburg in Prussia—centres of Protestantism—by this time outside the ambit of the tentacles of Rome.

Heavily influenced by Copernicus was John Kepler (1571-1630), who worked alongside a fellow Lutheran, Tycho Brahe (1546-1601), at the University of Prague. Fascinated by the hypotheses of the Polish mathematician, Kepler was determined to advance the cause of astronomy in order to verify the Copernican conclusions. The problem he faced was limited by a primitive telescopic technology, as yet struggling to meet the growing demands about to be made upon it. Nevertheless, he confidently affirmed the claims of the sun, as being central to life on planet earth, and while accepting universal cyclical motion, the gravitational attraction of two or more bodies seemed to suggest an (east to west) *elliptical* orientation, rather than strictly circular. Kepler's pantheistic view of the universe led him to conclude that as the world itself expressed God's being, the star 'followed' by the Magi to Bethlehem[321] was in fact the rare juxtaposition of planets Mars, Saturn and Jupiter giving rise to the celestial phenomenon, which by his calculation actually occurred in 6 BC, so much for the chronology of Exiguus.[322]

Such an intellectual inheritance did not elude Galileo, our inquisitive native of Pisa: he who was destined to be at the centre of our defining moment. As a teenager, he would be found marvelling at the architectural glories of his city, pondering the structural forces

---

[320] Joshua 10:12-14.

[321] Matthew 2:1-12.

[322] Dionysius Exiguus in the sixth century had calculated the beginning of the Christian era (AD) as New Year's Day, 25 March, the supposed date of the Annunciation. If Kepler were now correct, then Christ's birth would incongruously have been around 4 BC, about two years after the Magi had first witnessed the 'star in the east' (Matthew 2:2, 11); evidently the Holy Family was resident at Bethlehem in some kind of rented accommodation by the time the Magi finally arrived in Bethlehem possibly as much as another two years after that. The 'wise men' were most certainly never witnesses to the manger scene.

that combined functional pragmatism and aesthetic taste, such as were employed to construct its magnificent twelfth-century Gothic cathedral of white marble, with its elliptical dome soaring to a height of nearly two hundred feet and its detached (and leaning) campanile. It is quite probable that his observation of a swinging ray of light cast by a chandelier suspended from the lofty eminence of the cathedral excited his interest in the theoretical possibilities of the constancy of the pendulum;[323] probably apocryphal is the legend that his work on the forces of gravity was prompted by dropping objects from the Leaning Tower. Here, nevertheless, was someone with a mindset geared for empirical analysis. As he cast his eye heavenwards, past the manually crafted apex of the Dome, towards the glories of the esoteric night sky, he reflected upon the mathematical hypotheses for it all, so tantalisingly suggested by Copernicus and followed up by Brahe and Kepler. Yet to secure the verification that he convinced himself was there was initially beyond his reach: the planets were so distant and Kepler's primitive optical telescope was barely any more help than the naked eye. If only a more sophisticated mechanical device could come to his aid; nothing for it but to make one himself. Utilising a purloined organ pipe, Galileo improved on previous designs by attaching a convex object lens to one end and a concave eyepiece at the other, allowing the laws of refraction to produce an erect image magnified many times. He now had the basic tool at his disposal for the task. His teaching appointment at the University of Pisa between 1589 and 1591 had by now become controversial. His avant-garde ideas were at odds with the Aristotelian hierarchy there, wedded as it was still to the classical cosmological view. Crossing the Italian peninsular, Galileo finally pitched up at the University of Padua in 1592, where an improved version of his refractory telescope resulted in the most profound discoveries. By observation and induction, he published his *Siderius Nuncius* in 1610, whereby he was able to confirm many of the Copernican theories with the aid of his telescope. He had succeeded in witnessing for the first time the elliptical motion of the four 'moons' centred on planet Jupiter, such as that would be expected when *two* forces act upon a body simultaneously. He thus concluded that the moon associated with planet earth was subject to the same laws of motion. Indeed, as he examined the moon's surface, Galileo was able to *confirm* the substantial similarity between its surface and that of planet earth, and that the mysterious 'spots' on the moon were simply the shadows of plains and mountains, as cast by the same rays

---

[323] Galileo, in fact, never succeeded in the practical application of the pendulum principle to the clock.

of the sun experienced on the planet familiar to all of us. Furthermore, he reasoned on the basis of his observation that as Venus most certainly revolved around the sun, was it not empirically safe to conclude that earth acted likewise as Copernicus had suggested, given that the two were of the same imperfect galactic 'stuff'?

Galileo's conclusions were now boldly trumpeted by Cosimo II, grand duke of Tuscany at Florence, into whose service he was now summoned in 1610. The printing press duly had a field day in churning out his findings. His *Historia e Dimostrazioni Intorno Alle Macchie* unapologetically and unambiguously declared that planet earth was subject to the same natural and physical forces as the rest of the universe, nothing 'special' about it at all. It was this that rattled the church. The fact that Galileo further asserted that 'the astronomical language of the Bible was designed for the comprehension of the ignorant' assured the Pisan professor of an audience with the inquisitor. Arraigned by the scholarly Jesuit, Cardinal Robert Bellarmine (1542-1621) at the behest of Pope Paul V (1605-21), in Rome on 26 February 1616, Galileo was given, in fact, a surprisingly sympathetic hearing. Provided Galileo abandoned his Copernican theories (in public at least) and indeed regarded his own work as purely theoretical, then he was free to go. To reinforce the point, Copernicus's *De Revolutionibus* was placed on the Vatican's 'Index of Forbidden Books'.

For several years, Galileo figured that discretion dictated the biting of his tongue, but the relentless scientist in him could not keep his restless spirit bottled up. In a style that would have won the approval of Socrates and Plato, his *Dialogo del Due Massimi Sistemi del Mundo*[324] clearly enunciated the corroborated cosmological theories of Copernicus. His erstwhile friend Maffeo Barberini, now Pope Urban VIII (1623-44) with preoccupations of the Thirty Years' War (1618-48), and of the advocacy of the movement for Catholic Reform to consider, called him once again to answer to the Holy Office. By this time, there was little to be gained by a church, trying to claw its way back from the abyss, in attempting to accommodate a further troublemaker. This would be tantamount to a turning over of the applecart: much better to reassert the security of Aquinas, reiterating the omnipotence and ultimate incomprehensibility

---

[324] This work takes the form of an imaginary dialogue, wherein Salinati (a Copernican) and Simplicius (an Aristotelian) attempt to persuade a mutual acquaintance, Sagredo, of the validity of their respective cause. The conclusion suggests, enigmatically, Salinati's failure to win the argument unconditionally, although the line of attack pursued by Simplicius is shot through with unsubstantiated dogma.

The Church 159

of God. This time there was no kindly Bellarmine to offer any degree of sympathy either to Galileo's plight or to his plea that there had been a misunderstanding of the conditions attached to the 1616 sentence of the Holy Office. Although treated courteously, there was always the spectre of imprisonment hanging over him. He appeared in his white penitential garb as per our defining moment to recant in public and to bury his pride in private.

As it turned out, his punishment was not onerous, given the weighty import of the charge: mitigation for a timely Guilty Plea no doubt. The lifelong house arrest was to be served out at his not disagreeable residence at Acetri amidst its fountains, courtyard and olive groves overlooking the resplendent beauty of Florence, but with a requirement to recite the Seven Penitential Psalms once a week for three years. The real tragedy was the humiliation of an elderly sincere man of science being forced to deny for public consumption what *he* knew to be true: that 'the sun is the centre of the world and immovable, and that the Earth is not the centre and moves, to which he appended his reluctant signature'.[325]

Comforted initially by his elder daughter, Virginia, until her untimely death in 1634, Galileo busied himself during which time he published his famous treatise, *Dialogues concerning Two New Sciences,* on the theory of dynamics, which had so absorbed him earlier and whose manuscript was smuggled out of Italy for publication. 'Out of the shambles (of his plight)', so writes Arthur Koestler, 'modern physics was born'.[326] A synthesis of his scientific work was published in 1638 on dynamics, inertia, gravity, parabolic trajectory, etc. He died in 1642 in the company of friends and admirers, sadly and ironically by this time blind. It was the same year in which Isaac Newton (1642-1727) was born. It was as if the mantle of the founder of modern physics was being vicariously passed on to its greatest exponent, as recognised for three hundred years. Galileo's bones repose in the Parthenon of the Florentines, adjacent to those of Machiavelli and Michelangelo in their Church of Santa Croce.

Perhaps Galileo's supreme achievement was to break virtually any serious pretension the church might have had to a monopolistic interpretation of cosmological and for that matter scientific knowledge in general. In so doing, he had introduced the world to a totally novel way of looking at natural phenomena. The humanistic perception that so characterises the renaissance period led inexorably to the age of reason to which Galileo might well advance his archetypical claim. Theoretically,

---

[325] De Santillana, G.: *The Crime of Galileo,* Heinmann, 1961. The penitential Psalms are as follows: Psalms 6, 32, 38, 51, 102, 130, 143.

[326] Koestler, A.: *The Sleepwalkers,* Pelican, 1968.

advocated his contemporary Francis Bacon (1561-1626), there can be no limit to human capacity. Bacon, in fact, was to push Galileo's inductive process further, not simply to confirm mathematical theories, but to probe more deeply into the hitherto unknown. 'Measure', he asserted, 'what can be measured and make measurable what cannot be measured': a Tower of Babel before God had decided enough was enough![327] René Descartes (1596-1650) was to take such ideas to their ultimate whereby in his view, any dogma or presupposition is deemed alien to an honest assertion of existence. His *Cogito Ergo Sum*[328] serves as the quintessential 'ex posteriori' antidote to the 'a priori' assertion beloved of certain medieval scholastic churchmen: no room for an authoritarian church here. The individual human being is on his/her own; the centre of his/her own personal universe is how Isaac Newton saw it, as he pursued Galileo's pioneering work on inertia and dynamics to articulate the universal law of gravitation, that all bodies continue in a state of rest, or uniform motion, unless an external force acts upon them, which is a compelling rationale for the theory of heliocentricity. Newton's ideas were to hold sway in these areas until Einstein (1879-1955). Modern physics and chemistry were truly born, stripped of their alchemic mystique[329] or scriptural fundamentals. Despite Galileo's assertion that natural law was evidence enough of an omnipotent God, the church wasn't going to walk away without a fight. The problem for the church was that, since the reformation of the sixteenth century, it could not now invoke universality to its aid. No longer could the church mount a *united* front in the face of the apparent progressive claims of science and the

---

[327] Genesis 11:1-9.

[328] 'I think, therefore I am': The only certainty in which 'I' can be certain is that I exist because I have the power to think.

[329] Alchemy was prevalent throughout the European Medieval Period. Its practitioners followed the line that esoteric revelation to the initiated could lead to human control over matter. Transmuting base metal into gold was one of its more extreme aims and among its disciples were Roger Bacon (c.1214-94), Albertus Magnus (c.1200-80), Thomas Aquinas, while one, Paracelsus (1493-1541), asserted the claim that he had discovered the elixir of life. James Price in the eighteenth century claimed to have discovered the all-elusive 'Philosopher's Stone', but his assertions were overtaken by Robert Boyle (1627-91), whose leading role in the group of 'Natural Philosophers' led, in 1663, to the formation of the 'Royal Society', and as such is regarded as the founder of modern chemistry. He was the first to recognise the true nature of an element and to distinguish between a compound and a mixture: observation and investigation again.

The Church   161

inductive process. Luther, Zwingli, Calvin and Muntzer had seen to that, and in any case many Protestants, encouraged by their more freethinking inheritance, were willing to embrace and even advance the cause of science. Some Protestants, it is true, remained sceptical in the raw light of scripture, but with the Thirty Years' War tearing Central Europe apart, there was little appetite for a joint assault on the progressive ideas. While, on the whole, both the Iberian and Italian peninsulas tended to remain wedded to the Church of Rome and its inherent dogma, it was for the more liberal ambience of the disparate Protestant nation states—notably Sweden, the Netherlands and England—which tended first to embrace the progressive ideas of the 'age of reason', translate them into oceanic trade and thence to the Industrial Revolution. In France, where an aggressive dynasticism was being pursued by Louis XIV (1643-1714), the Roman Church as overseen by Bossuet (1627-1704) was pursuing its own idiosyncratic Gallican agenda: heavily Roman in theory and character, but equally weighted to function as the tool of the monarchy. As such it opened up an avenue through which the likes of Voltaire and the 'enlightenment' of the eighteenth century were to emerge to lampoon the establishment of the Roman Church for its arcane identity and its abuse of privilege.[330]

The defining moment centred on Galileo's assertion that, despite the forces arraigned against him, it was the earth that moved forcing the Roman Church in particular onto the defensive. Against the rationale staring at it in the face, the Vatican relied for the moment on a now discredited medieval cosmological perception that failed to square with the facts. Galileo's insistence on the inductive process of logical understanding in order to square with mathematical certainties made 'reason' the 'de facto' enemy of the church: a Rome out of touch and out of sympathy with the accompanying economic theories of 'laissez faire' and the apparently voracious appetite for science.

Galileo's legacy is a conundrum with which churchmen have been forced to come to terms ever since: how to reconcile the God of faith and scripture with the self-evident claims of modern science.

One academic had a go, early on. William Paley (1743-1805) postulated the theory of the 'grand design' as it pertains to the natural world.[331] Nevertheless, the application of the inductive process to advance the cause of knowledge led to a blossoming of academics in all

---

[330] Hill, J.: *Faith in the Age of Reason*, Lion Hudson, 2004.

[331] By using the analogy of a pocket watch, Paley postulates that nothing so intricate could be fashioned to achieve its desired ends without a designer. How much more, then, could the world, and the universe, be so constructed,

fields during the age of reason: Newton, we have already mentioned, nevertheless saw a non-Trinitarian God at work in sustaining natural laws. William Harvey (1578-1657), lecturing at the London College of Physicians, revealed the anatomical function of the heart, lungs and in particular the life-sustaining resource of the circulation of the blood. The patient work of Edward Jenner (1749-1823), experimenting at his surgical practice in Berkeley, resulted in the application of the first successful vaccine against smallpox and which ultimately purged the world of its dreaded scourge. The investigations of the Curies at the Sorbonne during the nineteenth century led to the extensive use of radiology in both diagnostic and treatment departments of modern medical science. The discovery of penicillin and its bacterial properties by Sir Alexander Fleming (1881-1955) is a classic model of investigative procedure: a combination of observation, patience and a fair slice of good fortune—to the relief of the suffering of many, the ubiquitous antibiotic.

With all these advances in medical science, most churches, Protestant or Catholic, could have little quarrel, given that despite its initial grudging acceptance of the process involved, the human condition seemed all the better for it.

More sinister in the long term as far as the church was concerned was the work of Carl Linnaeus (1707-78), the Swedish botanist, who laid the foundation of botanical classification. This was based upon the inherent character of organic structure rather than its relationship to human utility. Building on the research, Charles Darwin's *Origin of Species* (1859) went even further, much further, in explaining the human condition. He had collected multitudinous data from natural phenomena located on the isolated islands he visited while serving as naturalist on board the 'Beagle' in its survey of the Atlantic and Pacific Oceans between 1831 and 1836. Darwin (1809-82) concluded on analysis of this material that the human species, *Homo sapiens*, is but the culmination of the process of natural selection: the survival of the fittest. Chance evolutionary circumstances, he maintained, have ensured the survival of certain species as long as they could adapt and spelled the doom of others if they couldn't; thus the evolved cerebral capacity of *Homo sapiens* has secured its past, present and presumably its future. In a way, this evolutionary theory, if accepted, would put paid once and for all the medieval concept of creationism whereby each organic species was considered to be a specialist design, with a distinct purpose, as ordained

---

without a higher thought, in order to achieve a conducive environment for human experience?

The Church 163

by God,[332] the supreme architect of the universe. The debate has shown no sign of abating having, as it does, implications for education and politics as epitomised by the Scopes trial in Tennessee in 1925.[333] From the fundamentalist, Bible-based standpoint, Darwin's theory is a red herring thrown in to test the spiritual faith of the believer for whom the scientific and theological roots of humanity lie literally in the first two chapters of Genesis. To the confirmed atheist, Darwin's work (though not to Darwin himself) derides the idea of a Transcendent Being ('God') and that the honest humanist response is for humankind to utilise its innate nature and talents to secure its own individual and collective well-being. This is a strand of thought prefigured in the contractual governmental theories[334] expounded by Thomas Hobbes, John Locke and Jean-Jacques Rousseau, through the utilitarianism[335] of Jeremy Bentham (1748-1832) and John Stuart Mill (1806-73), to the out and out atheistic economic determinism of Karl Marx[336] as expressed in the areligious Soviet regimes in the twentieth century. Thus has evolved a purely materialistic view

---

[332] As per Genesis, 1:1-2:4 (a).

[333] The celebrated so-called 'Monkey Trial' in the USA in July 1925. John Scopes, a biology teacher in the state of Tennessee was accused in the courts of breaking the law by teaching the 'Darwinist evolutionary theory' as distinct from the state-approved curriculum, which held that the earth was specially created by God in six days as per Genesis 1. Scopes lost the case: He had broken the law in the face of hard line Protestant fundamentalism, but in fact his cause was given a boost by the high profile of the case.

[334] Hobbes (1588-1679) in part and Locke (1632-1704) and Rousseau (1712-78) certainly fundamentally agree on the need for a 'contract' to be respected between the governors of the state and the governed—for the well-being and security of both.

[335] The utilitarians held that government should be in the business of providing the greatest good for the greatest number: a crude expression of democracy.

[336] The dialectic of Marx (1818-83) articulated the inevitable triumph of the working person as the outcome of an ongoing class struggle. Ultimately the necessity of the state would wither away and human co-operation would express the highest recognition of the values of society. History was seen as an inexorable process, determined by economic needs, and as such he was following the footsteps of Gibbon, who saw history and historical outcomes in terms of the interrelationship of human causation, and the so-called Whig interpretation of history, which regarded the evolution of Liberal Democracy as its apotheosis: material means to a 'spiritual' end rather than the medieval concept of spiritual avenues from start to finish.

of the universe whereby human fortunes have been fashioned by the forces of environmental, political, social and economic circumstances impinging upon the human will.

The church itself, in its variety of guises, both Protestant and Catholic, has thus been forced to accept, reject or live alongside scientific factors now exposed as self-evident. Predictably, Darwin's *Origin of Species* was placed on the Vatican's 'Index of Forbidden Books' along with Rousseau's *Contrat Social* and Gibbon's *Decline and Fall*. Initially, the Vatican was dismissive of the darling of twentieth-century liberal Catholicism, the Abbé Hugues Félicité Robert de Lamennais (1782-1854), who sought to detach the church from the corrupting influence of the state and whose resonance has found fertile soil in the liberation theology movement of Gustavo Gutierrez (born 1928) in South America. He sought a kind of synthesis between Catholic traditionalism and Marxism determinism, whereby the church would choose to align itself with the plight of the poor and dispossessed, while standing up to any government that was regarded as aiding and abetting poverty in the first place. Around the world, Catholic bishops have become increasingly critical of state policy—notably the bishop of Bulawayo at the beginning of the twenty-first century in challenging in the name of the church the avarice of Robert Mugabe's regime in Zimbabwe: developments leading to the unravelling of the comfortable arrangement initiated by Constantine. Earlier on, there were those Christian thinkers loosely known collectively as 'deists', among whom Edward Herbert,[337] Blaise Pascal,[338] Locke[339] and Voltaire[340] are counted. They broadly accepted the rationalist

---

[337] Edward Herbert (1583-1648): aristocrat, diplomat, lover and philosopher, who propounded the idea that *all* religions have a similar core of ethical and eschatological beliefs, but which have been overlaid by human accretions such as to obscure the truth.

[338] Blaise Pascal (1623-62), a French theologian and mathematician. His 'Pensées' published in 1670 suggested that his scientific investigation convinced him that human existence is confronted by the need to accept or reject God. 'Better', he thought, 'to put one's money on faith in God'; that way he couldn't lose. 'The heart has its reasons of which reason knows not' is a famous phrase attributed to him.

[339] John Locke (1632-1704), philosopher and political thinker: the public apologist for the 'Glorious Revolution of 1688' and heavily influential in the ideas surrounding American Independence and its constitution.

[340] Voltaire (1694-1778), French philosopher, who, along with Rousseau, Montesquieu, Diderot and d'Alembert (1717-83), was the epitome of the age of enlightenment in the eighteenth century and whose ideas found

The Church 165

claims of Christianity, while rejecting the 'miraculous' accounts as of being of spurious authenticity. The Empiricist David Hume (1711-76) turned his back on Aristotelianism and scholasticism by rejecting the concept of causality as empirically unsound. While the existence of God is for practical purposes essential, any attempt to prove His existence is futile. Thus influenced, Emmanuel Kant (1724-1804) entered the foray in his 'discourse on reason', who held that God was incomprehensible to the finite, sense-oriented human mind and therefore any attempt to rationalise God or to reason Him into existence is bound to be frustrated—a dialogue of the deaf—certainly no room here for an 'a priori' presumption of God's existence. To Kant, it is the existence of morality itself that points to God's reality.

In the nineteenth century, the Unitarian movement prospered with its denial of a Trinitarian God, yet moved to social consequence by Christ's ethical and moral appeal. The scholarship of Rudolph Bultmann,[341] Albert Schweitzer,[342] Paul Tillich,[343] John Robinson[344] and others has attempted

---

expression in the *Encyclopaedia* of 1751, the germ of French Revolutionary ideas.

[341] Rudolf Bultmann (1884-1976), a German Protestant theologian, very influential in progressive thought in his day. His 'demythologising' of Christ seeks to tease out the 'true' 'Jesus of history', stripped of much of the quasi-allegorical narrative found in the Gospels.

[342] Albert Schweitzer (1875-1965): Protestant German musician, theologian, physician and philanthropist whose pioneering hospital in Gabon, West Africa, became world famous. He was similarly moved to find the 'historical Jesus', maintaining that in fact Christ, initially, expected an end to the material world to be imminent. When this was perceived as mistaken, He then saw the necessity to submit His body to suffering in order to spare the tribulation of His people.

[343] Paul Tillich (1886-1966): German Protestant theologian, sought to accommodate theology with secular philosophy. He taught that God, 'the Ground of our being', is encountered not in the strict observance to structural creeds, but through human experience. God's presence cannot be 'proved' on the same terms as the existence of material phenomena. Therefore, God's existence must be regarded as 'other' and not a reality in the humanly accepted sense.

[344] In the tradition of the 'demythologisers', John Robinson (1919-83), an Anglican bishop, tried to debunk the theory of the 'God of the Gaps' in his *Honest to God*, SCM, 1968, by suggesting that the Almighty cannot simply exist in order to explain the inexplicable. Science has been shown to reveal previously hidden secrets and presumably will continue to do so.

166   But It Does Move

to square their undoubted faith with the incontrovertible evidence thrown up by modern science. The work of Stephen Hawking (born 1942) in his *A Brief History of Time* at the University of Cambridge has furthered our understanding of the astrophysics of Albert Einstein[345] and the nuclear physics of Ernest Rutherford.[346] This research throws fresh challenges confronting revealed theology in the face of explicable natural forces.

In an increasingly westernised secular and materialistic world, it does appear that traditional spiritual values have become eroded. An increasingly prosperous and growing 'middle class' sees little need to turn to 'faith' for its sustenance; those beneath the poverty line see little to be gained by adhering to a 'church' whose values, where they exist, are seen to reflect theological subtleties from which they feel alienated. The rationalists, as exemplified by Galileo, and those who came after them have proffered intellectual reinforcement in support of this outlook. The old 'a priori' medieval certainties as held sacrosanct by a universal, all-pervasive church seem to have moved over in favour of scepticism in the light of the sensual evaluation of appearances on the ground floor. The reality of an HIV (AIDS) pandemic in several parts of the world has raised the stakes. Is the belief in the sanctity of a life God-given on *His* own initiative, as the Catholic Church would contend, commensurate with the desperate need to encourage 'safe sex' whose by-product would potentially inhibit the creation of new life or, for that matter, to induce the cessation of a life already in existence? The papal encyclical of Paul VI (1963-78), *Humanae Vitae* (1968), explicitly forbids the intervention of any artificial barrier calculated to prevent conception whether inside or outside the sacrament of marriage.[347] Protestants generally take a softer as a result of sexual intercourse may well be admissible on the

---

[345] Albert Einstein (1879-1955): the true successor to Newton in the field of physics. His famous theory of relativity, $E = MC^2$, postulates that the universe itself is constantly expanding and contracting; that time is a co-ordinate of space and that distances in space are relative. Stephen Hawking's work, *A Brief History of Time*, utilises this material.

[346] Sir Ernest Rutherford (1871-1937), the New Zealand physicist, whose researches at Cambridge recognised the nuclear nature of the atom and the structure of matter.

[347] Specifically and significantly, the encyclical *Humanae Vitae* forbids the use, by Catholics, of the condom as an artificial barrier to conception during intercourse. This view is considered by liberals as irresponsible in so far it is a relatively inexpensive means in combating the infection of the HIV virus. The devastation caused by the disease in less developed countries, in Africa particularly, has forced the Vatican to modify its stance on the matter, and

The Church 167

grounds that every child should be a wanted child. All Christians seem to be agreed that euthanasia or assisted suicide as well as induced abortion be the least acceptable means of the disposal of life, although even here there are differing shades of opinion. The cloning of modern stem cells for the purpose of saving, or improving, the life quality of existing beings is an area where the church has been faced with an inherent moral dilemma. How far do the ends justify the means? It does appear that the dilemma for the church and for Christians is going to intensify rather than diminish, as ethical considerations on life/death issues have to come to terms with the reality of certain perverse advances in medical science such as Mary Shelley's *Frankenstein* (1818) and Robert Louis Stevenson's *Jekyll and Hyde* (1886) could only hint at.[348]

The world and the human condition took on a new perspective such as that occasioned our defining moment by unlocking the hidden treasures of empirical science and exposing the power of humanity's capacity to harness them. Galileo had wrecked the symbolism of medieval theology, authoritarian that it was, yet liberated thinkers and activists in the name of the church could now stand up to perverse secular regimes and so redeem its sense of purpose as Jonathan Hill suggests.[349] Nevertheless, it took the Roman Church three centuries to concede that Galileo might well have been right. On 31 October 1992, Pope John Paul II (1978-2005) went as far as to declare that fundamental theological errors had been made at Galileo's trial and that the verdict was consequently 'unsafe'. While stopping short of admitting that the church was wrong in the heresy conviction, in its own eyes, the case was finally closed; Galileo's stance was now officially accommodated if not condoned. His bones could now repose in the Church of San Croce undisturbed by papal imprecations. The only movement they now experience will be that which is common to us all as fellow travellers on the earth's axiomatic revolution around the sun.

---

to permit such usage, provided the motivation is infection prevention, and not as a backdoor avenue to contraception.

[348] Both these nineteenth-century stories throw up the vision of the limitless (and possibly perverse) possibilities opening up in the world of science: the alteration of the persona and the human creation of life itself.

[349] Hill, J.: *Faith in the Age of Reason*, Lion Hudson, 2004. The Christian teaching and example of the Protestant Pastor Bonhoeffer (1906-45) in fearlessly denouncing the Nazi regime in Germany during the 1930s and 1940s cost him his life. A similar fate befell the Catholic Liberation Theologian Bishop Oscar Romero of San Salvador (1917-80) in his criticism of Latin American totalitarianism in the late twentieth century.

Chapter 16

John Wesley preaching at Epworth market cross

MY HEART STRANGELY WARMED

Running due north of St Paul's Cathedral in the city of London, the thoroughfare of St Martins-le-Grand gives way to Aldersgate Street, whose name recalls the site of one of the historic entrances to the walled community.

During the Blitz of 1940, the entire area fell victim to heavy bombing. The subsequent reconstruction is now dominated by the multidimensional Barbican Centre occupying sixty acres on Aldersgate's eastern periphery. Characterised by its variety of concrete complexes linked by risqué flyovers and walkways, this modern residential amalgam coexisting alongside the home of the Royal Shakespeare Company, the London Symphony Orchestra, the Barbican Art Gallery and Library, the Pit Theatre, concert hall, conservatory and assorted exhibition venues would render the vicinity virtually unrecognisable to the eighteenth-century figure who stands as central to our defining moment. During his residence in London, the serious, dapper, diminutive, trim figure of John Wesley would have, nevertheless, been familiar with the nearby church of St Giles-without-Cripplegate, now restored, where Shakespeare (1564-1616) had been attendant on the baptism of his nephew and where Oliver Cromwell (1599-1658) had been married in

The Church

169

1620; John Milton, poet and puritan (1608-74), is buried here while the church testifies to its association with the likes of Frobisher (1535-94), John Foxe (1516-87), Bunyan (1628-88) and Defoe (1660-1731). The Museum of London, located at the south-eastern intersection of Aldersgate Street and London Wall, opened in 1981, reinforces the historical importance of this area: In the adjacent Nestleton Court, there stands a fifteen-foot tall replication of an entry in Wesley's journal,[350] which bears witness to the site representing not only a landmark in this remarkable individual's life but also a watershed in the fortunes of the church worldwide and something of a pivot in the evolution of Britain's social and political life.

Let Wesley's own words, as etched in this memorial culled from his journal, speak for themselves.

Wednesday 24 May 1738.

. . . In the evening I went very unwillingly to a society in Aldersgate Street where one was reading Luther's Preface to the Epistle to the Romans. About a Quarter before Nine, while he was describing the change which God works in the Heart thro' Faith in Christ, I felt my heart strangely warm'd. I felt I did trust in Christ, Christ alone for Salvation: And an assurance was given me. That He had taken away my Sins, even mine, and saved me from the Law of Sin and Death.

This was the genesis of a life reborn, and action packed, not that life for this rising thirty-five-year-old had hitherto been dull. Born in 1703, the son of Samuel Wesley, rector of the Lincolnshire parish of Epworth, and his redoubtable wife Susannah, he was the fifteenth of a battery of nineteen siblings. At the age of five, Wesley had been saved in dramatic fashion from the blazing inferno of the rectory, possibly the unwitting victim of the local community aiming to redress some perceived shortcomings exhibited by John Wesley's father, the well-meaning albeit

---

[350] Wesley's journal is the record of his active life. Originally produced in twenty-six volumes, only a portion has ever been published. It is a remarkable document embracing the social ambience of all parts of the United Kingdom during the seventeenth century. 'No one lived nearer the centre (of life) than John Wesley', wrote Alexander Burrell, K. C., in his *Appreciation of John Wesley's Journal.* The edition used here is edited by Parker, P. L., STL Productions.

insensitive cleric, who had the unfortunate tendency to ruffle a few parochial feathers.

'A brand plucked from the burning' was his mother's prescient declaration on her son's good fortune. Subsumed within the context of the established Church of England—Charterhouse, Christ Church Oxford and Fellow of Lincoln College—bright, conscientious and sincere, there had been no reason to suspect that Wesley and his younger brother Charles (1707-88), a fellow Oxford man and cleric, would not follow the conventional career as a clerk in Holy Orders. Yet there was restlessness in the spirit of this young priest. Like Luther before him, he was desperate to secure the assurance of God's acceptance of his sinful nature. In pursuit of this aim, John and Charles Wesley had gathered around themselves in Oxford like-minded Christians, James Harvey, Benjamin Ingham, the influential George Whitefield (1714-70) and others, into what was known pejoratively by contemporaries as 'The Bible Moths', the 'Holy Club' or simply the 'Methodists': a group dedicated to a study of the scriptures and a practical outreach to prisoners, the indigent and the illiterate. Wesley's missionary zeal was subsequently fuelled by an invitation to minister to the settlers and indigenous people of Oglethorpe's recently founded American colony of Georgia in the 1730s, which he and Charles accepted, yet which was to materialise in a period of two years there distinguished in the main only by frustration, disappointment and a sense of failure. A characteristic romantic trauma was the straw that had broken his heart,[351] but more seriously, 'I who went to America', he lamented, 'to convert others was never myself converted to God'. This was at the root of his dilemma and yet the colonial experience provided him with the germ of hope. In America, he had come into contact with another group of missionaries—the Bohemian/German Moravian[352] Christian Brotherhood of Count

---

[351] In Georgia, Wesley's naiveté in affairs of the heart revealed itself in his relationship with Sophie Hopkey. She having married another man, Wesley then denied her communion, thus rendering him persona non grata in the eyes of her uncle who happened to be the chief magistrate of Savannah. Wesley's departure from the colony quickly ensued. Later, back in England, he fell in love with Grace Murray over whom Wesley dithered while taking stock of his brother Charles's warning that she was 'beneath his station'. She then married a fellow Methodist. Wesley's subsequent tempestuous marriage to Maria Vazeille is well documented. By contrast, Charles Wesley's marriage, and family life, was one of sublime felicity.

[352] The Moravians: a quasi-Lutheran group based in Germany with Bohemian roots. They had strong missionary ideals; Wesley visited them, meeting Count

Zinzendorf and Herr Spangenberg, their man on the spot. They possessed what Wesley knew that he himself lacked: a personal joyful assurance of salvation. Back in London, Wesley came into contact with Peter Böhler (1712-75), a leading member of the Moravian brotherhood there. He encouraged Wesley to 'preach faith until you have it and then because you have it you will preach faith'. Wesley was on his way. Having established another small religious community in Fetter Lane, Wesley's enthusiastic preaching in and around the city of London, with its emphasis on God's love for all people, was not necessarily congruent with the prevailing spirit inside the establishment of the Church of England. He was increasingly denied access to its pulpits. It was in this sterile atmosphere that Wesley, intellectually inspired, yet emotionally drained, set off on his 'unwilling' stroll round into Aldersgate Street and to the heart-warming response to Luther's preface to the Romans: 24 May 1738, our defining moment.

This was to signal a further fifty years of ministry—unconventional, yet spirit filled. By the time of his death in 1791, Wesley had become the reluctant founder of a dynamic nonconformist denomination destined to become the largest disestablished Protestant Church in the world. As a professed and unapologetic priest of the Church of England to the end, he was to challenge many who remained within its embrace to espouse an evangelical sense of mission and whose fortunes since the beginning of the reign of Elizabeth I (1558-1603) we must now briefly consider.

Of all the Western churches founded since the reformation, few have exhibited a more enigmatic profile than the established Church of England. Founded on the altar of divorce proceedings,[353] it has traditionally set its face against the remarriage of divorcees. Rejecting the authority of Rome, it nevertheless holds fast to its inheritance of the Catholic apostolic succession of St Peter. As the state-sponsored church, the Middle Way as expressed in Elizabeth's Act of Settlement in 1559 had been intended to embrace those of both Catholic and Protestant wings and all in between with the monarch as its supreme governor and guarantor. While most were prepared to work within the spirit of the settlement, there were many who most patently were not. The uncompromising Romanists were to find themselves marginalised and deprived of their civil rights during Elizabeth's reign, while a strong

---

Zinzendorf (1700-60), and was inspired by their zeal and organisation, much of which found its way into Methodism.

[353] Henry VIII's dispute with Pope Clement VII over his marriage to Catherine of Aragon. See chapter 13.

Protestant puritan element sought to distance itself from anything tainted by its Roman inheritance or indeed any Constantinian identification between church and state. Roman Catholic recusancy during this period is the stuff of Jesuit apologia—priest holes and pimpernels—but it is the growth of the independent non-conformist Protestant church groupings to which our attention should be drawn: those who could not accept state patronage and the constraint and control of their religious principles. Disappointed by James I's reinforcement of episcopacy at the Hampton Court Conference in 1604,[354] the influence of these communities led directly to the foundation of the Plymouth Colony in America with the encouragement of John Robinson and the sailing of the Pilgrim Fathers aboard the 'Mayflower' in 1620; to the increasing intensity of hostility towards Archbishop Laud's[355] High Church policy in the 1630s and 1640s, the English Civil War (1642-49) and to the execution of King Charles I in 1649; and to the Puritan Commonwealth of Oliver and Richard Cromwell, (1649-60). This ephemeral puritan supremacy was cut short by the restoration of Charles II in 1660 and the rigorous application of the Clarendon Code[356] (1660-65) in restoring the Church

---

[354] Despite his Presbyterian associations, the Scottish James VI on becoming James I of the United Crowns of England and Scotland summoned a meeting of leading bishops and puritans to Hampton Court to discuss the issue of church governing practice. He came down heavily on the side of those in favour of retaining the historic episcopacy, 'No bishop, no king'. This frustrated the wishes of the puritans who thought their time had come. One direct result of the conference was the commissioning of the 'authorised' ('King James') version of the Bible.

[355] Archbishop of Canterbury, 1633-41, who alienated puritan sensitivities by issuing directives ordering absolute obedience to his policy of reinstating Roman Catholic ritualism, while holding fast to the Church of England. The Long Parliament impeached him and he was executed in 1645.

[356] A series of laws passed by the Restoration Parliament determined to restore Anglican supremacy. The Corporation Act (1661) reserved membership of municipal corporations to Anglicans. The Act of Uniformity (1662) established a slightly modified edition of the Elizabethan Book of Common Prayer, whose use was to be compulsory in all churches. The Conventicle Act (1664) declared all religious assemblies of five people or more, not held in accordance with the BCP to be illegal, and the Five Mile Act (1665) forbade all priests unable to abide by he Act of Uniformity to live within five miles of the nearest corporate town or to teach in schools. These laws were supplemented by the Test Act (1673), which required, among other things, that all office holders under the crown must receive the sacrament of Holy

The Church 173

of England with its active repudiation of both Roman Catholicism and Protestant Dissenters alike. James II's failed attempt to re-Romanise England (1685-88) paved the way for the historic enactment into law by William III and Mary (1688-94-1702) of the Bill of Rights and the Toleration Act[357] of 1689, which was a recognition in law that religious bodies other than that of the established church had the right to exist. This toleration was granted to Protestant nonconformists in return for their support in opposing James II's Catholic policies and was of course not extended to Roman Catholics. This and the childless marriage of the royal couple as well as Queen Anne's failure to produce a surviving heir (1702-14) paved the way for the incontrovertibly Protestant Hanoverian succession in 1714, which, despite the Jacobite Catholic uprisings in 1715 and 1745, was to secure the primacy of the Anglican Church in the state. It is therefore surprising that puritanism and nonconformity, not to mention Romanism, had survived in England. Emigration to the newly acquired lands in America had been one way out. Reference has already been made of the founding of Massachusetts by the Pilgrim Fathers. Disaffected Catholics had established the Maryland colony in 1634 and William Penn (1644-1718) founded the Quaker settlement of Pennsylvania in 1682.

For those who had stayed, life had been difficult. Those who favoured 'believers' baptism'[358] and a more democratic approach to church government, rather than the episcopal hierarchy imposed by the state, ran the risk of imprisonment for propagating their views. John Bunyan had been incarcerated in Bedford Jail during the seventeenth century, while another fervent Congregationalist, Thomas Helwys (1550-1616), ran the gauntlet by opening the first Baptist Church in London in 1612. Of particular note was George Fox (1624-91) whose quest for sanctity led him to the assertion that truth is the experience of a personal and individual response to the inner voice of the Spirit of God. Not for him and his 'friends' or Quakers, as they came to be called, the Book of

---

Communion according to the established Church of England practice and to make a declaration against transubstantiation.

[357] The Toleration Act effectively repealed the *religious* disabilities of Protestant nonconformists, freeing them from the restrictions imposed by the Uniformity, Conventicle and Five Mile acts, outlined in note 356 (above), although until the repeal of the Test and Corporation Act of 1828, they were still deprived of public office. Catholics were restored to full religious and civil rights by the controversial Catholic Relief Act of 1829.

[358] The validity of baptism only recognised when the individual fully understands the significance and accepts the commitment.

Common Prayer and its imposed liturgy; imprisoned yet undaunted his movement took hold. Although not attracting a wide swathe of adherents, its distinctive unstructured meetings for reflection spawned some of the great philanthropic movements of the nineteenth century with whom the names of Elizabeth Fry (1780-1845), Joseph Lancaster (1774-1838), Joseph Rowntree (1836-1925) and George Cadbury (1839-1922) are associated.

Thus, until 1689, Protestant dissenters had had a tortuous and tenuous existence: zealous, occasionally vociferous, yet numerically relatively small.

Wesley, then, he of our defining moment, an Anglican priest to his dying day was, paradoxically, to give birth to the Methodist movement and, as such, destined to give Protestant nonconformity a truly dynamic force during the nineteenth century. It was to give the nonconformist cause clarity, wide acceptance and respectability throughout the British Isles and around the world.

'I look upon all the world as my parish', claimed Wesley, 'thus far in whatever part of it I am, I judge it meet, right and my bounden duty to declare unto all that are willing to hear, the glad tidings of salvation'.[359]

This was a movement driven initially by the desire of this inherently conservative man to unleash the Holy Spirit into areas long ago forsaken by an established church increasingly complacent and elitist in its focus.

What made Wesley's heart-warming experience so profound was the fact that he could not luxuriate in self-indulgence at his own discovery. Its very nature compelled transmission on the world service. In Wesley's words,

> All need to be saved.
> All may be saved.
> All may know themselves saved.
> All may be saved to the uttermost.[360]

His brother Charles, the hymn writer of the Methodist movement, echoes this theme in several of his compositions. Soaked in scripture and sublime in poetry, he wrote in celebration of his own conversion as well as that of John.

---

[359] Wesley, J.: *Journal*, op. cit. Entry for Monday 11 June 1739.

[360] Quoted in *How Great a Flame*, Methodist Publishing House, London, 1987. It is undoubtedly Wesley's response to the great evangelical text, John 3:16.

The Church

... O how shall I the goodness tell,
Father, which Thou to me hast showed?
That I, a child of wrath and hell,
I should be called a child of God,
Should know, should feel my sins forgiven,
Blest with the antipast of heaven ...

... Outcasts of men to you I call,
Harlots, and publicans, and thieves!
He spreads His arms to embrace you all:
Sinners alone His grace receives:
No need of Him the righteous have:
He came the lost to seek and save ... [361]

Or in a later hymn as follows:

For all my Lord was crucified
For all, for all my saviour died.[362]

Such sentiment sat uneasily upon the soul of the established church of the day and Wesley's pre-conversion exclusion from some pulpits in London intensified around the country commensurate with the zealous persistence of his mission. Influenced by his Oxford friend, the celebrated open-air evangelist, George Whitefield, Wesley took the conscious decision in 1740 to compensate for his failure to secure access to the vaulted and buttressed edifices of worship by resorting to a ministry constrained only by the canopy of the skies, the hedgerows, rivers and streams of rural England and the walls of its ancient cities and boroughs: his pulpit, the open field, the village smithy, the town square, a paddock, a barn.

---

[361] Verses 2 and 4 of Charles Wesley's hymn: 'Where shall my wondering soul begin?' Number 706 in *Hymns and Psalms*, Methodist Publishing House, London, 1983. Known as the Wesley Conversion Hymn, Charles Wesley records it in his own journal as having been sung 'with great joy' on the evening of John's Conversion, 24 May 1738. It expresses so much, so succinctly, the quintessence of the Wesleyan movement. The extract printed here draws heavily on Matthew 9:12-13; 21:31-32; Luke 19:10; Romans 8:16; Ephesians 2:1-10.

[362] From Charles Wesley's hymn 'Let Earth and Heaven agree', Number 226, Hymns and Psalms, op. cit.; John 3:16 again.

The details of John Wesley's travels are well documented in his journal as well as in several biographies.[363] In all, Wesley travelled on foot, on horseback and in later years by carriage, a distance in excess of a quarter of a million miles and the delivery of some forty-two thousand sermons, many of them delivered at 5:00 a.m. in order to reach the agricultural labourers and quarrymen before work. (Wesley's unhappy marriage to Maria Vazeille, who frankly couldn't stand her husband's frenetic tension and pace, could well stand as advancing the case for clerical celibacy.)

His reception, like the vagaries of the British climate, was mixed, but there can be no question as to his drawing power. At Givenny Pit in Cornwall, the ten thousand folks of mining stock[364] flocked from far and wide to listen to him. At Epworth, having been denied the use of the Parish Church pulpit, he preached from atop his father's grave, while at Pensford a frenzied mob, at the behest of the local squire, set an enraged bull on him.[365]

At Bath, he had a celebrated exchange with Beau Nash, fop, flirt and frivolous doyen of the frippery of the fashionable spa in which Wesley's exposition of the eternal values of the Holy Spirit laid bare the veneer of sophistication and decadence, symbolic of the pretensions of contemporary genteel society. From the Shetland to the Channel Islands, from Galway to East Anglia, the British Isles were very much Wesley's parish. Although reluctant to do so, Wesley felt obliged to 'ordain' Dr Thomas Coke in 1784 as 'superintendent of the Societies in America', who would otherwise be denied access to the sacrament of Holy Communion there[366]—a move on his part of doubtful legality as far as the Church of England was concerned and an action that presaged the complete separation of the Methodist movement from the Anglican Church.

---

[363] There have been several from the hagiographic Bevan, F.: *The Story of John Wesley*, Alfred Holness, 1896, to the objective study by Hattersley, R.: *John Wesley*, Abacus, 2003.

[364] According to Wesley himself in his *Journal*, op. cit., entry for Tuesday, 20 September 1743. A subsequent entry, dated Sunday, 2 September 1770, speaks of a crowd of twenty thousand gathered to hear him in the amphitheatre at Gwennap.

[365] *Journal*, op. cit. Entry for Tuesday, 5 June 1739.

[366] As a result of many in the newly independent USA rejecting the authority of the Church of England. Coke in turn ordained Francis Asbury (1745-1816) to lead Methodist work in America, while Coke (1747-1814) himself became legendary in the Caribbean field.

The Church   177

Had Wesley been a mere itinerant evangelist as Whitefield undoubtedly was, firing people into an emotional stratosphere and moving on, it is doubtful whether his success would have been so profound. Although wary of institutionalism, he was concerned to leave behind him local societies whereby their newly rediscovered faith could be nurtured. Thus evolved a structure that has characterised Methodism for two hundred years. Each Methodist 'society', as its numbers grew, would appoint 'class leaders', who would be responsible for the material and spiritual well-being of their 'class' of, say, ten to fifteen members. Societies themselves would be grouped into geographical circuits superintended by Wesley's 'travelling preachers': those responsible to 'Mr Wesley himself'—'in full connection'- and who could be assigned to an area of the country at his discretion. Within the circuits evolved another feature, local preachers—laymen empowered to preach in response to the growing demand for worship services, for which the shortage of ordained clergy was unable to satisfy. In order to give his movement some coherence, Wesley invited those lay preachers and ordained clergymen who supported him to a conference in 1744: the first annual meeting of Methodism's supreme governing body. Having opened his first building, a disused armaments factory, the foundry in London, four years earlier,[367] the first purpose-built meeting house for Methodists was opened in 1741 as the 'New Room' in Bristol.

What, then, was distinctive about Wesley's persona and his message, which moved so many to respond? We have already touched on the *inclusiveness* of Wesley's interpretation of the Gospel. *Everyone* was made to feel valued and wanted, from prince to pauper—that in true Lutheran tradition, a person is saved by faith, which is God's gracious gift to all and which He wishes all people to experience.[368] By extension, Wesley put much emphasis upon what he termed the attainment of Christian perfection, that state of being which diffused the state of 'inward holiness'—that assurance of a person's undeserved forgiveness—into the realm of social concern and action: 'enabling us to walk as Christ walked'.[369] This was the very practical side of Wesley's impact, not for him and the early Methodists the permanent retreat into self-indulgent contemplation. It was to meet the challenges of a society in the grip of profound agrarian changes and the Industrial Revolution. His was a message that spoke to the hearts of individuals who were caught up, it seemed, powerless in

---

[367] This was replaced by Wesley's Chapel in nearby City Road in 1778.
[368] Ephesians 2:8; Acts 15:11.
[369] Quoted in Deane, P.: *Know Your Methodism*, Nassau, Bahamas, 1980.

the grip of rampant unchecked capitalism. 'His wide view of Christian social obligations urged him to denounce political corruption, attack smuggling, condemn the 'distilling of spirituous liquors', claim work for the workless'.[370] The last letter he wrote, in the year of his death, 1791, was to William Wilberforce (1759-1833), encouraging the latter not to cease in his efforts to end the evils of the slave trade. In a letter to one of his leaders, Wesley expressed himself very clearly:

> I want you to converse more, abundantly more, with the poorest of souls, who if they have not taste, have souls, which you may forward in their way to heaven. And they have faith and the Love of God in a larger measure than any person I know. Creep in among these in spite of dirt and a hundred disgusting circumstances . . . Do not confine your conversation to genteel and elegant people.

Wesley appealed to a class of people relatively untouched by the Church of England. He did it by appealing not only to their hearts, and by the conviction of his preaching, for he was a very practical man, opening opportunities for deserving young people by founding Kingswood School in Bath for the education of the poor, first in a chain of Methodist schools in the country and around the world.

He was something of a dilettante in the field of medicine, offering advice on the alleviation of physical pain, palliative care for the chronically ill and other perhaps more questionable elixirs on which he published many tracts. Medical dispensaries were set up at the foundry and in Bristol. Clothes were distributed to the poor while at the foundry, soup kitchens were started and work found for destitute women. Books on English grammar were published as well as his translation of hymns from German. Much of this boundless energy stemmed from his overwhelming belief in the capacity of the human spirit to *respond* to God's grace and for it to make a material difference. In this regard, he split doctrinally from Whitefield, whose Calvinistic insistence on election and reprobation was at variance with what Wesley, in the Arminian tradition, believed to be the merciful dimension as innately expressed in an 'all-just God'. There remain, however, particularly in Wales, paradoxical echoes of Whitefield's Calvinist influence within the context of Methodism.[371]

---

[370] Quoted in Deane, P.: *Know Your Methodism*, Nassau, Bahamas, 1980.

[371] Deane, P. op. cit.

The Church   179

It is generally acknowledged that Wesley's influence pervades much of the social development of the nineteenth-century Britain. The origins of the Trade Union Movement have been traced to an open-air meeting of a group of working people at Mow Cop in the potteries in 1807—the primitive Methodists led by Hugh Bourne (1772-1853) and William Clowes (1780-1852). These were people who were moved to seek redress of the degrading and insensitive working conditions to which circumstances had condemned them, by co-operation and mutual self-help. As they channelled their energies into an interpretation of the Wesleyan doctrine of Christian perfection, so the evolution of the ubiquitous Methodist Chapel in towns and villages of Victorian Britain and the Central Hall of the cities became the focal point for a cultivation of universal holiness and social action. Thus the British Isles, it has been suggested, moved towards a democratic state in a spirit of gradualism under the influence of the Methodist spirit and the evangelical revival, which paradoxically was to reinvigorate the Church of England itself. As such, perhaps, Britain escaped the revolutionary excesses that, since the events in France in 1789, were to engulf the continent throughout the nineteenth century and steered the Labour movement away from extreme atheistic and Marxist principles. Roy Hattersley in his biography of Wesley certainly seems to think so.[372]

Shortly after Wesley's death, and despite his most fervent wish, the Methodist movement split from the Church of England, its members thereby being excluded from civic leadership until the repeal of the Test and Corporation Acts in 1828. The movement itself divided into various traditions of its own. The Methodist New Connexion was formed in 1797 to ensure a greater reserve of lay leadership within the church; the Bible Christians were very active and vociferous particularly in the West Country. Mention has been made of the establishment of the Primitive Methodist Church with its emphasis upon cultivating working class membership and influence. In 1932, these strands and branches voted to harness their energies in conjunction with the mainstream Wesleyan Church to form the Methodist Church of Great Britain, and its branches throughout the world, taking its place as a strand in the Western catholic tradition.

John Wesley himself would have lamented his movement's break with the church into which he had been born and to the polarised chapel versus church culture so characteristic of the nineteenth century. Yet he would have rejoiced that, in part, he and his fellow Methodists

---

[372] Hattersley, R. op. cit.

breathed new life into it. The Sunday School phenomenon of Robert Raikes (1735-1811) and Hannah More (1745-1833), the leading role played by the Church of England in primary education and the work of the Earl of Shaftesbury (1801-85) in securing the passage in parliament for legislation to ameliorating conditions for both adults and children in the satanic mills immortalised by Blake (1757-1827)[373] are testimonies to this. Wesley's heart would have danced had he lived to see the final abolition of slavery throughout the British Empire in 1838. How he would be praying for the success of the tortuous negotiations currently under way for a rapprochement and organic reunion of his Methodists and the church they chose to leave![374]

Intentional or not, Wesley gave Protestant Nonconformity both in Britain and in the mission fields around the globe a respectability and a force to be reckoned with. That warmed heart of our defining moment facilitated the breathing of a new dynamic spirit that would serve to revive the fortunes of Christian witness and its call to mission.

---

[373] From the poem 'Jerusalem' set to music by Charles Hubert Parry (1848-1918), 'Hymns Old and New' Kevin Mayhew, 1996, number 31. The acts of parliament referred to here include 'The Ten Hours' Bill', 1847, and 'The Factory Act', 1874, for which Shaftesbury was largely responsible.

[374] An attempt at organic reunification foundered in the 1960s, but restarted in 2003.

Chapter 17

Napoleon Crowns Josephine, Notre Dame, Paris. By J.L. David

VIVE L'EMPEREUR

Roughly five hundred years separate the completion dates of two iconic symbols of Paris, the Eiffel Tower and the Cathedral of Notre Dame. If the former embodies the future as envisaged by nineteenth-century industrialists, then the latter, reposing in its dedication to 'Our Lady', represents a kind of spiritual barometer of the French nation and its capital. Here it stands in its thirteenth-century Gothic 'eminence' sometimes *grise*, often *brillante*, but *toujours là*. For well over half a millennium, it has presided over the Ile de la Cité, coexisting in tenuous harmony with the Palais de Justice and the sinister Conciergerie, flanked by the flowing Burgundian waters of the Seine. The twin Gothic towers, guarding the cathedral's Western facade like the Pillars of Hercules, appear to cast a timeless philosophical maternal benevolence over the capital, its people and their relationship to the fortunes of the Roman Catholic Church in whose name it was called into being. Indeed from the standpoint of the hunchback of Victor Hugo's conception as he cavorted with the gargoyles in its upper echelons, the edifice was, in terms of its stained glass, its stone foliage, its colossal towers, the Parisian roar, 'the Universe; nay more, it was Nature itself'.[375]

A painting by Jacques-Louis David[376] on the neoclassical grand scale, some twenty-seven feet by eighteen now hanging in the Louvre, barely a few blocks downstream from Notre Dame on the right bank of the river, takes us vicariously inside the cathedral and to our defining moment. Captured in this stage-managed tableau, played out in front of the high altar, David depicts the Pope, Pius VII (1800-23), somewhat detached in what was, after all, the latter's prime demesne in France: not centre stage, but a forlorn, sullen profile of a man, an emasculated figure in the role of a supine returning officer, there to proffer his official imprimatur over proceedings for which he exhibited a demonstrable lack of enthusiasm. Viewed through the eyes of the artist, the shining star is, in fact, Napoleon Bonaparte and for once there is little reason to doubt the testimony of this obsequious painter as to the main thrust, if not the finer detail, of the imperious occasion. Bonaparte, having hijacked the coronation ceremony, had bypassed the Pope's prerogative by positioning the golden representation of a Roman's victor's laurel wreath over his own head as emperor of the French, the congregation signifying its apparent approbation in its 'Vive l'Empereur' rendition. Thus regaled in the classical imperial purple, emblazoned with the mystical bees of the old Frankish Merovingian kings,[377] David depicts Napoleon conferring the consort's dignity upon his first wife, Josephine.

By concentrating the beholder's gaze on the unfolding drama, one is left to contemplate the gargantuan edifice that was serving as hostess for the occasion: the cathedral by this time a crumbling, neglected elegance—a fertile target for any person seeking to make a mark in a latter-day health and safety executive. Its high altar, no less, had been hastily rehabilitated to some semblance of religious dignity for the occasion in the wake of its desecration a decade earlier at the height of the revolutionary terror. The long-term restorative efforts of Viollet-le-Duc (1814-79) on the very gargoyles frequented by Quasimodo were to await another half century. Hence, for Napoleon's coronation

---

[375] Hugo, V. (1802-85): *Notre Dame de Paris*, 1831.

[376] David, J-L (1748-1825), a painter in the neoclassical tradition whose representations of significant events of the French Revolutionary and Napoleonic era, such as *The Tennis Court Oath*, *The Death of Marat*, *Napoleon Crossing the Alps* and *The Coronation of Napoleon*, have provided us with an indelible, if idealised, portrait of the time.

[377] The bee was of particular significance to the Merovingian dynasty such as Clovis (481-511) and Dagobert II (656-679).

The Church   183

on 2 December 1804, the interior blemishes were discreetly veiled by brightly hung tapestries. Yet on this day nothing, however, could dispel the numinous, inspired as it was by the lofty grandeur of the vaulted stone roofing and by the incomparable rose windows, parading their exquisite talent upon a pontiff summoned from Rome, upstaged and subordinated to a self-styled emperor in the tradition of Charlemagne, a Caesar nouveau and an Alexander in prospect. This, then, is our defining moment—the ominous spectre of Napoleon Bonaparte—one destined to cast a long shadow across France, the European continent and upon the Western Church itself.

Napoleon, of course, was very much a product of the French Revolution by any standard a pivotal episode in world history, such that the ethos of academe has been awash with interpretations, Marxist and Revisionist and all in between, as regards the events surrounding the years 1787-94.[378] This drama needs to be considered.

In May 1789, the inept Louis XVI, 'the most Christian king' (1774-92), had summoned to his palace at Versailles representatives of the historic orders of France in a last-ditch attempt to stave off financial meltdown. All this ill-fated decision succeeded in doing was to lay bare the festering wounds of a land floundering under the burden of administrative inefficiency and injustice, having coincidently suffered a particularly bad harvest and the resultant high price of bread, straining the resources of the Parisian poor to the limit of their patience. The once powerful monarchy was no longer up to the job of sorting it all out: lampooned by the likes of Voltaire, Montesquieu (1687-1755), Rousseau, Quesnay (1694-1774) and Diderot—they of the eighteenth-century 'enlightenment'[379]—who collectively thought of the Roman Catholic

---

[378] Many and varied are authors and commentators on the French Revolution from such historians as Rudé, G., Lefebvre, G. and Soboul, A., taking the Marxist perspective to the work of Cobb, R. offering a more revisionist approach. A balanced summary of research done on the subject is found in Doyle, W.: *The Origins of the French Revolution*, OUP, 1989, while his *The Oxford Book of the French Revolution*; Sutherland, D. M. G.: *France 1789-1815: Revolution and Counter-revolution*, Fontana, 1985, and Cobban, A.: *A History of Modern France*, vols. I and II (Penguin, 1957) are useful for a consideration of both the revolution and Napoleon. Blanning, T. C. W.: *Aristocrats versus Bourgeois*, Macmillan, 1987, is a useful synthesis of research. Without doubt, Schama, S.: *Citizens*, Penguin 1989' is the best read for any interested investigation.

[379] The enlightenment, as applied particularly to eighteenth-century France, was an intellectual elite, whose ideas were common currency in the

184 Vive l'Empereur

Church and its devotee, the French king, as displaying an obscurantist resistance to reason and science.

The upshot of Louis's indecision, vacillation and failed leadership at the States General in May 1789 was the fall of the Bastille in July and to his execution in 1793 followed that of his wife Marie-Antoinette (1755-93) a few months later: the downfall of the monarchical principle in France and indeed the assumptions upon which France and the West—church and state in partnership—had been sustained for centuries. In its place, a tenuous republic had been established in September 1792, a logical outcome of the proclamation of the Rights of Man and the Citizen (August 1789),[380] the rule of the Jacobins,[381] the Guillotine and the formal abrogation of any religious justification for the existence of the state. The historic notion of a monarch's divine right to rule was consigned to the scrap heap. Sovereignty was handed to the people—in reality the radical elements of the sections of Paris and their representatives-en-mission despatched to the provinces to ensure compliance—during these tumultuous days encompassing the years 1792-94. The revolutionary Fouché[382] was adamant that death was not a rite of passage but simply 'an eternal sleep', and the 'Committee of Public Safety'[383] headed by people

---

fashionable Parisian salons of the period. Their views, collected by Diderot between 1751 and 1765 in his monumental *Encyclopaedia*, tended to reject 'revealed theology' as traditionally taught by the church in favour of a more deist-oriented 'natural theology' in which natural law implied natural human rights, in the tradition of John Locke and Thomas Jefferson, president of the USA,1801-09). Its influence, therefore, on both the American and French Revolutions is clear.

[380] A proclamation of the self-styled national assembly.

[381] A loose grouping of radical politicians, including Danton (1759-94), Robespierre (1758-94), Couthon (1755-94), Saint-Just (1767-94), Hebert (1757-94), Fouché (1759-1820), all of whom met in the Jacobin Club in Paris, who prosecuted and executed Louis XVI, leading to their domination of the 'Committee of Public Safety', 1793-94. It is they who are associated incontrovertibly with the 'Reign of Terror' and the Guillotine.

[382] See footnote 381.

[383] A committee of the national convention or 'parliament' ostensibly to oversee the defence of the state from threats to the revolutionary gains from internal and external sources, synonymous, however, with the extreme measures undertaken to secure this objective.

The Church 185

such as Robespierre,[384] Saint-Just[385] and Couthon[386] offered many the opportunity to put this claim, prematurely, to the test, as heads rolled with abandon in Paris, bodies swallowed up by the waters of the Loire at Nantes[387] or simply mown down by shot in Lyons[388] at the slightest hint of counter-revolutionary sentiment.

Thus, the whole edifice of Bourbon[389] absolutism had been toppled, and for the first time for over a millennium, a Western European state publicly flaunted its non-Christian, if not atheistic, credentials in the face of the church. As Edmund Burke[390] had predicted in 1790, the outcome would be war on a European scale and a reversion to dictatorship. Napoleon's coup d'état of 1799 fulfilled the prophecy.

Such a brazen attack upon the church, and its partial rehabilitation by Napoleon, was, it must be conceded, not altogether unprovoked. Under the regime of the Bourbon dynasty and secure in its Gallican Liberties,[391] the Roman Church in France enjoyed a virtual monopoly of religious observance and expression, especially since Louis XIV had revoked earlier undertakings to respect Protestantism by repealing the edict of Nantes in 1685.[392] In terms of its influence and privilege, the church had pervaded nearly every segment of French life, spiritual, social, economic and political. It owned 10% of the land; its clergy enjoyed the material benefits of the tithe as well as tax exemptions and its own ecclesiastical courts dealt exclusively with the men of the cloth in the disposal of disputes and discipline. Despite this general assertion, J. H. Shennan[393] insists, for example, that a distinction should be drawn between the

---

[384]   See footnote 381.

[385]   See footnote 381.

[386]   See footnote 381.

[387]   Prosecuted by Carrier (1756-94), a Jacobin zealot.

[388]   Instigated by the zealots Collot (1750-96) and Fouché.

[389]   The dynasty of French kings: Henry IV (1589-1610), Louis XIII (1610-43), Louis XIV (1643-1715), Louis XV (1715-74), Louis XVI (1774-92) and the brief restoration under Louis XVIII (1815-24) and Charles X (1824-30).

[390]   Burke, E.: *Reflections on the French Revolution*, 1790.

[391]   The Gallican Liberties of the French Church had been negotiated with the papacy in a former Concordat signed in 1516, which granted the French Monarchy considerable independence from Rome in ecclesiastical matters, including, interestingly, the king's right to nominate bishops.

[392]   Henry IV had guaranteed the rights, security and privileges of the French Protestants, the Huguenots, in 1598. It was this act that Louis XIV revoked in 1685, much, it is claimed, to the detriment of France.

[393]   Shennan, J. H.: *France before the Revolution*, Routledge, 1995.

186   Vive l'Empereur

lordly prelates—bishops and cardinals—royal favourites whose access to Crown patronage and the stereotypical village priest—the curé—who frequently fared little better than the peasantry among whom he lived and to whom many of the latter clandestinely adhered during the intense persecution of 1793-94. In fairness, the church in France had performed many duties on behalf of the crown and the people, in the provision of poor relief, education, hospitals, registration and the publication of official policy.[394] Unfortunately, it was its abuse of its historic privileges, which by the mid-eighteenth century had obscured the philanthropic enterprises and classified the Ecclesiastical Establishment alongside the aristocracy, that other bastion of outmoded privilege, the rationale for whose existence had long since expired. Such was portrayed by Dickens (1812-70) in the caricature of 'Monseigneur in Town and Country' and his tormentors in the guise of Madame Desfarges, the Vengeance and the Jacquerie,[395] as also penned by Baroness Orczy (early 1900s) who declaimed with tongue in cheek that the old noblesse had crushed the people 'under the scarlet buckled shoes'.[396]

Thus after the fall of the Bastille, 14 July 1789 and the humiliation of the crown thus symbolised, it is scarcely surprising that the French Church should represent a common target in the carve-up of its wealth and ultimately justified by ideological revenge: the doors of equality having been prised ajar, the Parisian mob burst through.

In August 1789, the Constituent Assembly[397] voted to end the privileged status of the church in France: tithes and pluralism were abolished, tax exemptions curtailed, 'non-productive' monasteries wound up, their land seized as security for a revamped national currency and civil rights extended to Protestants. Apart from the last named, the

---

[394]   Townson, D.: *France in Revolution*, Hodder and Stoughton, 1996.

[395]   Dickens, C.: *A Tale of Two Cities*, Penguin, 1994. All the names, of course, are fictional. However, *jacquerie* was an accepted term for people of revolutionary inclinations, especially in the run-up to the outbreak.

[396]   Baroness Orczy: *The Scarlet Pimpernel*, MDS/Mediasat, 2004, first published 1913. This story is a romantic and romanticised piece of fiction extolling the virtues of the fictional Sir Percy Blakeney in his attempts to rescue beleaguered former French aristocrats and to welcome them to the British shores.

[397]   In June, The states general determined to sit as one chamber instead of the traditional three orders separately, known initially as the national assembly, and subsequently as the constituent assembly in July 1789 charged as it was with formulating a new constitution.

The Church 187

clergy by and large acquiesced: reality dictated that it was scarcely politic to defend the indefensible.

Carried away by the sweet scent of success, and an apparent mania for a fundamental rationalisation of everything within its competence, from the metric system of weights and measures through the election of the judiciary to the neat arrangement of the 'department' as the unit of local government, the constituent assembly enacted, in 1790, the 'Civil Constitution of the Clergy'. Touted by some as a mere 'tidying up exercise' to go hand in hand with other reforms, this has been branded the most divisive piece of legislation in the entire revolutionary programme. Herein lie a 'cause celebre' and a catalyst for those opposed to the principle or practice of the revolution: the court, the papacy of Pius VI (1775-99), provincials who resisted the dictates of Paris, the émigrés[398] and, of course, many of the clergy themselves, all adjudged fairly or unfairly, as opposing the mantra espoused by the revolutionaries of liberty, equality and fraternity. Under this act, in its zeal to subordinate religious affairs to the needs of the state, as well as to achieve a symmetrical coalescence of the new departmental administrative districts, the church became a ministry of state. Bishoprics were now to be coterminous (and 'ipso facto' reduced in number) with the new departments and the papal veto on such appointments was to cease. All ecclesiastical offices, including that of the village curé were to be salaried civil servants of the state in return for their loss of income from church land, confiscated as it had been by the government in its endemic search for property and cash. At a stroke, the French Church was split. While the king reluctantly signed the legislation into law—he had no choice given his precarious circumstances—Pope Pius VI in far-off Rome had no such qualms in condemning it outright, officially suspending the so-called 'constitutional clergy' as schismatic, heretical and treacherous, while pitting against them the 'non-jurors'—those clerics who refused to take the new oath and who refused to be part of the new arrangements.

As International Conflict (declared April 1792)[399] and Civil War (in La Vendée, 1793-96) threatened the domestic advances made during the first flush of reforms, so more radical measures were required in their

---

[398] Émigrés: those aristocrats who fled France during the revolution in the hope of restoring the Ancien Régime and their personal fortunes when more propitious times returned.

[399] France declared war on Austria on 20 April 1992 in defence of its rights to determine its future without external interference and Prussia declared war on France a month later in defence of traditional rights and institutions.

defence and attacks now on the Constitutional Church were motivated by further demands for war material—church plate sold off and bells melted down for canon—justified by atheistic fanatics such as Hébert and Fouché, who saw in any hint of traditional religious observance evidence of revolutionary doctrinal heresy. An orgy of iconoclasm swept the country such as put Carlstadt's efforts in Wittenberg in the 1520s and Edward VI's English reformers during the early 1550s into the shade. Heads and bodies, as we have seen, were no longer sacrosanct, let alone the abstract concept of God.

All Christian inferences were expunged from the national consciousness. A new calendar, drawn up to coincide with the dawn of the republic, came into being as year I, on 22 September 1792. The twelve months, each of thirty days, were renamed to denote the seasons of the agrarian year (florial, thermidor, brumaire, etc.) and each week comprising ten days, ignoring traditional Sunday observance and religious festivals: a day of rest every *tenth* day and the five days remaining at the end of the year as workers' playtime—hardly a recompense for the holidays lost, yet well worth the sacrifice, apparently, if the safety of the revolution were to be assured. By May 1793, the municipal administration of Paris, the Commune, had ceased paying clerical salaries, and by November, all Parisian churches had been closed; we have noted the Cathedral of Notre Dame, desecrated and reconstituted as the Temple of Reason. Its high altar, playing hostess to its 'goddess' who had been escorted thus 'by wind music, red nightcaps and the madness of the world', danced no longer to the tune of Our Lady, nor to the Fruit of Her Womb, but to the vengeful spirit of the atheistic ideologues and the ready acceptance of the Parisian Sans-Culottes. The rest of France was expected to follow suit and the *Armées Révolutionnaires* attempted to ensure that it did. In an attempt to appease the increasing reaction directed against such draconian methods, Robespierre, 'the incorruptible', fearing that the backlash had gone too far, back-pedalled in an attempt to underpin support for the revolution. Danton, his fellow Jacobin and one-time friend, was upbraided for being too soft and Hébert for being too extreme. The result was the same: heads in the basket! Robespierre was prepared instead to acknowledge a transcendental divinity of sorts and to replace the abstract worship of reason, albeit without the trappings of any institutional church. Thus the 'cult of the Supreme Being' was celebrated in gaudy and grandiose style on the 'Champs de Mars' in Paris, in July 1794. Here, from the elevated set orchestrated by the ubiquitous David, Robespierre 'descended from the mountain like some Jacobin Moses, parting the ways of tri-coloured patriots, and graciously received the burst of orchestrated applause

The Church

that broke over his head'.[100] This was Robespierre's final throw of the dice. That summer he went to the guillotine as terrified colleagues and enemies alike conspired against him fearing for their own lives at his discretion: a case of 'Do unto him before he doeth unto us'. The sans-culottes, the mainstay of his support, many still hungry, had finally deserted him.

The end of the reign of terror saw a gradual, albeit furtive (and still technically illegal) reopening of churches across France, during the reactionary period of the Directory, 1795-99.[101] For the Church of Rome, however, this might have been something of a respite, but it was scarcely a regeneration of fortune. France, at war with pretty well everybody at some stage during this period, was turning its attention once more towards intervention in the complexity of the divided Italian peninsula where success engineered by Bonaparte in the field of battle would inevitably, sooner or later, confront papal authority in its own backyard. By the Treaty of Campo-Formio in 1797,[102] Ferrara, Bologna and Romagna became client states of the French, Rome itself subsequently occupied and declared a republic by 1798. Pope Pius VI ended his ill-starred reign and was punished for his recalcitrance and resistance to Bonaparte's demands, incarcerated in various secure strongholds until his death in 1799. His successor to St Peter's chair, the aforesaid Pius VII, was destined to be at the helm of a church, whose character was to mutate in response to the Napoleonic imprint.

Bonaparte recognised, however, that on becoming First Consul of France in 1799,[103] some sort of rapprochement would have to be made with the church if his prospects for sustained power were to be assured. Like Robespierre, he appreciated the power of the religious spirit in the hearts of humankind. As we have noted, many people were drifting back to their despoiled churches, despite the paucity of adequate religious guidance and psychologically increasingly looking to the constitutional structures for authority. The historic concordat signed between Bonaparte and the new pope, Pius VII in 1801, accordingly reflected the First Consul's need to harness the power, prestige and mystique of the ancient church in much

---

[100] Schama, S.: *Citizens*, Penguin, 1989.

[101] A quasi-reactionary era under which France was governed by a body of five directors; largely discredited as corrupt and inefficient, it was overthrown by Napoleon in the coup d'état of Brumaire, 1799, when he established the Consulate, with himself as First Consul.

[102] Signed between Napoleon and the Holy Roman Emperor Francis II (1792-1806).

[103] See footnote 391.

190 Vive l'Empereur

the same cynical fashion employed by Charlemagne one thousand years earlier. In short, Bonaparte needed this measure to wean the religious cause away from opposition to what was still a nominally revolutionary regime into at the very least a tolerance of it. 'People need religion', he is reputed to have said. 'I must rebuild the altars. This religion must be in the hands of the government'. Under its terms, the concordat was to re-establish Catholicism as the 'religion of the majority of Frenchmen', while freedom of worship for all denominations was to be guaranteed. Bishops were to be nominated by Napoleon, but formally appointed by the Pope, while the state was to undertake to pay the stipends of bishops and clergy—an arrangement tantalisingly analogous to the 1790 Civil Constitution of the Clergy. Despite Bonaparte's unilateral moves to tighten further state control over the church in France through the so-called 'Organic Articles' of 1802, the pragmatic approach to religious matters did much to pave the way for Bonaparte's assumption of the imperial dignity as Napoleon I on 1804 and to the symbolic gesture of his coronation on that December day in the same year: Napoleon in charge and the papacy in its (subordinate) role, where the new emperor wanted it. As a cosmetic gesture, Napoleon restored to Notre-Dame the Holy Relics of Christ's passion filched from Sainte Chapelle by zealous revolutionaries: no matter to him that they might well be forgeries.[404] He could now afford to restore to France, without fanfare, the Christian calendar by 1806. After all, what harm would it do?

The coronation had far greater implications than the mere domestic concerns of France. In contrast to David's obsequious opportunism, Beethoven (1770-1827) reacted in disgust by excising the original dedication to Napoleon from his newly composed 'Eroica' symphony in E^b. On the military and diplomatic front, following a third defeat at Napoleon's hands in 1805,[405] the Habsburg Francis II surrendered the position and title of Holy Roman emperor the following year, officially winding up the office that had jointly symbolised the historic political and spiritual axis initiated by Charlemagne and the Pope in AD 800.

---

[404] The Holy Relics, bought by King Louis IX (St Louis), at great expense had been housed in the fine chapel he had built for the purpose in the thirteenth century. The possession of a portion of the 'true cross of Christ', and in particular the 'authentic' crown of thorns supposedly reinforced the Capetian legitimacy to the throne of France. They would have been natural targets for republican revolutionaries. Those that Napoleon 'returned' to the church are doubtless fakes, but it was the gesture that counted. They are now housed in the treasury at Notre-Dame.

[405] The Battle of Austerlitz over the Austrians and Russians.

The Church 191

One thousand years of history flushed down the tubes; no room in Napoleon's mind for *two* emperors striding the European stage—at least two with ultramontane pretensions. In a letter to Pope Pius shortly after crowning himself as king of Italy in Milan, 1805, Napoleon made his position with the papacy quite clear: 'As far as the Pope is concerned, I am Charlemagne . . . I therefore expect the Pope to accommodate his conduct to my requirements. If he behaves well I shall make no outward changes. If not, I shall reduce him to the status of a Bishop of Rome'.[406] Napoleon's subsequent military career is well known—Trafalgar, Austerlitz, Iena, Borodino, Leipzig, Waterloo, not all of which feature on the Arc de Triomphe: yet some attention now needs to be paid to the consequences for the church.

Further spats with Pope Pius VII leading to an invasion of the Papal States and imprisonment of the humiliated pontiff in 1809 merely reinforced the papacy's proclivity for impotence. The papal territories were incorporated into Napoleon's Italian kingdom. In attempting to eclipse the achievements of Charlemagne, Napoleon was demonstrably shattering the religious foundations upon which the Europe of the 'Ancien régime' had been built.

While Napoleon's ambitions thus built on the growing cynicism with the Roman Church in the eighteenth century expressed by the 'enlightened' theorists, as indeed attempted in reality by the Emperor Joseph II (1780-90)[407] and embraced by the French revolutionaries, the seeds were unwittingly sown for the growth of nationalism, industrialisation, materialism and intensified spirit of enquiry, which characterised nineteenth-century Europe. Even Napoleon could not, however, completely divorce his ambitions from the legacy of Europe's Christian past. By divorcing Josephine in 1809, Napoleon was now free to marry the daughter of 'Emperor' Francis II, Marie-Louise in 1810. Having proclaimed their son as king of Rome in time-honoured imperial fashion, Napoleon was, subconsciously perhaps, through the Habsburg bloodline, attempting to synthesise the mystical past in order to legitimate his future direction, yet as an avowed product of the revolution.

However much Metternich, the Austrian Foreign Minister (1809-48), and the other signatories to the Treaty of Vienna in 1815 bringing the Napoleonic Era to a close, might have wished to return the continent to its 'legitimate' roots, the genie of a future built on scientific enquiry

---

[406] Quoted in Stiles, A.: *Napoleon, France and Europe*, Hodder and Stoughton.
[407] The Habsburg Holy Roman emperor and ruler of the hereditary lands in Austria had attempted enlightened reforms in those family possessions, but that were characterised by spectacular failure.

was irrevocably out of the bottle. The rise of powerful nation states in the nineteenth century, which Napoleon perhaps indirectly and unwittingly did much to promote, was bound to sideline still further the influence of a papacy, and national churches in Europe, into the position of spectators rather than players in the international quest for supremacy in a new world order. In France, the 1801 concordat outlived Bonaparte's empire and it survived sustained anticlerical attacks until its final abrogation under the Separation Law of 1905 when the divorce between church and state was declared absolute: no more state subsidies to religious institutions, church buildings to be held 'on trust' from the state by 'Associations for the Public Worship' and any remaining privileges held by the church rescinded, and complete freedom of worship to all replaced it. This was initiated by the socialist politicians Aristide Briand (1862-1932) and reinforced by the anticlerical Emile Combes (1835-1921), Jean Jaurès (1859-1914) and Georges Clemenceau (1841-1929). Under the chancellorship of Bismarck (1871-90), Protestant and Catholic Germany were finally united in 1871 as the 'Second Reich', his policy of 'kulturkampf' weakening the hold of the church on its people still further in the face of a state built not on spirituality but forged ominously by 'blood and iron'. In his own backyard, the Pope's position was bound to be compromised further in the wake of Italy's reunification—the 'Risorgimento'—the loss of the Papal States by 1861, reducing him by 1870 to the status of 'prisoner in the Vatican'. The Habsburg Dual Monarchy of Austria-Hungary, the heir, if anything, to the medieval imperial ideal, stumbled on until the debacle of World War I finally put paid to it, while the Ottomans in the Balkans—the 'sick man' and residual irritant to Christian Europe—were to provide the immediate backdrop to the 1914-18 war. Tsarist Russia—Holy Russia to its people and bastion of the Eastern Orthodox faith—the self-assumed heir of Byzantium, jealous guardian of Constantine's heritage, became increasingly embroiled in nationalistic struggles of states in the West and blundered imperviously yet inexorably towards a revolution of its own, but with world shattering repercussions in 1917. Meanwhile, the British Isles were preoccupied with their own brand of national advancement, focusing upon industrial enterprise and empire, while finding space for religious activity in the fields of education, trade unionism, missionary opportunities overseas, the Tractarian Movement, the expansion of nonconformity, the Salvation Army and Roman Catholic Emancipation. Thus, while in the nineteenth century, the organised, structured church lost ground, the growth of the Romantic view of religion, in its variety of guises both in Europe and the USA, was a recognition of a spiritual

The Church

193

awareness and yearning. In the Iberian Peninsula alone, did the Roman Church remain fossilised, in fact, at the expense of social, economic and political progress.

From the perspective of history, our defining moment at Notre Dame in 1804 may be regarded as a pivotal symbol of the culmination of the direction to which eighteenth-century thought and events were pointing—the enlightenment and the social, political and economic tensions in France, which spilled over into revolution, and the rise of a superstar from the phoenix of chaos. It was confirmation that the Roman Church, despite its long and accepted position, was no longer a major player in a Europe usurped by an upstart emperor with medieval instincts but whose influence, direct and indirect, was to push materialism, nationalism and reason to the forefront of humankind's struggle for liberation. After all, how many battalions does the Pope command? Louis XVI had lost his head defending a church and a tradition, which was clearly out of touch, in many people's minds, with the cause of Christ to whom it owed its existence. Napoleon had invited that same church back, but on his terms and to serve his own ends. The Eiffel Tower completed in 1889 remains as a towering edifice, perhaps to some people a monumental folly reflecting the nineteenth-century vision of a future built on the adulation of coal, iron and steel astride the revolutionary shrine on the Champs de Mars. Notre Dame, an enduring symbol in stone of Europe's religious heritage, now restored to its former splendour. David's depiction of Napoleon's coronation—our defining moment—provides, arguably, a link between the two. Which, if either, of these two Parisian icons is destined for immortality?

Chapter 18

Pope Pius IX

PRISONER IN THE VATICAN

The spa resort of Ems punctuating the river Lahn in the modern German province of North Rhine-Westphalia represented throughout much of the nineteenth century a genteel summer focal point for the fashionable elite. Here there existed an opportunity to chance one's arm at the Casino and to derive the health-giving sustenance offered by its waters: the Prussian version of Tunbridge Wells or Bath where Jane Austen (1775-1817) or a Beau Nash (1674-1762) would have felt very much at ease. This was an ancient town of around ten thousand inhabitants, at a discreet distance from the growing urban sprawl of Koblenz: a place where traditional industries such as lead and particularly salt mining were giving way to more leisured pursuits as patronised by the great and the good of the Prussian establishment.[408]

On the morning of 13 July 1870, King William I of Prussia (1861-88) emerged from his royal suite so as to fulfil his obligatory constitutional

---

[408] Prussia was one of the several German nation states prior to unification in 1871. It was around this powerful entity that the modern Germany evolved. Its king, of the Hohenzollern dynasty, was proclaimed Kaiser of Imperial Germany (1871-88) in that year.

The Church   195

on the Brunnen Promenade to absorb the balmy summer breezes, themselves doubtless edified by the distinctively august ambience generated by the gracious patronage of His Majesty and entourage. Likewise, the French ambassador to the Prussian Court, Count Benedetti (1817-90), taking advantage of the salubrious blessings accruing to Ems, and with a prescience derived from a familiarity with the accepted routine of the town's worthies, waylaid the king in the course of his stroll such as would render twitchy any twenty-first-century security minder susceptible to any predisposition to apoplexy.[109] Benedetti had a purpose in this peremptory affront to ritual—a matter of pressing diplomatic import. France, its own imperial pretensions having been rejuvenated by the tinsel town elegance of Napoleon III (1851-70), was becoming edgy at recent successful Prussian brushes with Denmark (1864) and Austria (1866), and *now* there was the worrying issue of the vacant crown of Spain having been offered to a kinsman of the Hohenzollern king of Prussia: the French feared circumscription by degrees. Benedetti accordingly demanded from the king an assurance that a well-publicised rejection in principle of Spain's offer by the Prussian authorities be guaranteed in both fact and perpetuity. In response to Benedetti's somewhat brusque interruption of His Majesty's progress that morning, it would seem that the king bit his tongue by confirming, politely, that as far as he was concerned, the matter of the Hohenzollern candidature was now closed: that he had nothing more to add, and if he may be excused, he would be grateful if his morning's arrangements could be allowed to continue unhindered. A somewhat miffed Benedetti felt that he had been given short shrift.

Later in the day, the king telegraphed his bellicose, ambitious and impatient chancellor, Bismarck, now back in Berlin, to apprise him of the encounter with Benedetti. This now celebrated Ems Telegram provided the occasion and circumstance upon which Bismarck seized, spoiling as he was for a showdown with the French emperor. The unscrupulous chancellor ruthlessly edited the contents of the king's objective account of the morning's events. Bismarck's amended version of the king's communication was then syndicated for worldwide consumption. The new text made it *appear* as though William had exceeded all diplomatic niceties in executing a calculated snub to France by declining 'to receive the French Ambassador again'.[110] As Bismarck anticipated, this

---

[109]   Although, according to Leslie, R. F., in *The Age of Transformation*, Blandford Press, 1964, a meeting between the two men was expected at some stage.

[110]   Translation of the text as quoted in Henrison, A.: *Bismarck and the Unification of Germany*, Edward Arnold, 1977.

provocation unleashed a wave of hysteria in the French capital. Napoleon III, his Foreign Minister the Duc of Gramont (1819-80) and the legislative assembly all responded appropriately by falling for it: 'Prussia insults us', 'Let us cross the Rhine' and 'The soldiers are ready' were sentiments bandied around in parliament; 'To Berlin!' bleated every shepherd and sheep from Bayonne to Dunkerque, from Strasbourg to Brest. It was of little consequence to them that, in fact, the soldiers were not ready: The moral outrage far outweighed such practical considerations, as their righteous indignation propelled the country into a Declaration of War on 19 July; Paris had played right into Bismarck's hands. Within two months, on 2 September, a humiliated French emperor and army capitulated to superior Prussian forces at Sedan; at Versailles, a united Germany under Prussian leadership was triumphantly proclaimed, as a new French Republic tortuously struggled to rise from the ashes, bent ominously upon revenge.

For the Church of Rome, this defining moment was to portend the decisive conclusion to its temporal interests in Italy and was to deal a mortal blow to any lingering pretence its bishop might have entertained to consideration as a secular player on the European stage. The French decision to go to war forced its mercurial emperor to put his national interests before his religious duty. A considerable French military garrison had been stationed in Rome for some twenty years previously to protect papal integrity in the face of rising radical and nationalistic sentiment across Europe in general and throughout Italy in particular. Napoleon now required all available military resources to engage in his struggle with Prussia. If that meant leaving Rome defenceless, then sorry, but needs must: not the first time he had reneged upon a solemn agreement. A hapless pontiff was now exposed to the confident steamroller of the Italian 'Risorgimento'.[411] The power vacuum left by the departing French presence from Rome was triumphantly filled by the Piedmontese army of King Victor Emmanuel.[412] The all but complete cause of a unified Italy was, as a result, a fait accompli.

Pope Pius IX (1846-78) was one of the most remarkable men to have occupied the see of St Peter in terms of both the longevity of his tenure and for his handling of the consequences of our defining moment. He

---

[411] The Risorgimento: The name given to the movement for Italian national unity in the nineteenth century.

[412] Piedmont/Sardinia: A state based in north-western Italy under the monarchical dynasty of the House of Savoy and around which the unified kingdom evolved. Victor Emmanuel, king of Piedmont (1849-61), of Italy, 1861-78.

The Church 197

had been caught up in the aftermath of the revolutionary and Napoleonic wars, 1792-1815, and the valiant yet ultimately unsuccessful attempts by Metternich[413] to turn back the European clock to the pre-revolutionary era. As the continent was to face up to the tensions of conservatism and liberalism, it was in Italy that the movement for unity whose cause, the first Napoleon had unwittingly fostered, was gaining ground. Here the idealism of Mazzini,[414] Garibaldi[415] and Cavour[416] would challenge the old presuppositions of the past; the peninsula was not to escape the winds of change gathering strength north of the Alps. Pius IX, elected in 1846, had been given the nod partly in recognition of his liberal sympathies and apparent espousal of the principle of a unified Italian state. Indeed, his first two years in office witnessed such sentiments being realised across the extensive Papal States straddling Central Italy. The year 1848, however, was a turning point. As revolutionary fervour engulfed much of continental Europe, Italian aspirations in favour of expelling Austrian influence in the peninsula boiled over. The Pope's refusal to commit papal resources to supporting the Piedmontese-led war effort against the Habsburg Empire cost Pius dearly in political terms. He could, to be fair, scarcely be seen to be taking up arms against one of the most Catholic monarchies in Europe. In response to his negative approach, revolutionary Italian partisans besieged and occupied Rome from which Pius beat a hasty retreat to the relative safety of Gaeta in the south. Here, his appeal to the Catholic states met a sympathetic response from Napoleon in France, ever anxious, as his uncle had been, to harness Catholic support at home; hence, Pius was duly reinstated in Rome in 1850, his position guaranteed internally and externally by the French garrison. For Pius, his dalliance with liberalism and constitutionalism was now uncompromisingly terminated. With

---

[413] Prince Metternich (1773-1859): Austrian foreign minister and was the key figure on the continent, following the defeat of Napoleon I and the ensuing peace conference at Vienna. He is known for his iron will and determination to reinstate the conservative pre-revolutionary systems throughout Europe.

[414] Giuseppe Mazzini (1805-72): The inspired Italian patriot and author whose 'Young Italy' organisation inspired the movement towards unity.

[415] Giuseppe Garibaldi (1807-82): A heroic figure of Italian patriotism. His down-to-earth skills and pragmatism did much to secure the success of the cause of unity.

[416] Camillo Cavour (1810-61): Prime minister of Piedmont/Sardinia, whose political strategy paved the way for the expulsion of the Austrians from Italy and whose work complemented that of Mazzini and Garibaldi.

Napoleon's help, the Austrians were expelled from Lombardy in 1859 at the expense of the acquisition of Savoy and Nice by France; in 1860, other states in Northern Italy threw in their lot with Piedmont and most of the Papal States in Central Italy—Romagna, Umbria and the Marches—were absorbed with mere token resistance in the same year. From the South, meanwhile, the romantic, yet rugged idealist, Garibaldi, and his rough-and-ready band of Red Shirts were in the process of liberating Naples and Sicily from foreign rule and turning them over to King Victor Emmanuel of Piedmont/Sardinia in a heavily symbolic gesture at Naples. Cavour, prime minister and diplomat, warned Garibaldi to keep his hands off Rome itself—for the moment—and said there was no need to turn Napoleon against the fledgling kingdom of Italy at this critical juncture. Thus Pius was left intact with just the rump of his once extensive possessions, the city of Rome and its rural hinterland, by the grace of God, the exigencies of political expediency and courtesy of the French presence, while it lasted. The expulsion of the Austrians from Venetia and its accession to the Italian state in 1866 further strengthened the hand of the nationalist cause and the withdrawal of the French Garrison from Rome presented King Victor Emmanuel with the opportunity to take over and proclaim the city as the predestined capital of the unified state in 1870. As Pius saw it, this was a further instance of Napoleon's perfidy,[417] and by way of retribution, the Pope resorted to invoking the only psychological armoury left to him by excommunicating Victor Emmanuel while enjoining Italian Catholics to be less than co-operative with the new state. In a measure of magnanimity tempered perhaps with concern for his own soul, the king offered the Pope a 'Law of Guarantees'—a pension, the inviolability of his person and security in his possession of St Peter's Basilica and the Vatican properties in Rome. The offer was unceremoniously and ungraciously rejected by the Pope who preferred, calculatingly, to present himself to the world as an unwilling martyr to the eternal cause, sidelined in a perpetual sulk—a self-proclaimed prisoner in the Vatican. Thus was abandoned the last vestige of papal pretension in the temporal destiny of Italy, which had endured, with short intermissions, since the fourth century. The papacy as a political force on the peninsula was now, recognisably, a spent force in direct consequence of our defining moment in faraway Ems. Yet paradoxically perhaps, on the back of these

---

[417] In 1867, French troops who had guaranteed Napoleon's hapless client, the Emperor Maximilian of Mexico (1864-67), abandoned Mexico City, leaving him exposed to the radical forces of Juárez and to his subsequent execution by firing squad.

The Church 199

secular misfortunes, a renewed impetus for the church was occasioned and to this we must now turn.

It is perfectly plain that Pius was out of his depth in the treacherous shoals of contemporary European diplomacy. Nonetheless he was increasingly focused upon spiritual opportunities that were now open to him. It was his stamp and legacy that was to set the tone of the Catholic Church and its relationship with other denominations for the next one hundred years. The experience of his 1848 exile from Rome had left an indelible imprint upon his own thinking and upon the direction he would take his church. In his own mind, he recognised the dangers posed by scientific 'enlightenment' and the concomitant knock-on menace these ideas represented to a world seething with radical political idealism, nationalist fervour and industrial advance. Pius regarded these progressive movements and indeed religious laxity as a threat not only to traditional Catholic authority but also to its doctrine as well: a cancer eating away at the very church attacking it both internally and externally, a church over which he had been called to preside.

In Catholic eyes, the church, by virtue of our Lord's commission to Peter,[418] 'becomes the Body of Christ'.[419] As such it follows that it is the very expression of Christ's being and 'ipso facto', infallible. Of course, *how* that infallibility was to be executed had exercised the minds of academics for centuries. Pius, again with bitter memories of his own ill-starred flirtation with constitutionalism, was to seek to incorporate that authoritarian sense of infallibility into his own person, as far as spiritual matters were concerned. This was his response to liberalism and, by extension, to anarchy and fragmentation. The groundwork for some kind of official statement on this proceeded throughout the 1850s and 1860s as the momentum for 'Risorgimento' in Italy gathered pace. He aimed to rein in the forces within the church, which seemed to him to be reinforcing local particularism,[420] and which threatened a breakdown in discipline. In 1854, Pius proclaimed the dogma of the 'immaculate conception of the Blessed Virgin Mary' in his bull *Ineffabilis Deus.* Supplication through the Mother of Christ had always been a significant plank of Catholic devotion, but medieval scholars had disagreed over its theological foundation. Duns Scotus and the Franciscans generally

---

[418] Matthew 16:18-19. See chapter 1.

[419] Ephesians 3:6; 1 Corinthians 12:27.

[420] For centuries, there had been a struggle between 'national churches', known in France as the Gallican Liberties, and the centralisation of Rome. Pius now wanted to settle this in favour of the latter once and for all. See chapter17.

promoted Mary as the one 'Highly Favoured'[421] and as the instrument through whom fallen womanhood[422] was reinstated. This school of thought advanced Mary's claim to pole position in the cult of sainthood, concluding that through the merits of her son and her alleged purity symbolised by her 'perpetual virginity', she had been cleansed from original sin when conceived. However, other scholars, notably Aquinas and the Dominicans, had taken the contrary view in respect of her conception on the grounds that *any* natural conception was *necessarily* tainted with original sin, as Augustine of Hippo had insisted in the days of the early church. Pius accordingly saw the opportunity to make his mark by pronouncing decisively on the issue and to determine the reality of his authority especially as the popularisation of the Marian Cult was gaining considerable currency within the Roman Church. The promulgation of the 'Immaculate Conception' must, in its own terms, be judged a success, for certainly the cult of Mary blossomed significantly throughout the nineteenth century. Only four years later, in 1858, the fourteen-year-old Bernadette Soubirous claimed to have had mystical visitations from 'the Beautiful Lady' at Lourdes in Southern France at which the said 'Lady' identified herself as the 'Immaculate Conception':[423] the genesis of subsequent mass Catholic pilgrimage to the spot, where miraculous cures have been reported. The 'shrine of Our Lady' at Walsingham in Norfolk—a medieval resort of pilgrimage—has seen a similar revival of popularity in the late nineteenth and twentieth centuries as have other Marian shrines across the world. In 1950, Pope Pius XII built on the dogma of the 'Immaculate Conception' by proclaiming the doctrine of the 'assumption of the virgin', whereby Mary was allegedly 'assumed into heavenly glory', body and soul at the conclusion of her earthly existence.[424]

Encouraged by the response to *Ineffabilis Deus*, Pius IX went further in 1864. In promulgating his 'Syllabus Errorum' (Syllabus of Errors) and its encyclical *Quanta Curia*, he was throwing down the gauntlet to all manifestations of European liberalism—political, philosophical and theological. This was an uncompromising invocation of traditional conservative Catholic dogma in response to the supposed attacks from socialism, Marxism, freemasonry, absolute rationalism, liberal

---

[421] Luke 1:28.

[422] Genesis 3:15.

[423] Under rigorous examination, Bernadette stuck tenaciously to her story and mainstream Catholicism has accepted that this visitation was, in fact, that of the Virgin Mary.

[424] The proclamation of *Munificentissimus Deus*.

The Church   201

clerical attitudes and unabashed anticlericalism. Despite this, he had temporised by signing concordats with individual Catholic states and, in 1850, had restored a Roman Catholic hierarchy in England. Pius was in fact preparing for his greatest gamble yet: the summoning of a Vatican council, intended to stamp his authority over the Universal Church incontrovertibly, once and for all.

Encouraged by the success of missionary activity in Africa and elsewhere in the developing world, Pius formally opened the Vatican council in Rome on 8 December 1869, whose eight hundred or so delegates, nevertheless, were overwhelmingly drawn from the prelates of Italy. It was obvious from the outset that the related issues of papal infallibility and the linked theory of ultramontanism[425] were to dominate the proceedings. In a broadside aimed at scientific liberalism, the council accepted in *Dei Filius* that any presumptions that science might proclaim were trumped by the church's claim that the 'revelator of mysteries' (God) is, by His very nature, the very author and creator of reason.

With increasing tension looming between the French and the Prussians, and its possible implications for Rome, the council worked feverishly to secure agreement on a definition and recognition of papal infallibility. Less than a week after our defining moment at Ems, on 18 July 1870, just one day before the outbreak of the Franco-Prussian War, and with the French garrison in Rome on the point of departure, the council accepted with only two dissenting voices the constitution *Pastor Aeternus*: when the Pope decrees 'ex cathedra' on matters of faith and morals, his word is binding and final. In effect this laid to rest any lingering doubt in the Catholic context, as to whether the bishop of Rome exercised full and supreme jurisdiction over its worldwide adherence in such matters of spirituality and ethics; here, the Pope 'cannot err', given the divine aid promised to Peter by Christ in the first place[426] and the guidance of the Holy Spirit at the first Christian council in Jerusalem.[427] Ultramontanism had triumphed in the face of a significant and voluble minority of bishops opposed to the definition and who left the council rather than placing themselves in the invidious position of voting against the Pope. Inevitably, there were defections from the church, notably in Germany, where the 'Old Catholics' presented themselves as a minor branch in communion with Anglicanism and the Catholic theologian J. Dollinger (1799-1890) was excommunicated in consequence.

---

[425] Ultramontanism: The idea that decisions taken by the Curia in Rome take precedence over policies adopted by purely national or local hierarchies.

[426] Matthew 16:19.

[427] Acts 15:28.

202   Prisoner in the Vatican

This turned out to be the apex of the Vatican council's work. It never completed its full agenda: the Franco-Prussian War saw to that. With the city of Rome now in the hands of the Italian military, Pius prorogued the assembly and it never reconvened. Thus, the events of July 1870 stand out as a pivotal paradox in papal fortunes. Pius, now an embittered reclusive self-imposed prisoner in the Vatican, shorn of what remained of his political and temporal authority in Italy, was at odds with the kingdom that had grown up around him. Yet—within the context of his church approaching ¾ billion adherents worldwide, he was a man of supreme moral significance whose spiritual influence could not now be ignored by even the most hardened of statesmen. In some ways, the proclamation of Rome as the capital of a secular kingdom of Italy could be seen as a final, welcome reversal of a Constantine's Edict of Milan of 313, which had identified the symbiotic fortunes of church and state. This was not a totally new experience for Catholics—they had suffered persecution and discrimination at Protestant hands in the British Isles and in the robust anticlericalism of Revolutionary France. Now, it was at the heart of the faith itself. The consequence was to require, among Catholic clergy and lay people, a resolve to stand up and be counted in the face of an establishment, which was prepared to mount a challenge to privileges once enjoyed by the church. This was particularly true in Italy, of course, and manifest in Bismark's 'Kulturkampf'[428] policy in Germany as well as the French Third Republic of the socialist leaders Briand and Clemenceau,[429] whose 'Law of Separation' (1905) facilitated by the anticlerical Emile Combes, president of the council, finally eradicated the remnants of church/state collusion that Napoleon I and Pius VII had cobbled together back in 1801.[430]

Pius IX died in 1878. His successors were left to cope with his inheritance as best as they could. Leo XIII (1878-1903) attempted to engage with the process of social reform, urging, unsuccessfully as it turned out, the conservative rural French clergy to accept the French Republic, who had had to come to terms with the execution of the archbishop of Paris at the hands of Paris Communards in 1871. Leo tended to be more willing than his predecessor to accommodate

---

[428] Kulturkampf: the programme designed by Bismark to promote, decisively, the state's interest over any pretensions of the Catholic Church.

[429] Georges Clemenceau and Aristide Briand: towering French anticlerical politicians at the turn of the century, whose role in the World War I and its aftermath was significant.

[430] See chapter 17.

The Church 203

medieval Thomist dogma with nineteenth-century political, social and material progress. He at least recognised the grievances that had led to working-class movements taking root in the first place and sought to work cautiously towards a definition of 'social Catholicism', such as was to bear fruit towards the end of the twentieth century.

The opening years of the twentieth century were clouded by the build-up and outbreak of World War I. Here the Roman Church and its pontiffs—successively Pius X (1903-14) and Benedict XV (1914-22)—were caught in a virtually impossible position in which in the secular world Catholic was to be pitted against Catholic. Benedict, for example, tended to pronounce in favour of universal Catholicism whenever he could. He viewed (Catholic) Austria's policy towards (Orthodox) Serbia as 'understandable', while the (Protestant dominated) German violation of (Catholic) Belgium in 1914 was seen as legally indefensible. The isolation of the Catholic Church from other Christian denominations that Pius IX's pontificate engendered was being distinctly felt. Despite Benedict's well-intentioned attempt at mediation during the 1914-18 conflict, his impoverished political status and his neutral stance cost the papal office dearly in his relations with the belligerent powers. Accorded no role in the Paris Peace Conference (1919), as the statesmen representing the victorious powers drew up a new map of Europe, his work behind the scenes on behalf of prisoners of war scarcely rewarded, as the newly created League of Nations assumed greater responsibility for tidying up the social problems that are the legacy of war.

Pope Pius XI, pontiff from 1922 to 1939, was faced with the aftermath of World War I and the events leading to World War II. This was a Europe of a bitter, humiliated Germany, its Weimar Republic[131] foisted upon a sceptical public following the collapse of Bismarck's imperial system and a paranoid French Republic with unfinished business to attend to. The successor states carved out of the old Austro-Hungarian Empire in Central Europe were either weak or unstable:[132] the Soviet Union, a menacing prospect in the East. Italy itself, beset by endemic economic problems, post-1918, and a marginalisation of its interests at the Peace Settlements in 1919, succumbed to Mussolini and his Fascist thugs, 1922-43. In the latter, though, was a man with whom the Pope recognised he might . . . just might . . . be able to do business.

---

[131] On the abdication of Kaiser Wilhelm II in 1918, a newly democratic Germany was created, known as the Weimar Republic. It was never popular with Germans at large, associated as it was with the humiliation of the Versailles Peace settlement, 1919.

[132] Czechoslovakia, Poland, Yugoslavia, Austria, Hungary.

Accordingly, a solution was found to the Roman question, festering since 1870, following negotiations between the papal Curia and the Italian state. The agreement signed—the Lateran Treaties of 1929—allowed the papacy to enjoy full sovereign powers over St Peter's Basilica and its administrative and cultural appurtenances to be known collectively as the Vatican City State, an area of approximately one hundred acres, with extra territorial privileges over the Lateran Churches in Rome and the papal summer residence at Castel Gondolfo: a flag and a recognised international status. Catholicism was to be accorded privileged status in terms of religious observance, education and rites of passage. In return for this, the Pope was to recognise the legality and integrity of the Fascist Italian State; after fifty-nine years, the prisoner in the Vatican walked free, but his legacies remained. The Pope was seen to temporise with a regime of questionable morality and which on the surface appeared also to cosy up to Hitler and the German Nazi Regime (1933-45) as a consequence of the Wall Street Crash and the inability of the League of Nations to halt aggression and rearmament throughout the 1930s. The morality of the concordat between the Catholic Church and Nazi Germany in 1933-34 has been much debated. Perhaps, though, in his defence, as a result of our defining moment, the pontiff was caught between a rock and a hard place. He felt a genuine need to protect the numerous members of his Catholic flock within their respective countries as well as seeing the fascist dictatorships as bulwarks against the even greater threat posed by Stalin's brand of atheistic communism in the Soviet Union. As war loomed, however, even Pius XI perceived the inherent dangers of secular totalitarianism from whatever source, left or right. His moral criticism of its effect as well as his pronouncements on human rights tended to draw him closer to the Western democracies.

It was during the pontificate of Pius XII (1939-58) that the full effects of our defining moment of 1870 were fully realised. By initially defining what the church now stood for, Pius IX and his more liberal successors had tentatively adapted to a changed set of circumstances. As World War II (1939-45) engulfed the planet, so the Pope could now regard himself as a spiritual leader of considerable substance, totally detached from the material conflict in a position to work quietly to help shape minds capable of working towards a just and lasting peace. Of course he has been much criticised for not taking a more ostentatious and strident stand against the self-evident inhumanity of Nazi ideology and practice when individual Christians, such as the high-profile cases of Catholic Priest Maximilian Kolbe and the Protestant Pastor Dietrich Bonhoeffer paid the supreme penalty for their defiance of Hitler. Again, though, many would argue that Pius XII did his best under trying conditions. He denounced aggression and, in the end, the extreme nationalism to which it gave rise. While falling short of endorsing outright socialism, he did endorse the rights of working people, individual worth and the concept of liberty. He sought to promote a more equitable secular society by playing his full part as a member of the post-war United Nations through his support for its agencies on famine relief and sponsorship of Catholic Charities designed to this end: all this, against a background challenged by the atomic bomb and the cold war.

Thus as a consequence of our defining moment, the Vatican and its church had emerged through some severely testing times. In many ways, it had navigated them with skill. Bereft, as we have seen, of any residual political pretensions, the church could now exercise more authoritatively the spiritual and traditional values and so command greater respect, if not agreement, in terms of its moral purpose. Governments and individuals, Catholic and non-Catholic will listen, if not necessarily heed. The personal calibre of the pontiffs from Pius IX onwards has been high—their sincerity, perceived piety and a desire to reflect Christ's genuine concern for the individual of whatever station has been palpable, if not always popular.[133] Certainly, the underlying experience and influence of Pope John Paul II (1978-2005) played a not insignificant role in the downfall of communism and the revival of active Christian participation in the societies of Eastern Europe during the 1980s. Prior to 1870, the papacy was still trying to discern its path and re-establish a role since the failed bid by Napoleon I to become a second Charlemagne. After Vatican I, the papacy has evolved as a spiritual resource, heavily influential, yet itself battling with overzealous progressivism and a determined conservative backlash. Vatican I reinforced the division between Protestant, Orthodox and Catholic and, as such, was in the mould of the Tridentine tradition. It was to take a Second Vatican Council (1962-65) to change all that. The outpouring of grief, from all religions and none, at the passing of Pope John Paul II in 2005 is testimony to the prestige to which the office has been elevated, which but for our defining moment on the Promenade at Ems, it might cease to command.

---

[133] Conservative attitudes to such issues as birth control and women in the priesthood have drawn considerable criticism.

Chapter 19

Sistine Chapel, Rome

WINDOWS OPENED

As Angelo Giuseppe Roncalli, archbishop of Venice, mingled with his fellow 'Red Hats' in the Vatican's Sistine Chapel, some sixty odd of them, he would have been conscious, during mid-October 1958, that this could well be his final visit to fulfil his cardinal's duty of casting a vote in the process of electing a new pope: the upper age limit was eighty. He had less than four years to go. His prescience was destined to be well founded, but for reasons that neither he nor, for that matter, others could have foreseen: momentous. Few, if any, would have put money on *this* jovial prelate emerging from the conclave by the end of the month as the Holy Pontiff, vicar of Christ, pope, head of the Roman Catholic Church, in succession to St Peter and to the controversial Pius XII. For Roncalli, the most kindly, simple and pastoral of cardinals, his very presence in the fabled repository of some of the finest frescoes of the high renaissance must have evoked a measure of incongruity in his soul. In the eyes of this son of tenant farmers from the Milanese village of Bergamo, the Sistine ambience was resonant of another world: of a sixteenth-century church as much concerned with its secular veneer as of the pious symbolism evoked by the masterpieces adorning walls

The Church 207

and ceiling. The lives of Moses and Jesus running in parallel along the eastern and western walls, respectively, would have reminded him of the significance of the occasion for which he had been summoned. Not least Perugino's (1446-1524) panel of 'Christ giving the Keys to Peter'[434] complemented by Botticelli's 'Punishment of the Rebels'[435] directly opposite elicited a sense of the awesome power the church had intended to wield: the classical humanism designed to emphasise its temporal and spiritual aspirations. Casting his eyes to the ceiling, Roncalli would have been aware of the beginnings of it all: Michelangelo's depictions of the Genesis account. Here is a representation of God, frenetic as He gives vent to His creative genius: a larger than life figure completing the building block of humanity as He summons Eve from the corpus of the man.[436] This is the central panel flanked by the contrasting tableaux: on the one side, Adam, new, naked and naive in formation perfectly contoured receiving the divine spark of wholeness from his maker's outstretched finger;[437] on the other, a visibly shaken couple fallen from grace in abhorrence of their wilful disobedience and in anticipation of the due punishment for which their original sin called.[438] Yet for all the power exhibited by these scenes directly above him, the old man Roncalli's line of vision would have been lowered, drawn more comfortably and inexorably towards the high altar, its central candle inviting him to contemplate Michelangelo's monumental frescoed altarpiece on the Western wall—the 'final judgement': Christ, the central figure dispensing justice in the heavens, dynamically assured, as the dead are torn from their graves and the damned, after the style of Dante (1265-1321), cast into the clutches of the demons in hell,[439] daring any Catholics seduced by the sixteenth-century reformation to challenge the church at their peril. Perhaps, though, Roncalli was more focused on the suffering of crucified Christ at the base of the fresco, at eye level, as being more in tune with his grass roots sympathies.[440]

With the door to the chapel firmly locked at the appointed hour, the windows blacked out, the Swiss Guards posted to ensure that the gathered prelates were incommunicado with the outside world, the secret

---

[434] Matthew 16:19.
[435] Exodus 32:19-33.
[436] Genesis 2:21-23.
[437] Genesis 2:7.
[438] Genesis 3:20-24.
[439] Revelation 20:11-15; 33.
[440] Matthew 27:27-50; Mark 15:37; Luke 23:44,48; John 19:30.

protracted process to elect a new pope was now solely in the hands of the cardinals. Modernisers were pitted in almost equal numbers against the conservatives; deadlock, until on Tuesday, 28 October, the patience of the pilgrims gathered in anticipation, packed into Bernini's colonnaded Square of St Peter, was rewarded as they witnessed the symbolism emanating from the Sistine chimney. The white smoke from the ritually burning ballot papers supervised far below by the Swiss Guards in the squat rounded stove equipped for the purpose snaked upwards into the view of an expectant world. The delight of the multitude outside was tempered when the identity of the newly signified incumbent became apparent as Roncalli assumed centre stage on the balcony of St Peter's Basilica for the first time. To most thinking people, here was the best compromise available for the time being: a caretaker pope, with a limited expected lifespan, to hold the reins, while preparations were being made for the real thing next time. To the humble soul of Roncalli, who assumed the title role as John XXIII, it was as if his own roots were being torn from beneath him. Too trusting and traditional to shirk the prompting of the Holy Spirit, the implicit sentiments expressed in his *Journey of a Soul*[141] reflect the new pope's overwhelming sense of duty and a new direction. 'Will I ever see my beloved Venice again?' would be his diffident reaction to the awesome realisation of responsibility. This man of humble origins was destined to serve barely five years in office, yet this was to prove no mere stopgap. His election was no less than a defining moment.

The world of 1958 was one in which the old certainties were passing away and a political/ideological struggle between East and West was threatening its very existence. Two World Wars had come and gone as had the rapid rise and fall of the European Empires; the terrors of a potential nuclear Armageddon had been triggered by the visitation of atomic devastation upon Hiroshima and Nagasaki in 1945; mutual assured destruction was the pessimistic formula that undergirded Superpower foreign policy at the height of the cold war. Just prior to Roncalli's election, the launch of the Soviet Union's Sputnik in 1957 signalled humankind's breakthrough into space. The Treaty of Rome in 1958 had spawned the embryonic European Union.

For the church, the very speed at which this world was evolving was such as to put the spotlight upon the inadequacies of the conservative outcome of Pius IX's Vatican Council (1869-70)[142] and Catholicism's capacity to respond to such radical shifts. Under the pontificate of his

---

[141] Roncalli, A.: *Journey of a Soul*, London, 1980.
[142] See chapter 18.

The Church

209

immediate predecessors the church had been tainted with, at best, inertia in its corporate stance towards Nazism, Fascism and anti-Semitism, while, at the same time, pursuing a vicious vitriolic campaign against communism and anything that smacked of its tendencies. Even the Worker Priest Movement within the church itself had not been above suspicion. At best, under Pius XII, the church was seen by many of the faithful as a fortress and refuge for those seeking comfort and spiritual succour in a bewildering sea of change. By the late 1950s, however, the youth of the Western world were about to embrace a more secular response to their own perceived needs. To them, the liberal message sent out by Bill Haley, Tommy Steele, Elvis Presley, the Rolling Stones, the Beatles, et al., was a conviction that the future belonged to them and with it a cynical dismissal of all things traditional—political, social and ecclesiastical.

In the immediate aftermath of World War II, non-Catholics had already faced up to the need to speak up collectively on social and spiritual issues with the foundation of the ecumenical World Council of Churches at Amsterdam in 1948. Recognising the need to pronounce with some kind of authoritative clarity in the shadow of one of the world's most soul destroying conflicts, it defined itself as a 'fellowship of churches that accept our Lord Jesus Christ as God and saviour'. Away from institutional sound bites, the selfless sacrifice of such high-profile churchmen as Maximilian Kolbe[443] and Dietrich Bonhoeffer,[444] during the conflict of 1939-45, spurred many in the worldwide church to rediscover its prophetic mission in the context of international instability. Bonhoeffer himself had reiterated, during his distinguished academic career, Reinhold Niebuhr's[445] insistence on Christianity's

---

[443] Maximilian Kolbe (1894-1941), a Franciscan friar imprisoned under the Nazis at Auschwitz, volunteered in 1941 to substitute himself for a married family man, a fellow inmate, who had been selected to be starved to death. Kolbe was subsequently canonised in 1982.

[444] Dietrich Bonhoeffer (1906-45), a leading Protestant in Germany during the Nazi period. During the war, he organized covert operations aimed at eliminating Hitler. He was discovered, arrested and hanged a few weeks prior to the end of the war, leaving behind his inspirational *Letters and Papers from Prison*.

[445] Reinhold Niebuhr (1892-1971), an American Lutheran pastor was also one of the foremost political philosophers of his generation in the mid-twentieth century. He believed that the sensitive application of science and education to religion would progressively eliminate society's evils. This would be fostered by means of an awareness of group dynamics, which were

210 Windows Opened

social imperatives, going so far as to accuse certain aspects of organised religion with individualistic smugness and its almost indifferent regard for corporate humanity.

This seemed to be at variance with the mystical emphasis embraced by some Christian exponents, including that of the influential Karl Barth's[446] earlier vision of God as the 'wholly other'.

Within two years of his election, John XXIII astounded many by announcing his intention to call a new assembly of the church—a Second Vatican Council. Herein lay the actions of a man not content to sit his pontificate out while the world moved on. Rather, in a mood of 'aggiornamento', he recognised the need for dialogue and sensitivity towards the world and the 'separated brethren' of other Christian denominations. This envisaged gathering would involve the assembly of some twenty-eight hundred bishops from around the globe, many of whom shared the Pope's concerns and many of whom did not. It was, for the Pope, a leap in faith, but it was a decision taken in the recognition that the confrontational stance adopted by the incomplete Vatican I was incommensurate with the needs of the present age. It was his hope that the 'modernisers' among the prelates would ultimately prevail: those who shared his vision of adopting an evolutionary concept of the church as a living organism rather than one that was to be left to fester under the weight of a conservative, self-serving, bureaucratic treadmill as an increasingly marginalised metaphysical irrelevance.

The opening session, in October 1962, was awesome. The tiered ranks of bishops regaled simply in white, twelve rows deep and flanking the entire length of St Peter's Basilica were focused upon the lonely figure of the Pope dwarfed in the shadow of Bernini, whose bronze canopy towered above the papal presence. The Pope's message was clear and lucid. He sought to equip the church to meet the needs of a rapidly changing world: he sought to preside over a church characterised by a smiling benevolence, palpably reflected in his own countenance. Having addressed the plenary session, Pope John was content to allow the Holy

---

far more potent than the employment of 'changed individuals' to secure social amelioration.

[446] Karl Barth (1886-1968), like Bonhoeffer, had been a leading figure in Germany's Protestant Confessing Church in the Nazi era, but moved to Switzerland, where as professor of theology at Basel, he proclaimed a traditional Gospel message. *Scripture*, he maintained, is the human word *becoming* God's word when God Himself speaks *through* it, bearing witness to Christ as God's son. It is the individual response to this, which makes the difference.

The Church   211

Spirit to direct its course, by means of its deliberations in the various committees. Indeed, the Pope was not destined to see the council through to its conclusion. Pope John, 'the good', died in 1963, lamented by many a Catholic and non-Catholic alike. Yet the essential values characteristic of John were to be espoused by his successor, Cardinal Montini (Paul VI, 1963-78). His support for the council sustained this 'most revolutionary Christian event since the Reformation'[447] ensured its significant impact. In the course of four sessions between 1962 and 1965, several major issues were discussed, documents approved and ultimately promulgated. Its main findings can be outlined as follows.

An increase in active lay participation in the life of the church was reflected in its dogmatic constitution[448] *Lumen Gentium* in which both laity and clergy were to recognise the aspiration to spiritual holiness. This was to find practical expression in the pastoral constitution *Gaudium et Spes*, whereby all Catholics were urged to meet Christ by co-operating with other agencies and other Christian denominations in establishing a more humane global community. Together, these two constitutions conceded the validity of spiritual experiences outside the context of the Catholic Church. Here the influence of Catholic theologian Hans Küng,[449] whose line on justification by faith leaned towards the Protestant viewpoint and the Jesuit Karl Rahner's[450] controversial proclamation of 'Anonymous Christianity' was marked. The council went on to negate, albeit somewhat ambiguously, the bull *Unam Sanctam* promulgated by Boniface VIII in 1302,[451] which had decreed that there could be no salvation in 'rival churches'.

---

[447] Duffy, E: *Saints and Sinners: A History of the Popes*, Yale University Press in association with S4C, 1997.

[448] The major pronouncements of the council are officially entitled constitutions. They are broadly classified as dogmatic—those dealing with theological and doctrinal statements, and pastoral—whose emphasis is upon the practical outcomes.

[449] Hans Küng (born 1928), although appointed by John XXIII as an official theological adviser to Vatican II and influential in liberal Catholic circles, increasingly fell foul of the Vatican as his views *appeared* to veer towards agnosticism.

[450] Karl Rahner (1904-84) held the view that in the world there could be many 'anonymous Christians': those whose salvation is assured in so far as they have experienced the grace of Christ without necessarily acknowledging or even realising it. Such a position was ultimately bound to bring him into conflict with the Vatican's stance on the matter.

[451] See chapter 10.

Now, while Vatican II saw the Church of Christ as 'subsisting' within Roman Catholicism, it did not equate to it: a tacit acceptance that a resort to salvation could be satisfied elsewhere, it further advocated scholarly co-operation with other denominations to enquire further into the divine purposes. This was little short of a resolve to engage in dialogue with a world outside the Vatican in contrast to its hitherto bull-nosed suspicion and objection to it. Thus the pastoral constitution *Dignitatis Humanae* turned its back on the religious persecutions, enforced baptism and coerced conversion inflicted by the historic church; now, it was prepared to accept the mistakes of the past. In terms of future policy-making, the role of bishops was to be reinforced and reinvigorated in tune with the practice of the early church. Ultimate papal primacy was retained as a concession to Vatican I, but 'episcopal collegiality' was pronounced in so far as decisions taken were to be seen as a collective deliberation of all the prelates. It was in this mood that the Jewish people as a whole were to be absolved from responsibility for the death of Christ.[452]

Perhaps the most visible influence of Vatican II was spelled out in the dogmatic constitution *Sacrosanctum Consilium*, whereby the sacraments were to involve far greater participation of the laity: priestly initiative—still—in the celebration of the mass, for example, but with significant lay assistance in its administration and communion in 'both kinds'—bread and *wine* to be available to all. The liturgy was now to be conducted by the priest celebrating mass in the vernacular facing the congregation, rather than turning his back on it, eschewing the universal impersonal Latin requirements that went back centuries. Folk traditions were to be encouraged during the services—guitars, even rock groups were to play their part: the toning down of exotic priestly vestments and a relaxation of the rules relating to monastic habits. Guitar-toting priests and nuns discarding their severe apparel in favour of make-up were all open signals that the church was to present a far less stuffy image.

One must not assume, of course, that all these resolutions went through on the nod. There were heated debates and some passed the council with slender majorities. Not least among these, of course, were fundamental issues that had split the church some 450 years previously. For some representatives, their tender prejudices and consciences were sorely tested. The issue of the source of Holy Truth, which had been so divisive, historically, generated much heat in debates. Finally, in the dogmatic constitution *Dei Verbum*, divine revelation asserted that the

---

[452] See, for example, Luke 22:52-54, 66; 23:6-23. In particular, Luke, the Gospel writer and a Gentile, is at pains to emphasise the Jewish initiative in this matter. See also Acts 14:2, 19: Luke again—the author of Acts.

The Church 213

Gospel as contained in scripture is to be the touchstone of truth and that the interpretation of its precepts is to evolve as scholars continue to explore the texts. Here, the influence of the progressive Catholic theologian Teilhard de Chardin and his dalliance with a kind of 'process theology'[453] was brought to bear. Scripture, tradition and an evolving interpretation were no longer seen, as some had opined, to be mutually exclusive.

Any attempts to elevate the status of the Virgin Mary even further were resisted as being too offensive to Protestant sensibilities. Rather than viewing her as Co-Redemptrix, as many traditionalists wished, she was instead to be specially honoured as one who had willingly and unequivocally co-operated in the bearing the incarnate son of God.[454]

John XXIII doubtless anticipated a somewhat bruising experience resulting from his opening of Pandora's box. The inherent divisions within the Catholic Church were now to be exposed during the course of impassioned debates, as the influence of a conservative Italian Curia pitted itself against the increasingly vocal bishops from the developing world. It wasn't the case, however, of the Pope simply lighting the blue touch paper and then watching with some kind of disembodied interest as the church removed its cloak of mystery and aired its linen very publicly. Two major encyclicals issued during John's brief reign made it clear where he stood. 'Mater and Magistra' had really set the tone early on in which he sought a way whereby the church itself could play a part in taking the heat out of national and class struggles, which had so bedevilled international security with such devastating consequences over the previous century. He urged a more intense programme of communal and interpersonal co-operation, enjoining richer nations to place their technical resources and expertise at the disposal of the developing world. In similar vein, his encyclical *Pacem in Terris* issued shortly before his death emphasised his own aspiration towards a more loving, less confrontational approach focusing upon reconciliation and a recognition of individual well-being. This was his response in the wake

---

[453]   Teilhard de Chardin (1881-1955), a French Jesuit made some attempts to square Christology with Darwinian evolution. He viewed creation itself not as a static, once for all event, but as an evolutionary organism with God actively and positively involved in the process. The climatic 'omega' point will be reached in humanity's experience of the 'total Christ'. This view represents a more pantheistic approach to God who coexists with nature and expressed in his concept of 'process theology' by A. N. Whitehead (1861-1947).

[454]   Luke 1:26-56.

of a world pushed to the brink as he reflected on the implications of the Cuban Missile Crisis of 1962. In moves to promote the ecumenical movement as he felt Christ Himself sought,[455] so much a feature of Vatican II, Pope John invited observers from other denominations to the council. 'We do not intend to conduct a trial of the past', he announced to his guests. 'We do not want to prove who was right and wrong. All we say is let us come together . . . 'With similar sentiments, he despatched delegates to sessions of the non-Catholic World Council of Churches. Within the Vatican Curia, he established a state secretariat for the promotion of Christian Unity.

Paul VI, successor to Pope John, was wedded to seeing the Vatican Council through to a successful conclusion. His was going to be the unenviable task of holding the fabric of the church together in the light of its radical and controversial decisions. In a few cases, he certainly intervened, diplomatically, in drafting the final reports of the council, where he foresaw that papal inaction would allow cracks to evolve into rupture. In the end, he promulgated the council's findings in 1965 as the authoritative will of the Roman Catholic Church.

The church had finally disposed of its fortress facade and windows were opened upon a world it was commissioned to serve. The new pope was keen to exploit many aspects of this new liberal approach and the increased facilities to see the world at first hand. Paul VI travelled widely, his visit to the Holy Land being a particularly memorable venture. Yet he was not afraid to stem the liberal trend on such fundamental issues as the sanctity of life. He courted controversy by holding the line on matters of marital and sexual morality. Amid calls from the liberal wing from his own church and clamours from almost every quarter elsewhere to address the problems of a burgeoning population explosion and large dysfunctional families, Paul VI stuck to his principles by issuing the encyclical *Humanae Vitae* in 1968. All forms of artificial means of human contraception were stated to be incommensurate with a Godly Catholic lifestyle: a matter of extreme personal significance for otherwise sound Catholic families whose own principles were to be sorely tested (and frequently found wanting) and to those in countries ravaged by the scourge of HIV/AIDS.

There have been casualties of Vatican II. On the conservative wing of the church, rebel bishops and priests have defied authority by leading a movement designed to perpetuate the observance of the unchanged Tridentine (Latin) mass in some parishes. They, and other recalcitrants, have, on occasion, been severely upbraided. At the other end of the

---

[455] John 17:21.

spectrum, liberal theologians who both helped shape Vatican II and who were fertilised by it have been censored and stamped on. Karl Rahner whose radical views have already been noted probably verged on heresy, increasingly tilted the balance of Christian experience away from the spiritual to a measure of secular responsibility. He survived, just, but Hans Kung did not. His sympathy with overtly Protestant doctrine apparently got out of hand, but it was his speculation on the justification for papal infallibility and even upon the existence of God, which led Pope John Paul II to withdraw church sponsorship of his professorship at the University of Tübingen. The Protestant initiative in terms of liberation theology has been taken up by such high-ranking Catholic priests as Camillo Torres (1929-66) and Gustavo Gutiérrez in South America,[456] whose identification with the oppressed working classes, and left-wing political movements, has met with a less than enthusiastic endorsement from the Vatican. Its Marxist and revolutionary overtones have frequently been too much for the Curia to swallow.

So the tensions remain. On the whole, though, the response within the church to Vatican II, and in the outside world at large, to Pope John's initiative has been positive. The numerical strength of nominal Catholicism has not appreciably diminished except, perhaps, in parts of Latin America, though attendance at mass, and the volume of young men coming forward for the priestly vocation most certainly has, at least in the West. While some might put this down to disillusionment with the outcome of Vatican II, still more would argue that the decline in the church would have been far more drastic without it. Catholic-sponsored aid, in all its forms, has certainly been more visible. The success of CAFOD working in conjunction with Christian Aid and Oxfam has made the Roman Church a significant player in the International Development programme. The volunteer work sponsored by the Catholic Institute for International Relations in the UK and the Papal Volunteers

---

[456] Although a Latin American phenomenon, the concept of liberation theology has had a worldwide exposure. It attempts to portray salvation as inextricably tied up with political liberation. It draws some of its inspiration from Marxist dialectic and the class struggle on a continent, which up until the late twentieth century, had been identified with brutal capitalistic dictatorships. To a liberation theologian, the classification of history into discreet secular and spiritual concerns is spurious. The church's commitment *must* be to the poor, the disadvantaged, the voiceless and the oppressed. Gustavo Gutiérrez (born 1928), author of *A Theology of Liberation* (1971), is regarded as its philosophical guru: a theme echoed by the Anglican archbishop of Cape Town, Desmond Tutu (born 1931).

to Latin America based in the USA has highlighted the practical application of Catholic spirituality. Mother Teresa (1910-97) and the work of her 'Sisters of Charity' in India and elsewhere have developed an iconic status of their own. The church's willingness to comment more outspokenly on secular issues, without necessarily receiving the wholehearted endorsement of the Vatican, has tended to take the sting out of purely secular socialist movements or indeed to engage as catalyst to promote opposition to ruthless dictatorships whether on the left or the right. Lech Walesa's (born 1943) Solidarity Movement in Poland was underpinned by an unshakeable Catholic spirituality, which ultimately led to the fall of communism in Eastern Europe, while Father Oscar Romero's (1917-80) martyrdom in challenging the right wing Sandinista regime in Nicaragua in the 1980s hastened its demise there. As far as the European Union is concerned, Vatican pronouncements have vacillated from a guarded endorsement, seeing its enhanced role as providing some spiritual cement, to dire warnings that the union was evolving into Godless mammon of elephantine proportions.

In Protestant circles, organic church union has taken place worldwide—in India, Australia and in Canada a little earlier, uniting churches has become reality, and in England, the former Presbyterian and Congregational denominations joined forces as the United Reformed Church in 1972. The much hoped for unity between Catholicism and the rest of Christendom, however, still seems a long way off. Nevertheless, the mood engendered by the spirit of Vatican II has been pregnant with hitherto unthinkable symbolic gestures. In 1960, Pope John XXIII welcomed Geoffrey Fisher, archbishop of Canterbury (1945-61), to the Vatican and in 1961 he extended the same courtesy to Queen Elizabeth II (assumed the throne, 1952) in an attempt to reverse the negative climate occasioned by Pope Pius V's excommunication of her ancestral namesake in 1570. This was followed up by a joint act of spiritual reconciliation between Pope John Paul II and the prime archbishop, Robert Runcie (1980-91), at the shrine of Thomas a Becket in Canterbury Cathedral. However, fundamental obstacles to organic unity remain: the recent ordination of women and the ordination of openly gay priests in the Anglican Church have proved a contentious issue between Rome and Canterbury, two communions inherently at one on the concept of apostolic succession.

In an act of magnanimity, the Orthodox and Catholic hierarchy lifted their thousand-year mutual excommunication in 1965 in response to Pope Paul VI's meeting with Patriarch Athenagoras (1886-1972) in Jerusalem shortly before. Here too, though, theological and practical factors pose stumbling blocks to closer union.

The Church

Meanwhile, at local level, the pragmatic desire for the laity and clergy from churches of all denominations to work together positively in areas where they have agreement has made considerable progress since Vatican II. Co-operation and suspicion have given way to an appreciation of the strengths of others rather than a disparagement of their apparent weakness or of their perceived differences. Ecumenical projects such as that of Corrymeela in Northern Ireland,[457] the increased popularity of the ecumenical retreat founded by Frère Roger (1915-2005) at Taize in France and the strong personal co-operation between the Anglican bishop of Liverpool, David Sheppard (1975-97) and his Catholic counterpart Derek Worlock (1976-96) have all been symptomatic of the new mood. Across the UK and beyond, 'churches together' in towns and cities are pooling their resources in a common desire to harness a regenerated spirit. The words of the Camerlengo in Dan Brown's novel perhaps reflect the yearnings of many of the faithful of all denominations when he passionately implores others to look 'beyond the ritual of (our institutions, and see) a modern miracle . . . a brotherhood of imperfect, simple souls wanting only to be a voice of compassion in a world spinning out of control'.[458]

Perhaps the simple soul, elected at that defining moment in October 1958, has been the formal embodiment of this change in the spiritual landscape among the ordinary people of God. What is certain is that the momentum is there to come to grips with the secular challenges and, in particular, with the hostility encountered between the world's major faiths. Herein lay difficult and tortuous channels to navigate as the twenty-first century unfolds. A rise in militant Islam and the dangers of conservative Christian reaction will require sensitive handling. The church has pulled through before. What is certain is that the Catholic Church of which John XXIII was the caretaker for five brief years has had its windows opened and its siege mentality lifted. The Sistine frescoes, which bore witness to his election have, as a consequence, been released from the narrow and authoritarian atmosphere, which originally inspired them; they can now speak to us of a reinvigorated spiritual renaissance such as that has been facilitated by the Godly peasant from Bergamo.

---

[457] A much heralded breakthrough in Protestant/Catholic relationships in the traumatised province of Northern Ireland. Corrymeela was a social and educational joint enterprise catering for the needs of anyone in the community, regardless of religions affiliation, the demand for which came from moderate lay people tired of the sectarian violence at the height of the 'Troubles'.

[458] Brown, D.: *Angels and Demons*, Corgi Books, 2001.

Chapter 20

Rev. Florence Li Tim-Oi with Archbishop of Canterbury,
Robert Runcie in the 1980s

BLACK CHRISTMAS

25 December: by anyone's calculation, a date invested with the aura of pivot and definition; by convention, if not in reality, herein lies the annual observance of the saviour's birth and Charlemagne's coronation eight centuries on. Customarily the urbane, handsome, Old Etonian apogee of the British colonial establishment in Hong Kong, His Excellency the governor, Sir Mark Young, would be hosting one of the obligatory receptions at Government House. Here it would be customary for the Hong Kong worthies to make their way to this tropical Georgian pile set amidst extensive gardens on the ridge between Upper and Lower Albert Roads with its commanding views across the harbour to the district of Kowloon on the mainland. Not today they wouldn't, not Christmas Day, 1941. Instead of presiding at the traditional bash, Young and his colonial secretariat would be beating a forlorn pathway to the third floor of the historic Peninsula Hotel on Salisbury Road, Kowloon; room 336, where he was to sign the instruments of surrender of himself and the colony to the triumphant Japanese invaders—the latest twist in the unfolding catalogue of disasters encountered by the British since Chamberlain's Declaration of War on Germany, 3 September 1939: the fall of Britain's first colonial possession to the Far Eastern enemy since Japan's indecent

The Church   219

foray into the conflict on the 'Day of Infamy': 7 December 1941: Pearl Harbor. As Prime Minister Winston Churchill (1940-45, 1951-55) back home braced himself for more bad news in the Pacific, General Takashi Sakai (1881-1946), commander of the victorious Japanese imperial forces, led his exultant troops along Queen Street on Boxing Day and handed over the Civil Command of Hong Kong to Rensuke Isagai, the colony on the threshold of full participation in a new era: the Japanese euphemistically self-styled 'South East Asia Co-Prosperity Zone'.

For the previous seventeen days, the rag, tag and bobtail garrison under Major General Christopher Maltby (1891-1980) comprising British, Canadian, Indian and Hong Kong forces had fought and given ground, as the superior Japanese 23rd Division had crossed the Chinese border into Hong Kong's New Territories and had fully exploited their numerical 5 to 1 superiority. Gindrinker's line on the mainland was held briefly, after which Hong Kong Island itself withstood a five-day siege, until the final assault on Victoria Harbour and the taking of the strategic Wong Nai Chung Gap, which split the remaining allied forces on the island into two. On Maltby's advice, further suffering was pointless. The governor had little choice but to bow to the inevitable and to throw in the towel. For Mark Young himself and the surviving allied combatants (there had been forty-five hundred casualties out of a garrison of fifteen thousands), it was to mean imprisonment. For expatriate citizens, it was to presage internment. For most residents of the colony, this was destined to be known as 'Black Christmas', as they prepared to endure what turned out to be three years and eight months of humiliation, rape, deprivation, starvation, repression and premature death at the hands of the Japanese occupiers, so much for the concept of 'co-prosperity'. For the Western Church, it was to be a defining moment.

As it happened, during these momentous days, the Anglican bishop of Hong Kong and South China, in the ecclesiastical province of Chung Hua Sheng Kung Hui, was on official business in the USA. While there he learnt that the core of his diocese had been wrenched from his grasp like a thief in the night, occupied by uninvited squatters determined to rid the territory of its Western imperialistic religious influence, and had been replaced with a stamp of its own. While this prevented Bishop Hall's (1932-66) return to Hong Kong, he did have various bolt holes to which he could resort in the parts of South China outside the control of the Japanese forces.

The then Portuguese colony of Macao lay just thirty-five miles across the Canton Estuary to the south of Hong Kong. This anomalous entity was still technically neutral and therefore 'free' in terms of the armed conflict. Within its ten square miles, Macao's indigenous population of Sino-Portuguese extraction had been augmented to immense proportions as an influx of Chinese refugees flooded the tiny territory in a stampede to escape the horrors being perpetrated on the mainland. It was here that a deaconess from Hong Kong, Florence Li Tim-Oi, was already ministering to the small Anglican community with the peripatetic support of priests who would periodically issue forth from Hong Kong to administer the sacraments. With the fall of the British colony, the young woman was then in sole charge of her flock, cut off as she then was from the nerve centre of her church. No longer could Anglicans in Macao receive Holy Communion due to the prohibition on travel and the absence of resident clergy.

Bishop Hall, his cathedral in Hong Kong having been desecrated and revamped as a social club for Japanese soldiers and the diocesan schools having been metamorphosed into military hospitals, had relocated to Zhaoqing in Free China on his return from America, some seventy miles west of Guangzhou (Canton) on the Xi Jiang River. He was eventually contacted by Florence Li Tim-Oi, who had by then become conscious of the fact that she had been obliged, 'de facto' and unofficially, to preside over the Eucharist. She clearly recognised the sacramental deprivation inherent in her non-priestly status and her highly irregular practice, questionably efficacious in an Anglican context. Hall, as a high church Tractarian, was mindful of such irregularity and was faced with a painful choice: continue with the status quo and allow the sacrament to be administered by a lay person or to ordain the woman as a priest. The sheer spirituality and courage displayed by Florence helped him make up his mind. As far as he was concerned, the exigencies of the situation justified his momentous decision. After a long, hazardous journey, Florence arrived in Zhaoqing, where Bishop Hall consecrated her as priest in Holy Orders at the Anglican Church of Xsinxing in Zhaoqing on the feast day of the conversion of St Paul, 25 January 1944. Bishop Hall had broken decisively with Anglican and Catholic traditions and practice and with canon law that for centuries had reserved ordination to males. William Temple, archbishop of Canterbury (1942-44), was at best equivocal on the learning of Hall's actions 'ex post facto'. Temple's successor, Geoffrey Fisher, as primate of the communion, was actively hostile. After the war pressure was put upon the Chinese House of bishops to censure Hall for his actions. Indeed, Florence unselfishly surrendered her licence to administer the sacraments in order to spare Hall the ignominy of his enforced resignation. Nevertheless, she remained within 'Holy Orders', serving as a teacher, social worker and factotum at the Cathedral of Our Saviour in Guangzhou in the years immediately after the end of the war. During the Chinese Cultural

The Church 221

Revolution (1958-74), Florence was deemed a counter-revolutionary by the Maoist authorities, her life threatened and sickeningly humiliated in the process of her 're-education'. Eventually she found refuge in Canada during the 1980s at which time she was relicensed initially in Montreal and subsequently in the Diocese of Toronto, where she died in 1992.[459]

As Mark Young was reinstalled as Hong Kong's governor and Bishop Hall set about regenerating his mission, in the wake of the Japanese capitulation in August 1945 and the nuclear controversy associated with it, the Anglican Communion at large would now have to come to terms with—and address—Ronald Hall's actions in ordaining Florence Li Tim-Oi in the first place. He had violated the hitherto male preserve by admitting a female into the realms of sacramental authority. The 1948 Lambeth Conference of the global representatives from the Anglican Provinces solemnly declared that her ordination be not regarded as a precedent and refused to recognise the ordination retrospectively. Nevertheless, a precedent *had* been set; she had been ordained by a bishop in good standing, and despite censure, in good standing he remained. The issue was destined to have huge implications for the future direction, structure, authority and the very nature of the worldwide Anglican Communion, its capacity to cope with the vexed issue of sexuality and genderism at large as well as the implications for its relationship with its partners in the apostolic tradition, Catholic and Orthodox. By the end of the millennium, the post-war breeze pervading the Anglican Church had assumed the dimensions of a force-eight hurricane, a leaning tower teetering on the brink.

As the role of women in secular society during the second half of the twentieth century was re-evaluated towards a broad acceptance of social and economic equality in the Western world, and as reflected in legislation to give it effect, the church was bound to be caught up in its wake. Hitherto the churches had rested relatively securely in its male-centred power bastion, its comfort zone reposing in the cultural conventions of preceding centuries. No longer could its smug presuppositions be kept under wraps. On the face of it, if one turns to the Canonical biblical texts, there does seem to be considerable evidential support for a subordinate role for women in the religious hierarchy. The Jewish priesthood of the Old Testament, for example, appears to have been a male prerogative. Even the 'saintly' Deborah, the

---

[459] Her own story is told in Li Tim-Oi (1907-92), *Raindrops of My Life*, Anglican Book Centre, Toronto, 1976.

judge and prophetess in Israel,[460] was not accredited with the possession of the priestly preserve of the 'kohen' caste, translated into Greek as 'hiereus',[461] as one authorised to 'come near to Yahweh', interceding and offering sacrifice on behalf of the people.[462] Such priests, after the tradition of Aaron,[463] and, by implication, the Levitical priesthood, were all men.[464]

With the advent, in the New Testament, of Christ as the 'high priest', it is doubtful, initially, whether a Christian priesthood would be required, at least in the sacrificial or sacramental sense, for Jesus has fulfilled the role in His own Person.[465] However, as the church grew, and spread, some form of practical organisation would be necessary to ensure cohesion. The problem for subsequent church leaders and scholars has been one of translation and interpretation. In the life of the early church, its officers as described in the New Testament are referred to as presbyters (Presbuteros),[466]—literally 'elders', but often rendered into English as priests or even bishops. The term *Episkopoi* (literally an 'overseer') is applied to those called upon by the Holy Spirit to watch over the flock and nurture its spiritual well-being.[467] The other significant word of note is that of *Diakonos* (deacon), whose use is generally regarded as denoting a *servant* of the church.[468] Only once, in the New Testament, is this word used in its *feminine* form, with reference to Phoebe, who served the church at Cenchreae.[469] The problem, as we can see, revolves around the relative importance that one attaches to the orders to which the New Testament alludes and the interpretation one chooses to put upon them. An early Church Father, Ignatius (c.40-c.115), opined that the presbyter performed the *functions* of a bishop (including the celebration of Eucharist) so long as the presiding bishop gave his leave and performed such functions in his name. This was to lead to the evolution of the three 'major orders' common to the Orthodox, Catholic and Anglican traditions: deacon, priest and bishop in ascending order.

---

[460] Judges 4; 5.

[461] Exodus 19:6, 22.

[462] Numbers 16:43-50.

[463] Exodus 28:1.

[464] Numbers 3:2, 3, 6-10.

[465] See Hebrews 7:15-8:13 and especially. 7:26-27 and 8:8. See chapter 1 for a summary of the background to this.

[466] Acts 14:23; 20:17; Philippians 1:1.

[467] As used in Acts 20:17, 28.

[468] 1 Corinthians 3:5; Ephesians 3:7; Colossians 1:23, 25.

[469] Romans 16:1.

The Church 223

Cyprian (c.205-258), in the mid-third century, was more forthright. He associated presbyters with the concept of 'sacerdotes'—a sacramental function, although, like Tertullian he maintained that sacramental initiation derives from the bishop. As Christianity spread, it became increasingly apparent that bishops were to delegate their sacramental duties to the 'presbyters' as a matter of course. By the time of Aquinas, the term and function of priesthood in the thirteenth century had become inherently sacerdotal, a theory reinforced by the fact that many such priests were not necessarily linked to a benefice, but had specific liturgical functions to fulfil.

If we turn to the canonical Gospels, the priesthood referred to is almost exclusively descriptive of the Jewish orders,[470] as was the role of 'High Priest',[471] except that Jesus reserves that role exclusively to Himself in the new dispensation[472] and this is implied at His intimate gathering at the Last Supper,[473] while the writer to the Hebrews, as we have seen, comes right out in asserting this.[474] Much has been made of male predominance in the Gospels—Jesus chose twelve Apostles—all men apparently forming a closely knit band of brothers:[475] John the baptiser[476] and his father, Zechariah,[477] all pointers to an all-male Christian priesthood. Its detractors nevertheless will identify the pivotal role played by women in the unfolding of the drama: to Mary and Martha,[478] the women of the tomb,[479] the 'highly favoured' Virgin herself (but no priest),[480] not to mention Mary Magdalene[481]—she of the Nag Hammadi Gospels, much quoted doyen favoured by Leigh, Baigent and Brown et al. in their researches into the Sacred Feminine.[482]

The Apostle Paul could be quite strident in his apparent disdain for female equality, hardly an advocate for the European Convention

---

[470] See, e.g. Matthew 8:4; Mark 1:44; Luke 1:5; 5:14; 10:31.

[471] See, e.g. Matthew 26:3; Mark 2:26; Luke 22:50; John 18:13.

[472] See John 14:6.

[473] Matthew 26:26-28; Mark 14:22-25; Luke 22:19-20.

[474] Hebrews 9:11.

[475] Matthew 10:1-4; Mark 3:13-19; Luke 6:12-16; John 1:35-50.

[476] Matthew 3:1-17; Mark 1:1-11; Luke 3:1-22; John 1:19-34.

[477] Luke 1:5-25.

[478] Luke 10:38-42; John 11:1-7.

[479] Matthew 28:1-11; Mark 16:1-11; Luke 24:1-12; John 20:1-18.

[480] Matthew 1:18, 22-23; John 19:25-27; Luke 1:26-56; 2:1-51.

[481] Luke 8:1-3; John 19:25.

[482] Baigent, M., Leigh, B. and Lincoln, H.: *The Holy Blood and the Holy Grail*, Arrow Books, 1996; Brown, D.: *The Da Vinci Code*, Corgi Books, 2006.

on Human Rights. Women must not speak up in the congregation,[483] must 'cover themselves' with all due modesty and generally know their place,[484] although he does concede their role as invaluable facilitators of spreading the Gospel.[485] Indeed, David Dunn Wilson maintains that the early church offered women a way out of their previous pagan role as fodder for male sexual gratification by raising their status and self-esteem.[486] Down the ages, the example of women playing the part of exhorters, encouragers, teachers and exemplars is legion: Helena, mother of Constantine; Monica, mother of Augustine; Anthusa (c.330-374), mother of Chrysostom (c.347-407), the one-time archbishop of Constantinople: legendary preacher, liturgist and probably anti-Semite; Bertha (c.555-c.610), wife of King Ethelbert of Kent; Susanna Wesley (1669-1742), mother of John and Charles; Catherine of Siena (1347-80) and Mother Theresa spring to mind along with countless other nameless ones without whom the Christian story would have been vastly different. Yet they were not priests, not one of them.

To the reformers of the sixteenth century, the term *priest* had become repellent. It smacked too much to the Catholic mass, of sacrifice, authoritarian ritual and an abuse of power. Christ was the *one* intermediary through whom access to God is facilitated;[487] the *one* high priest[488] whose once and for all sacrifice is sufficient.[489] When it comes to that, Luther had argued, 'did not even the writer of the First Letter ascribed to Peter himself identify **all** believers as priests?'[490] Hence, the reformers have consistently preferred such terms as *minister* or *pastor* (shepherd)[491] to emphasise the caring, guiding principle when applied to church leaders, even to Christ Himself in order to play down the sacerdotal role and to identify with the apparent practice of the early church—presbyter, elder, deacon, as discussed above.

The position of the Anglicans has, not surprisingly, been ambivalent on the matter. Those of the Anglo-Catholic 'high church' wing have been more than happy to retain the name of *priest* and to refer to their incumbents as 'Father', while the 'low church' arm of Anglicanism is

---

[483] 1 Corinthians 14:34-35; 1 Timothy 2:11.

[484] 1 Timothy 2:9-15.

[485] Romans 16:1-12; see also Luke 8:1-3; Acts 16:14-15.

[486] Dunn-Wilson, D.: *A Mirror for the Church*, Eerdsmans Publishing Co, 2005.

[487] John 14:1-7, especially verse 6.

[488] Hebrews 7:26.

[489] Hebrews 7:27.

[490] 1 Peter 2:9.

[491] Psalm 23:1; Hebrews 13:20-21; 1 Peter 5:2-4.

The one consistent approach, however, even at the reformation and for many years subsequently, the concept of male ordination was unchallenged across the denominations. Certainly, the early Church Fathers tended to view women, at the very least, as the weaker gender. Capable, yes, of sharing in the Virgin Mary's victory as freeing the race of women from reproach, as Tertullian sees it, while Clement of Alexandria speaks of God's love in the feminine form and St Gregory reputedly regards Mary as the Mother of God, bringing to birth the new Adam, yet John Chrysostom's metaphor for sin is that of a hideous woman. Descended from the temptress, Eve,[493] small wonder is it that prejudicial resistance towards their ordination has been so sustained. Paul's apparent *scriptural* prejudices were sufficient to satisfy Protestants of the 'male only' injunction. Those of the Catholic, Orthodox and Anglican persuasion have relied more heavily on church tradition based upon pronouncements made at the Ecumenical Council of Laodicea (352), whereby women were specifically denied ordination to the priesthood or the right even to exercise the role of presbyter, while at the Council of Chalcedon (451), women 'under the age of forty years' were refused admission to the order of deacon. All of this suggests, of course, that prior to these decrees, *some* equality of gender in the issue of ordination *had* been practised hitherto or at the very least it had been a topic of contention. There is certainly evidence on the Mediterranean island of Thera that, according to a fourth-century epitaph, a woman, Epiktas, was referred as a 'presbytis' and there exists a third-century Egyptian inscription dedicated to Artemidoras, whose mother is referred to as a 'presbytera'.

It's hardly surprising, therefore, that given the somewhat speculative 'evidence' from the repository of early church ordinance and practice, any steps to promote women to formal ecclesiastical authority was bound to be tentative and gradual. Such moves as there were came initially from those churches that were free of state or hierarchical control, those which described themselves, loosely, as 'independent' community-based societies. So for example in 1853, Antoinette Brown was ordained pastor at her congregational church in South Butler, New York. From its inception, in 1865, William Booth's 'commissioned officers' in the Salvation Army have been drawn from either gender. The congregational church in England began ordaining women in 1917,

---

[492] See Matthew 23:9.

[493] Genesis 3:16-17.

while the burgeoning number of Afro/Caribbean churches in the USA and the West Indies have been practising female ordination for decades. The United Church of Canada had taken the step in 1936. The cults have been even bolder. The rise of Christian Science in the nineteenth century owes its foundation to the iconic Mary Baker Eddy (1821-1910) whose 'revelations' in her *Science and Health,* published in 1875 have, for her followers, an equivalence to Holy Scripture as far as doctrine and practice are concerned. Ellen White, the Seventh-Day Adventist visionary, is almost as highly regarded.

The 'apostolic' churches have been, inherently, the most resistant to change. Back in 1935, a commission appointed by the archbishops of Canterbury and York for the Church of England had concluded that there were 'no compelling theological reasons for, or against, the ordination of women', but at the same time, it somewhat paradoxically insisted on maintaining the priesthood as a male preserve. However, the very *nature* of the worldwide Anglican Communion with its loose association of quasi-independent provinces was to expose such pronouncements as non-binding observations. Specifically, it was the fall of Hong Kong, the defining moment, and the consequent pragmatic ordination of Florence Li Tim-Oi, which was to give hope to those anxious for change.

The post-1945 world was to hasten the increasingly vocal demand for changed attitudes inside the church and out. The campaign for civil rights in the USA was to embrace not just the question of ethnicity but was to branch out into the rights of workers of trade union activity and the feminist movement on both sides of the Atlantic. Inevitably, the church itself would be caught up in the cacophony, leaving the 1968 Lambeth Conference with little option but to address the vocal demands for women's ordination. Again, the precedent set by Bishop Hall and Florence Li Tim-Oi was cited; polarised opinions were stridently aired and the conference concluded that a *cautious* approach be adopted towards the issue and that the autonomous provinces postpone any decision pending the findings of the Anglican Consultative Committee. Its report, published in 1971, conceded, in fact, that as each province was a law unto itself, it was there that the matter should be decided for itself. In 1974, several women were ordained (irregularly) in Philadelphia but were recognised by the episcopal church in the USA as the Anglican Province is known there, and at the Lambeth Conference held in 1978, it was noted that, in addition, the provinces of Canada, New Zealand and South China (Hong Kong) had accepted women as ordained priests. Despite, or perhaps because of, all the pain that this realisation provoked, the conference was now forced to recognise the

The Church 227

'fait accompli', by acknowledging the 'legal right of each church to make its own decision about the appropriateness of admitting women to Holy Orders'. In reality, this resolution was more about preventing the increasingly disparate Anglican Communion from unravelling altogether.

For the senior partner in the Western apostolic tradition—Rome—the issue of women's ordination and indeed that of a married priesthood was bound to arise at some stage. Catholic bishops, despite their technical claim to collegiality, are nevertheless bound in canon law to the authority of the Pope, whose powers to exercise spiritual and ethical authority leave the archbishop of Canterbury standing.[494] The Vatican's effectively centralised Curia is able to impose religious sanctions upon dissidents wherever in the world they surface. Hence it was with considerable confidence that the Vatican's sacred congregation for the faith observed in 1976 that 'the church, in fidelity to the example of the Lord, does not consider herself authorised to admit women to priestly ordination' and in the pontiff's apostolic letter *Ordinatio Sacerdotalis* in the same year declared that 'the church has no authority whatsoever to confer priestly ordination on women'. It was now clear that, for the moment, Catholicism was holding the line, its integrity more or less in tact. However, there has been steady decline of candidates for the Catholic priesthood in the Western world with increasing numbers of parishes without a priest. Often it is a woman or women who are left to keep the local operations ticking over—echoes of the Florence Li Tim-Oi syndrome: just another time, place and circumstance. There is growing evidence of irregularities, however, as for instance, in the case of the 'ordination' of seven Catholic women 'somewhere on the river Danube' in 2002; secret ordinations have been reported elsewhere with the celebration of the mass presided over by an illicitly ordained female priest in 'house churches'—a throwback to the spirit of the early Christian experience.[495] It would seem, however, that Rome will not proceed with female ordination as a general principle nor, for that matter, will it countenance a married priesthood. That was certainly the stance adopted by Pope John Paul II and by Cardinal Ratzinger who as Benedict XVI succeeded him. For the moment, the issue for Catholics, while contentious, is not a serious threat to its corporate structure. In some respects, Rome's rigid position has been to its advantage. Given the 1978 Lambeth 'de facto' recognition of Anglican provincial autonomy, parishes and individual members of the communion—clergy and laity

---

[494] See chapter 18.
[495] Acts 2:46.

alike—were now going to wrestle with their consciences. When, in 1994, the Anglican Church of England finally got around to ordaining women, many clergy and laity of the high church Anglo-Catholic persuasion simply deserted to Rome: for them, Anglicanism had gone a step too far. Numbers of fundamental Anglicans, at the other end of the spectrum, likewise decamped for the same reason, adding their weight not to Rome, but to the 'populist 'community churches' which, while not recognising priestly functions, nevertheless retained the principle of male leadership as, in their eyes, scripture constrains. A fudge was worked out for those Anglican parishes and congregations who wished to remain inside the church, but who could not, in conscience, accept female ordination. Such congregations were granted 'extended episcopal oversight' or the 'flying bishop' principle, whereby their interests would be served, not necessarily by the bishop of the geographical diocese but by a bishop who would not be prepared, personally, to ordain a woman. Clearly the Anglican Church was paying the price for its historic inclusiveness: the broad (minded) church. On the matter of female ordination, social, pragmatic, economic and even populist forces were dictating its agenda against the more principled stance adopted by Rome and many of the evangelicals. The move further dismayed the ecumenical enthusiasts, for any kind of progress towards reunion of the two apostolic branches of Western Christendom—Canterbury and Rome—was bound to be frustrated on this fundamental point over which they so profoundly disagree.

Worse was to follow. The problem of women's ordination had rocked the Anglican Church although it could hardly be said to have invoked the sensitivities of common morality. However, it did pave the way to a broader debate on sexuality within the church, which most definitely would raise serious ethical issues. The reaction of the authoritarian Catholic hierarchy was to batten down the hatches: to rest in denial towards the scandalous cover-up concerning abuse of the young in its care by significant elements of the clergy in Ireland until public outcry prompted a peremptory summons of all the country's Catholic bishops to the Vatican for unprecedented 'consultation' in 2010. Yet for the Curia, Thomas Aquinas's principle of natural law *implied* male hegemony and a rejection of contraception, abortion, euthanasia, the remarriage of divorcees and homosexuality, all in the name of the sanctity of life. This principle was to be rigidly and uncompromisingly applied. Certain pressure groups from within the Catholic fold, it is true, have become increasingly vocal at the turn of the millennium. However, the unyielding stance on human non-interference in life and death as far as God's ultimate design and purpose is concerned is fundamental to Catholic

The Church 229

belief: 'The Lord gave, and now the Lord has taken away'[496] and there the matter rests.

There comes a point in the quasi-tolerant, forbearing, anything goes Anglican Church when the existing tensions within its ranks can no longer be sustained. The growing confidence of the Gay and Lesbian Movement in Western culture was inevitably going to spill over into theological debate and wherein emotions were bound to run deep. Like the Catholics, much debate centred around the *purpose* of the Creator when he created gender: what is the *prime* function of sexual relationships?[497] It's certainly true that some of the Old Testament pronouncements on homosexual behaviour are seemingly unnerving,[498] while in the New Testament mixed messages may be discerned. On the one hand, Christ Himself asserts that *all* who believe in Him shall inherit eternal life.[499] Michael Hampson argues forcefully that the very love extended to all of us by Christ supersedes the primitive understanding on the matter in Genesis and Leviticus.[500] Conversely, Paul is pretty harsh on same sex relationships.[501] He certainly condemns "sins of the flesh[502] and Jude comments upon the punishment meted out to Sodom and Gomorrah.[503] Both sides of the debate can make capital by selecting their preferred option. You pay your money, you take your choice.

Closet homosexuality among the laity and clergy—of all denominations—has been recognised as a plain fact down the centuries, but never openly acknowledged or sanctioned. Since the lifting of civil sanctions against the practice in most Western countries during the second half of the twentieth century, so a greater openness was to be expected from the church. The ordination of overt homosexuals was

---

[496] Job 1: 21.

[497] Bishop Ambrose (c.339-397), for example urged sexual abstinence except for the purposes of procreation. Augustine (354-430) took a similar position. However, it must be emphasised that this could well have been to distance Christian sexual ethics from the overt pagan rituals then prevalent rather than to promote theological principles 'per se'. Nevertheless, Catholic dogma has tended to 'ring fence' the principle.

[498] Leviticus 18:22; Genesis 19:1-29.

[499] John 3:16.

[500] Hampson, M.: *Last Rites: The End of the Church of England*, Granta Books, London, 2006.

[501] Romans 1:26-27; 1 Corinthians 6:9.

[502] 1 Corinthians 5:9; 6:9-10.

[503] Jude 1:7.

to become an issue. The prime initiator in the move to accept gay ordinands were sections of America's episcopal church, who pushed through a resolution at their general council in 1976 recognising that homosexuals are children of God and hinting at the imminence of ordaining gay clergy. This was met with a frosty reaction from the vast majority of the other provinces of the Anglican Communion, and as late as 1998, the Lambeth Conference was to declare that 'homosexual practice is incompatible with scripture'. Unsurprisingly, therefore, the ordination of Gene Robinson in 2003 as bishop of New Hampshire, USA, provoked a howl of protest from the conservative provinces, especially in Africa, whose spokesman, Bishop Peter Akinola, warned of a break-up of the communion. Even in the USA, opinions are polarised. The future appears far from rosy. Women bishops were first consecrated in the USA in 1989, a feature complicated still further by the fact that a woman bishop now presides (2007) over the episcopal province in the USA and the Church of England agonises if and when it will itself make its own decision on women bishops. While Archbishop Rowan Williams 'as first among equals' attempted to hold the Anglican Communion together nationally and internationally, its paucity of canon law makes his task difficult and unenviable. Such are the inconsistencies inherent within its make-up; his vacillation over the appointment of Jeffrey John, an openly gay priest, as bishop designate of Reading in 2003—and John's enforced offer to decline the post—serves to highlight the dilemma.

Meanwhile the world moves on and watches in amazement as the Anglicans tear each other apart and the other denominations face the future with unease. The church is often regarded as having become a pressure group (at best) as an irrelevance or as a malign influence (at worst), as Christopher Hitchens would try to persuade us.[504] Surely, the sceptics argue that, if it has *any* purpose, the church should be expending its energy on feeding the hungry, healing the sick, assisting the poor as enjoined by its respected founder.[505] The churches will reply that human sexuality lies at the very heart of the creative purpose[506] and all things must be seen within this spiritual context: a fair point.

As he walked despondently into the foyer of the Peninsula Hotel in Kowloon on 'Black Christmas' 1941 to surrender to the custody of the invaders, Mark Young could never have even dreamt that he was

---

[504] Hitchens, C.: *God is not Great*, Atlantic Books, 2007.

[505] Matthew 25:31-40; the position taken by Desmond Tutu, Nobel Prize winner and former archbishop of Cape Town.

[506] Genesis 1:27-28; 9:7.

unwittingly a player in this ecclesiastical defining moment: that it would catapult the 'Pink Bishop', Ronald Hall, into ordaining a woman priest within three years, and that a tenacious, saintly soul, Florence Li Tim-Oi, would become a catalyst for a revolution in church attitudes to sexuality and a pointer to more dramatic twists as the twenty-first century unfolds.

MM+

Kingdoms, states, empires have come and gone as the third millennium gets under way. Socially, culturally, politically the so-called Western world has mutated, yet the one feature that defines it—the church—has sustained its identity in the midst of all the changing scenes of life. Despite its fragmentation and its appearance in diverse guises and as implied by the twenty defining moments, the epicentre of church activity based upon Rome has been the one consistent structural feature: adapting, ducking, diving, scheming, weaving, accommodating, promoting, initiating . . . but hanging in there nevertheless. When all else appears to be intent on change, its remarkable tenacity is, perhaps, a testimony to the aspiration of the human spirit to access that mystical certainty that transcends the mere satisfaction of the material appetite.

As these pages have attempted to show, the church as presently known is no longer identifiable as one organic entity. In an age, when the democratic principle determines the West's politically correct moral high ground, with its justifiable emphasis upon individual human rights, the chances that the church will once again speak with one voice in the cause of the Gospel seem somewhat remote. 'That they may be One' (John 17:11) is a sentiment whose fulfilment in human terms seems a long way off. With such a variety of denominations, sects and cults, each peddling its own agenda and emphases as the 'right one', those seeking for truth are bewilderingly spoilt for choice. It is brutally clear that not one of these entities can, with clear conscience, boast of a past such as would bring unalloyed pleasure to the Founder Himself—least of all that of the Roman persuasion, although of course it has the longevity factor to multiply its propensities to weakness. That said and with the prospects of renewed proposals for a reintegration of the Methodists with the Church of England compromised by an Anglican Communion unravelling at the seams, the yearning for a spiritual dimension to life remains.

The Western world and indeed the millennia are defined by the birth of Christ. Despite its detractors, it is comforting to acknowledge the durability of the church, not only in human terms but also to recognise it as being beyond time and whose apotheosis is in the eternal realms. 'Behold', promises the Lord, 'I make all things new' (Rev. 21:5). By definition, this must include the church. Meanwhile, the human responsibility remains with us just as it was when Simon Peter was commissioned at Caesarea Philippi to uphold the values of the true Founder's Spirit and to participate in faithful stewardship until such time as 'the earth and everything in it will be laid bare' (2 Pet. 3:10).

Selected Reading List

The Bible is a constant reference point throughout this study. The New International Version is a reputable English translation and the Good News Bible is a useful colloquial edition. Nevertheless, some still prefer the majestic prose of the authorised (King James) version of 1611 or its derivative, the *Revised Standard Version*, despite their reliance on sources unavailable at the time of translation.

Many reference books exist, which cover the two millennia of church history in the West of which the following are recommended as worthy representatives of the period as a whole:

Davies, N.: *Europe: A History* (London, 1997).
Dowley, T. (ed.): *The History of Christianity* (Berkhamstead, 1977).
Cross, F. L. and Livingstone, E. A. (eds): *The Oxford Dictionary of the Christian Church* (Oxford 1996).
Lane, T: *The Lion Concise Book of Christian Thought* (Tring, 1984).
McManners, J. (ed.): *The Oxford Illustrated History of Christianity* (Oxford, 1995).

The following reference material is classified by chapter. In general, works cited in the body of the text are not included here. These will be found in the appropriate notes located therein.

Chapter 1

Barclay, W.: *Acts of the Apostles* (Edinburgh, 2003).
Barclay, W.: *Letter to the Hebrews* (Edinburgh, 2002).
Barclay, W.: *The Letters of James and Peter* (Edinburgh, 1965).
Brown, R. E. (ed.): *Peter in the New Testament: A Collaborative Assessment by Protestant and Roman Catholic Scholars* (Mineapolis, 1973).
Chadwick, H.: *The Early Church* (Harmondsworth, 1967).
Cleave, R.: *The Holy Land: A Unique Perspective* (Oxford, 1993).
Drane, J.: *Introducing the New Testament* (Oxford, 2000).
Dunn Wilson, D.: *A Mirror for the Church* (Cambridge, 2005).
Harnack, A.: *The Mission and Expansion of Christianity* (London, 1908).
Heussi, K.: *Die Romische Petrustradition in Kritischer Sicht* (Tubingen, 1955).
Keeley, R. (ed.): *Jesus 2000* (Oxford, 1989).
Kelly, J. N. D.: *A Commentary on the Pastoral Epistles* (New York, 1983).
Kelly, J. N. D.: *Early Christian Doctrines* (London, 1958).
Lietzmann, H.: *The Beginnings of the Christian Church* (London, 1937 ff).
Mounce, R. H.: *Matthew* (Carlisle, 1995).
Onilka, J.: *Petrus und Rom. Das Petrusbild in den ersten zwei Jahrhunderten in Kritischer Sicht* (Tubingen, 1955).
O'Connor, D. W.: *Peter in Rome: The Literary, Liturgical and Archaeological Evidence* (London, 1969).
Perkins, P.: *Peter: Apostle for the Whole Church* (Edinburgh, 2000).
Ridderbos, H. N.: *The Speeches of Peter in the Acts of the Apostles* (London, 1962).

Chapter 2

Baynes, N. H.: *Constantine the Great and the Christian Church* (Lecture to the Brutish Academy, London, 1972).
Chadwick, H.: *The Early Church* (Harmondsworth, 1967).
Dix, G.: *The Shape of the Liturgy* (Westminster, 1945).
Frend, W. H. C.: *Martyrdom and Persecution in the Early Church* (Oxford, 1965).
Jackson, A. and Neressian, V. N. (tr. and ed.): *The Gnostic Gospels* (London, 2007).
Jones, A. H. M.: *Constantine and the Conversion of Europe* (London, 1972).
Kelly, J. N. D.: *Early Christian Creeds* (Oxford, 1950).
Lietzmann, H.: *The Beginnings of the Christian Church* (London, 1937 ff).
MacMillan, R.: *Christianising the Roman Empire* (New Haven, 1984).
Norris, R. A.: *God and World in Early Christian Theology* (London, 1966).
Williams, R.: *Arius: Heresy and Tradition* (London, 1987).

Chapter 3

Battenhouse, R. W. (ed.): *A Companion to the Study of St. Augustine* (1955).

Brown, P.: *Religion and Society in the Age of Augustine* (London, 1972.

Burnaby, J.: *Amor Dei: A Study of the Religion of St. Augustine* (Norwich, 1991).

Chadwick, H.: *The Early Church* (Harmondsworth, 1967).

Dill, S.: *Roman Society in the Last Century of the Western Empire* (1899).

Fitzgerald, A. D. (ed.): *Augustine through the Ages: An Encyclopaedia* (Cambridge 1999).

Grant, R. M.: *Augustus to Constantine: The Thrust of the Christian Movement in the Roman World* (New York, 1970).

Marcus, R. A.: *Secularism: History and Society in the Theology of St. Augustine* (Cambridge, 1970).

Marcus, R. A.: *Christianity in the Roman World* (London, 1974).

O'Mara, J. J.: *The Young Augustine* (1954).

Przywara, E.: *Augustinus: Die Gestalt abs Gefuge* (Leipzig, 1934).

Chapter 4

Chapman, J.: *St. Benedict and the Sixth Century* (London, 1929).

Fry, T.: *The Rule of St. Benedict* (Collegeville, 1981).

Hamilton, B.: *Religion in the Medieval West* (London, 1981).

Hinnebusch, W. A.: *The History of the Dominican Order to 1500* (Staten Island, 1973).

Hunt, N.: *Cluniac Monasticism in the Central Middle Ages* (London, 1971).

Knowles, D.: *The Monastic Order in England* (Cambridge, 1963).

Lawrence, C. H.: *Medieval Monasticism* (London, 1984).

Leyser, H.: *Hermits and the New Monasticism* (London, 1984).

Moorman, J. R. H.: *A History of the Franciscan Order* (Oxford, 1968).

Southern, R. W.: *Western Society and the Church in the Middle Ages* (Harmondsworth, 1970).

Chapter 5

Brooks, N.: *The Early History of the Church of Canterbury* (Leicester, 1984).

Chadwick, N. K. et al.: *Studies in the Early British Church* (Cambridge, 1958).

Gameson, R. (ed.): *St. Augustine and the Conversion of England* (Stroud, 1999).

Hanson, R. P. C.: *St. Patrick: His Origins and Career* (Oxford, 1968).

MacQuarrie, A.: *Iona Through The Ages* (Breacachadh Castle, 1983).
Markus, A. R.: *Gregory the Great and his World* (Cambridge, 1997).
Mayr—Harting, H.: *The Coming of Christianity to Anglo-Saxon England* (London, 1972).
Meek, D. E.: *The Quest for Celtic Christianity* (Edinburgh, 2000).
Stenton, F. M.: *Anglo-Saxon England* (Oxford, 1971).
Thompson, A. H. (ed.): *Bede: His Life, Times and Writings* (Oxford, 1935).

Chapter 6

Barraclough, G.: *The Medieval Papacy* (London, 1968).
Cook, M. A.: *Muhammad* (Oxford, 1983).
Daniel, N.: *The Arabs and Medieval Europe* (London, 1979).
Fichtenau, H.: *The Carolingian Empire* (Oxford, 1957).
Heer, F.: *Der Heilge Romische Reich* (Bern, 1967).
McKitterick, R.: *The Frankish Church and the Carolingian Reforms 789-895* (London, 1977).
Ullmann, W.: *The Carolingian Renaissance and the Idea of Kingship* (London, 1969).
Ullmann, W.: *A Short History of the Papacy in the Middle Ages* (London, 1972).
Wallace-Hadrill, J. M.: *The Frankish Church* (Oxford, 1983).
Wallach, L.: *Alcuin and Chalemagne: Studies in Carolingian History and Literature* (Ithaca, New York, 1959).

Chapter 7

Barber, C.: *Figures and Likeness: On the Limits of Representation in Byzantine Iconoclasm* (Oxford, 2002).
Chadwick, H.: *East and West: The Making of a Rift in the Church* (Oxford, 2003).
Gero, S.: *Byzantine Iconoclasm during the reign of Leo III* (Subsidia, 1973).
Hussey, J. M.: *The Orthodox Church in the Byzantine Empire* (Oxford, 1986).
Mark, R. and Cakmak, A. S.: *Hagia Sophia from the Age of Justinian to the Present* (Cambridge, 1992).
Michel, A.: *Humbert und Kerullanos* (Paderborn, 1930).
Michel, A.: *Die Kaisernacht in de Ostkirche* (Darmstadt, 1959).
Runciman, J. C. S.: *The Eastern Schism* (Oxford, 1955).
Swift, E. H.: *Hagia Sophia* (New York, 1940).
Ware, K. T.: *The Orthodox Church* (London, 1963).

Chapter 8

Barraclough, G.: *The Medieval Papacy* (London, 1968).
Chenu, M-D.: *Introduction a l'Etude de Saint Thomas* (Montreal, 1950).
Clark, M. T. (ed.): *An Aquinas Reader* (London, 1972).
Cowdrey, H. E. J.: *Pope Gregory VII* (Oxford 1998).
Hamilton, B.: *Religion in the Medieval West* (London, 1986).
Lawrence, C. H.: *Medieval Monasticism* (London 1984).
Morris, C.: *The Papal Monarchy: The Western Church, 1050-1250* (Oxford, 1989).
Robinson, I. S.: *Authority and Resistance in the Investiture Contest* (Manchester 1978).
Robinson, I. S.: *Henry IV of Germany 1056-1106* (Cambridge, 1999).
Southern, R. W.: *Western Society and the Church in the Middle Ages* (Harmondsworth, 1970).
Tillman, H.: *Pope Innocent III* (Amsterdam, 1980).
Vicente. P.: *The Road to Santiago* (Leon, 1999).

Chapter 9

Barber, M. C. (ed.): *The New Knighthood: A History of the Order of the Temple* (Cambridge, 1994).
Daniel, N.: *The Arabs in Medieval Europe* (London, 1979).
Evans, G. R.: *Bernard of Clairvaux* (Oxford, 2000).
Kedar, B. Z.: *Crusade and Mission: European Approaches to the Muslims* (Princeton 1984).
Lewis, B.: *The Arabs in History* (London 1962).
Mayer, H. E.: *The Crusades* (Oxford, 1988).
Nicholson, H.: *The Knights Hopitaller* (Woodbridge 2001).
Partner, P. D.: *The murdered Magicians: The Templars and their Myth* (Oxford, 1982).
Powell, J. W. (ed.): *Muslims under Latin Rule, 1100-1300* (Princeton, 1990).
Prawer, J.: *The World of the Crusaders* (London, 1972).
Strayer, J. R.: *The Albigensian Crusades* (New York, 1971).

Chapter 10

Baumer, R. (ed.): *Der Konstanzer Konzil* (Darmstadt, 1977).
Chamberlin, R.: *The Bad Popes* (Stroud, 2004).
Kenny, A.: *Wyclif* (Oxford, 1985).
Labande, H.: *Les Palais des Papes et Les Monuments d'Avignon au XIVe Siecle* (Marseilles 1925).

240 Selected Reading List

Lambert, M.: *Medieval Heresy* (Oxford, 2002).

Menarche,S.: *Clement V* (Cambridge 1998).

Moore, R. I.: *The Origins of European Dissent* (Harmondsworth, 1977).

Oakley, F.: *The Conciliarist Tradition: Constitutionalism in the Catholic Church, 1300-1870* (Oxford, 2003).

Richard, J.: *Saint Louis, roi d'une France feodale, soutien de la Terre Sainte* (Paris, 1983).

Smith, J. H: *The Great Schism, 1378* (1970).

Ullmann, W.: *The Origins of the Great Schism* (London, 1948).

Chapter 11

Bossy, J.: *Christianity and the West, 1400-1700* (Oxford, 1985).

Brown, D. A.: *Leonardo: Origins of a Genius* (London 1998).

Diehl, C.: *History of the Byzantine Empire* (Oxford 1945).

Hitti, B. H.: *The History of the Arabs* (Basingstoke, 1964).

MacLagan, M.: *The City of Constantinople* (1968).

Oman, C.: *Art of War in the Middle Ages* (Oxford, 1960).

Pater, R.: *The Renaissance* (New York, 1959).

Penrose, B.: *Travel and Discovery in the Renaissance 1450-1670* (Oxford, 1952).

Runciman, S.: *The Fall of Constantinople* (1965).

Sears, E. (ed.): *The Sistine Ceiling* (Oxford, 2000).

Sherrard, P.: *Byzantium* (Nederland, 1967).

Talbot-Rice, D. *Byzantium—Istanbul* (1965).

Chapter 12

Bainton, R. H.: *The Reformation of the Sixteenth Century* (London, 1953).

Bossy, J.: *Christianity and the West, 1400-1700* (Oxford, 1985).

Cameron, E.: *The European Reformation* (Oxford, 1991).

Chadwick, W. O.: *The Early Reformation on the Continent* (Oxford, 2001).

Dickens, A. G.: *The German Nation and Martin Luther* (London 1974).

Du Bulay, F. R. H.: *Germany in the Late Middle Ages* (1983).

Elton, G. R. (ed.): *The Reformation, 1520-1550'* (Cambridge, 1958).

Elton, G. R.: *Reformation Europe, 1517-1559* (London, 1990).

Greengrass, M.: *The European Reformation, 1500-1618* (London, 1998).

Hopfl, H.: *The Christian Polity of John Calvin* (Cambridge, 1982).

Ozment, S. E.: *The Age of Reform, 1250-1550* (New Haven, 1980).

Potter, G. R.: *Zwingli* (Cambridge, 1976).

Randell, K.: *Luther and the German Reformation* (London 1993).

Scribner, R. W.: *The German Reformation* (London, 1986).

Williams, G. H.: *The Radical Reformation* (Philadelphia, 1962).

The Church 241

Chapter 13

Ayris, P. and Selwyn, D. (eds): *Thomas Cranmer, Churchman and Scholar* (Woodbridge 1993).

Bernard, G.W.: *The King's Reformation: Henry VIII and the Remaking of the English Church.* (Yale UP 2005)

Bindoff, S. T.: *Tudor England* (Harmondsworth, 1952).

Dickens, A. G.: *The English Reformation* (London, 1964).

Duffy, E. and Loades, D. M. (eds): *The Church of Mary Tudor* (Aldershot, 2005).

Elton, G. R.: *Reform and Reformation: England, 1509-1558* (1977).

Guy, J.; *Tudor England* (Oxford, 1988).

Hackett, F.: *Henry the Eighth* (London, 1946).

Haigh, C. (ed.): *The English Reformation Revised* (Cambridge 1987).

Lockyer, R.: *Tudor and Stuart Britain, 1471-1714* (Harlow, 1991).

MacCulloch, D. N. J.: *The Later Reformation in England, 1547-1603* (London, 1990).

Myers, A. R.: *England in the Late Middle Ages* (Harmondsworth, 1952).

Scarisbrick, J. J.: *The Reformation and the English People* (1991).

Smyth, C. H. E.: *Cranmer and the Reformation under Edward VI* (Cambridge, 1926).

Tjernagel, N. S.: *Henry VIII and the Lutherans: A study in Anglo-Lutheran Relations from 1521 to 1547* (St. Louis, 1965).

Voak, N.: *Richard Hooker and Reformed Theology* (Oxford, 2003).

Chapter 14

Belloso, J. M. R.: *Trento: Una Interpretacion Teologica* (Barcelona, 1979).

Delumeau, J.: *Catholicism between Luther and Voltaire* (London 1977).

Dickens, A. G.: *The Counter Reformation* (London, 1989).

Evennett, H. O. (ed.): *The Spirit of the Counter Reformation* (Cambridge, 1968).

Greengrass, M.: *The French Reformation* (London, 1987).

Hsia, R. P-c.: *The World of Catholic Renewal* (Cambridge, 1998).

Huizinga, J.: *Erasmus of Rotterdam* (London, 1952).

Jones, M. D. W.: *The Counter Reformation* (Cambridge 1995).

Mullett, M. A.: *The Catholic Reformation* (London, 1999).

O'Malley, J. W.: *The First Jesuits* (London, 1993).

Randell, K.: *The Catholic and Counter Reformations* (London 1990).

Rassow, P. and Schalk, F. (eds): *Karl V: Der Kaiser und seine Zweit* (Cologne).

Scarisbrick, J. J.: *The Jesuits and the Catholic Reformation* (London, 1988).

242 Selected Reading List

Shannon, A. C.: *The Medieval Inquisition* (Washington, 1983).
von Habsburg, O.: *Charles V* (London, 1970).
Wedgwood, C. V.: *The Thirty Years' War* (London, 1957).

Chapter 15

Bossy, J.: *Christianity and the West, 1400-1700* (Oxford, 1985).
Cragg, G. R.: *The Church in the Age of Reason* (London, 1960).
De Santillana, G.: *The Crime of Galileo* (Chicago, 1955).
Koestler, A.: *The Sleepwalkers* (Basingstoke, 1959).
Kuhn, T. S.: *The Copernican Revolution* (Cambridge, Mass, 1957).
Langford, J. J.: *Galileo, Science and the Church* (New York, 1966).
Norman, E. R.: *Christianity and the World Order* (Oxford, 1979).
O'Donovan, O. M. T.: *Begotten or Made?* (Oxford, 1984).
Ramsay, R. P.: *Ethics at the Edges of Life* (London, 1978).
Redondi, P.: *Galileo Eretico* (London 1988).
Ruse, M.: *Can a Darwinian be a Christian?* (Cambridge 2001).
Singer, C.: *A Short History of Scientific Ideas to 1900* (Oxford, 1959).
Templeton, J. M.: *The Humble Approach: Scientists Discover God* (London, 1981).

Chapter 16

Baker, F.: *A Union Catalogue of the Publications of John and Charles Wesley* (Durham, N. C., 1966).
Davies D. H. M.: *The English Free Churches* (HUL, 1952).
Davies, R. E., Rupp, E. G. and George, A. R. (eds): *A History of the Methodist Church in Great Britain* (1988).
Edwards, M. L.: *John Wesley and the Eighteenth Century: A Study of His Social and Political Influence* (1955).
McBeth, H. L.: *The Baptist Heritage* (Nashville, 1987).
Plumb, J. H.: *England in the Eighteenth Century* (Harmondsworth, 1963).
Pollock, J. C.: *George Whitefield and the Great Awakening* (London, 1973).
Routley, E. R.: *English Religious Dissent* (Cambridge, 1960).
Russell, E.: *The History of Quakerism* (New York, 1943).
Sell, A. P. F.: *Saints: Visible, Orderly, and Catholic: The Congregational Idea of the Church* (Princeton, 1986).
Thompson, D.: *England in the Nineteenth Century* (Harmondsworth, 1963).
Tuttle, R. G.: *John Wesley: His Life and Theology* (Grand Rapids, 1978).
Watson, S.: *The Reign of George III* (Oxford, 1960).
Woodward, L.: *The Age of Reform* (Oxford, 1962).

Chapter 17

Burke. E.: *Reflections on the Revolution in France* (Harmondsworth, 1969).
Cobban, A.: *The Social Interpretation of the French Revolution* (Cambridge, 1964).
Cobban, A.: *A History of Modern France* (3 vols) (Harmondsworth, 1965).
Dansette, A.: *Histoire religieuse de la France contemporaine* (1948).
Delacroix, S.: *La Reorganisation de l'Eglise de France apres la Revolution, 1801-1809* (1962).
Geyl, P.: *Napoleon For and Against* (London, 1964).
Hales, E. E. Y.: *Revolution and Papacy, 1769-1846* (1960).
Hobsbawm, E. J.: *The Age of Capital, 1848-78* (London, 2008).
Kohn, H.: *Nationalism: Its Meaning and History* (Princeton, 1965).
Latourette, K. S.: *Christianity in a Revolutionary Age* (London, 1963).
Lefebvre, G.: *The French Revolution from the Origins to 1793* (London, 1962).
Leslie, R. F.: *The Age of Transformation, 1789-1871* (London, 1964).
McKay, D. and Scott, H. M.: *The Rise of the Great Powers, 1648-1815* (London, 1983).
McManners, J.: *The French Revolution and the Church* (1969).
McManners, J.: *Church and State in France* (1972).
Schama, S.: *Citizens: A Chronicle of the French Revolution* (London, 1989).
Tackett, T.: *Religion, Revolution and Regional Culture in Eighteenth Century France: The Ecclesiastical Oath of 1791* (Princeton, 1986).
Townson, D.: *France in Revolution* (London, 1990).
Walsh, H. H.: *The Concordat of 1801: A Study of the problem of Nationalism in the Relations of Church and State* (New York, 1933).

Chapter 18

Binchy, D. A.: *Church and State in Fascist Italy* (Oxford, 1941).
Blet, P.: *Pius XII and the Second World War* (Hereford, 1999).
Falconi, C.: *Il Silenzio di Pio XII.*
Hasler, A. B.: *Pius IX (1846-1878): Papstiliche Unfehlbarkeit und I. Vatikanische Konzil* (Stuttgart, 1977).
Hobsbawm, E, J.: *Industry and Empire* (London, 1969).
Howard, M.: *The Franco-Prussian War: The German Invasion of France (1870-1)* (London, 1962).
Leslie, R. F.: *The Age of Transformation* (London, 1964).
Manning, H. E.: *The True Story of the Vatican Council* (1877).
O'Connor, E. D. (ed.): *The Dogma of the Immaculate Conception* (Notre Dame, Ind., 1958).

O'Gara, M.: *Triumph in Defeat: Infallibility, Vatican I and the French Minority Bishops* (Washington, 1988).

Pollard, J. F.: *The Vatican and Italian Fascism, 1929-32* (Cambridge, 1985).

Chapter 19

Branca, V. and Rosso-Massinghi, S. (eds): *Angelo Giuseppi Roncalli dal Patriacarto di Venizia alla Cattedra di San Petro* (Florence 1984).

Buhlmann, W.: *The Church of the Future: A Model for the Year 2001* (Slough 1986).

Busch, E.: *Karl Barth* (London, 1976).

Hastings, A. (ed.): *Modern Catholicism: Vatican II and After* (1991).

King, H.: *Christianity* (London 1995).

Lamberigts, M. and Kenis, L. (eds): *Vatican II and its Legacy* (Louvain, 2002).

Newbiggin, L.: *The Other side of 1984* (Geneva, 1983).

Novak, M.: *The Spirit of Democratic Capitalism* (New York, 1982).

Oliver, R. A.: *The Missionary Factor in East Africa* (London, 1952).

Rahner, K.: *The Shape of the Church to Come* (London, 1974).

Robinson, J. A. T.: *Honest to God* (London, 1963).

Robinson, J. A. T. and Edwards, D. L.: *The Honest to God Debate* (London, 1963).

Schall, J. V.: *Liberation Theology in Latin America* (San Francisco, 1982).

Sheehan, T.: *Karl Rahner: The Philosophical Foundations* (Athens, Ohio, 1987).

Templeton, J. M.: *The Humble Approach: Scientists Discover God* (London 1981).

Till, B.: *The Churches' Search for Unity* (Harmondsworth, 1972).

Whitehead, A. N.: *Religion in the Making* (Cambridge 1926).

Chapter 20

Buckley, R.: *The Road to 1997* (Cambridge, 1997).

Cortauld, C.: *The Hong Kong Story* (Oxford, 1997).

Fairweather, E. R. and Hettlinger, R. F.: *Episcopacy and Reunion* (London, 1953).

Harrison, T.: *Florence Tim Oi Li: Much Beloved Daughter* (London, 1985).

Kent, J.: *William Temple* (Cambridge, 1993).

Loades, A.: *Feminist Theology: Voices from the Past* (Oxford, 2001).

Sabourin, L.: *Priesthood: A Comparative Study* (Leiden, 1973).

The Church   245

Snow, P.: *The Fall of Hong Kong: Britain, China and the Japanese Occupation* (Yale, 2004).

Tse, H.: *Sweet Mandarin: The Complete Story of Three Generations of Women and their Journey from East to West* (Basingstoke, 2008).

Welch, A, C.: *Prophet and Priest in Old Israel* (Oxford, 1953).

Welsh, F.: *A History of Hong Kong* (London, 1993).

Witherington, B.: *Women in the Earliest Churches* (Cambridge 1988).

Appendices

Appendix I

THE ROMAN EMPERORS, 30 BC-AD 1453

JULIO-CLAUDIAN DYNASTY

31 BC-AD 14	Augustus
14-37	Tiberius
37-41	Caligula
41-5	Claudius I
54-68	Nero
68	Galba Otho
69	Vitellius
69-79	Vespasian
79-81	Titus
81-96	Domitian
96-8	Nerva
98-117	Trajan
117-38	Hadrian
138-61	Antoninus Pius
161-80	M. Aurelius*
161-9	Lucius Verus*

180-92	Commodus
193	Pertinax
193	Dedius Julianus
193-211	S. Severus
211-17	Caracalla*
211-12	Geta*
217-18	Macrinus
218-22	Heliogabalus
222-35	Alex. Severus
235-8	Maximinius
238	Gordian I
238	Gordian II
238	Balbinus*
238	Pupienus*
238-44	Gordian III
244-9	Philippus
249-51	Decius
251	Hostilianus
251-3	Gallus
253	Aemilianus
253-60	Valerian*
260-8	Gallienus*
268-70	Claudius II
270-5	Aurelian
275-6	Tacitus
276	Florianus
276-82	Probus
282-3	Carus
283-5	Carinus*
283-4	Numerianus*
284-305	Diocletian*
286-305	Maximian*
305-6	Constantius I*
305-10	Galerius*
306-12	Maxentius
308-13	Maxinus
308-24	Licinius (E)
305-37	Constantine I
337-40	Constantine II
337-50	Constans*
337-61	Constantius II*
361-3	Julian

363-4	Jovian
364-75	Valentinian I
364-78	Valens (E)
375-92	Valentinian II*
375-83	Gratian* (W)
379-95	Theodosius I
395-423	Honorius* (W)
395-408	Arcadius (E)
408-50	Theodosius II
421	Constantius III*
425-55	Valentinian III
450-7	Marcian (E)
455	Petronius (W)
455-6	Avitus (W)
457-61	Majorian (W)
457-74	Leo I (E)
461-5	Libius (W)
467-72	Anthemius (W)
472	Olybrius (W)
473-4	Glycerius (W)
474	Leo II (E)
474-5	J. Nepos (W)
474-91	Zeno (E)
475-6	Romulus Augustus (W)
491-518	Anastasius I
518-27	Justin I
527-65	Justinian I
565-78	Justin II
578-82	Tiberius II
582-602	Maurice
602-10	Phocas

HERACLIAN DYNASTY

610-41	Heraclius I
641	Constantine III*
641	Heracleonas*
641-8	Constans II
668-85	Constantine IV
685-95	Justinian II
695-8	Leontius
698-705	Tiberius III
705-11	Justinian III

250   Appendices

711-13	Philippicus
713-15	Anastasius II
716-17	Theodosius III

ISAURIAN DYNASTY

717-41	Leo III
741-75	Constantine V
775-80	Leo IV
780-97	Constantine VI
797-802	Irene
802-11	Nicephorus I
811	Stauracius
811-13	Michael I
813-20	Leo V
820-9	Michael II
829-42	Theophilus
842-67	Michael III

MACEDONIAN DYNASTY

867-86	Basil I
886-912	Leo VI
912-13	Alexander
913-19	Constantine VII
919-44	Romanus I
944-59	Constantine VII
959-63	Romanus II
963	Basil II
963-9	Nicephorus I
969-76	John I
976-1025	Basil II
1025-8	Constantine VIII
1028-34	Romanus III
1034-41	Michael IV
1041-2	Michael V
1042	Zoe and Theodora
1042-55	Constantine IX
1055-6	Theodora
1056-7	Michael VI
1057-9	Isaac I
1059-67	Constantine X
1067-8	Michael VII
1068-71	Romanus IV
1071-8	Michazel VII

1078-81	Nicephorus III

COMNENIAN DYNASTY

1081-1118	Alexius I
1118-43	John II
1143-80	Manuel I
1180-3	Alexius II
1183-5	Andronicus I
1185-95	Isaac II
1195-1203	Alexius III
1203-4	Alexius IV
1204	Alexius V
1204-22	Theodore I
1222-54	John III
1254-8	Theodore II
1258	John IV

PALAEOLOGAN DYNASTY

1258-82	Michael VIII
1282-1328	Andronicus II
1328-41	Andronicus III
1341-76,	
1379-91	John V
1376-9	Andronicus V
[1390	John VII]
1391-1425	Manuel II
1425-48	John VIII
1448-53	Constantine XI

* Joint Emperor; (W) Western Emperor; (E) Eastern Emperor

Appendix II

THE POPES: PATRIARCHS OF ROME

Peter, St, d. AD 64
Linus, St, c.66-c.78
Anacletus, St, c.79-c.91
Clement I, St, c.91-c.101
Evaristus I, St, c.100-c.109
Alexander I, St, c.109-c.116
Sixtus I, St, c.116-c.125
Telesphorus, St, c.125-c.136
Hyginus, St, c.138-c.142
Pius I, St, c.142-c.155
Anicetus, St, c.155-c.166
Soter, St, c.166-c.174
Eleutherius, St, c.174-89
Victor I, St, 189-98
Zephyrinus, St, 198/9-217
Callistus I, St, 217-22
[Hippolytus I, St, 217-35]
Urban I, St, 222-30
Pontian I, St, 230-5
Anterus, St, 235-6
Fabian, St, 236-50
Cornelius, St, 251-3
[Novatian, 251-8]
Lucius I, St, 253-4
Stephen I, St, 254-7
Sixtus II, St, 257-8
Dionysius, St, 260-8
Felix I, St, 269-74
Eutychian, St, 275-83
Gaius, St, 283-96
Marcellinus, St, 296-?304
Marcellus I, St, 306-8
Eusebius, St, 310
Miltiades, St, 311-14
Silvester I, St, 314-35
Mark, St, 336
Julius I, St, 337-52
Liberius, 352-66

[Felix II, St, 355-65]
Damasus I, St, 366-84
[Ursinus, 366-7]
Siricius, St, 384-99
Anastasius I, St, 399-401
Innocent I, St, 401-17
Zosimus, St, 417-18
Boniface I, St, 418-22
Celestine I, St, 422-32
Sixtus III, St, 432-40
Leo I, St, 440-61
Hilarus I, St, 461-8
Simplicius, St, 468-83
Felix III (II), St, 483-92
Gelasius I, St, 492-6
Anastasius II, 496-8
Symmachus, St, 498-514
[Lawrence, 498-9; 501-16]
Hormisdas, St, 514-23
John I, St, 523-6
Felix IV (III), St, 526-30
[Dioscorus, 530]
Boniface II, 530-2
John II, 533-5
Agapitus I, St, 535-6
Silverius, St, 536-7
Vigilius, 537-55
Pelagius I, 556-61
John III, 561-74
Benedict I, 575-9
Pelagius II, 579-90
Gregory I, St, 590-604
Sabinian 604-6
Boniface III, 607
Boniface IV, St, 608-15
Deusdedit (later Adeodatus I) St, 615-18
Boniface V, 619-25
Honorius I, 625-38
Severinus, 640
John IV, 640-2
Theodore I, 642-9
Martin I, St, 649-53

Eugene I, St, 654-7
Vitalian, St, 657-72
Adeodatus II, 672-6
Donus, 678
Agatho, St, 678-81
Leo II, St, 682-3
Benedict II, St, 684-5
John V, 685-6
Conon, 686-7
[Theodore, 687]
[Paschal, 687]
Sergius I, St, 687-701
John VI, 701-5
John VII, 705-7
Sisinnius, 708
Constantine, 708-15
Gregory II, St, 715-31
Gregory III, St, 731-41
Zacharias, St, 741-52
Stephen (II), 752
Stephen II (III), 752-7
Paul I, St, 757-67
[Constantine, 767-8]
[Philip, 768]
Stephen III (IV), 768-72
Hadrian I, 772-95
Leo III, St, 795-816
Stephen IV (V), 816-17
Paschal I, St, 817-24
Eugene II, 824-7
Valentine, 827
Gregory IV, 827-44
[John, 844]
Sergius II, 844-7
Leo IV, St, 847-55
Benedict III, 855-8
[Anastasius Bibliothecarius, 855]
Nicholas I, St, 858-67
Hadrian II, 867-72
John VIII, 872-82
Marinus I, 882-4

The Church

Hadrian III, St, 884-5
Stephen V (VI), 885-91
Formosus, 891-6
Boniface VI, 896
Stephen VI (VII), 896-7
Romanus, 897
Theodore II, 897
John IX, 898-900
Benedict IV, 900-3
Leo V, 903
[Christopher, 903-4]
Sergius III, 904-11
Anastasius III, 911-13
Lando, 913-14
John X, 914-28
Leo VI, 928
Stephen VII (VIII), 928-31
John XI, 931-5
Leo VII, 936-9
Stephen VIII (IX), 939-42
Marinus II, 942-6
Agapitus II, 946-55
John XII, 955-64
Leo VIII, 963-5
[Benedict V, 964]
John XIII, 965-72
Benedict VI, 973-4
[Boniface VII, 974, 984-5]
Benedict VII, 974-83
John XIV, 983-4
John XV, 985-96
Gregory V, 996-9
[John XVI, 997-8]
Silvester II, 999-1003
John XVII, 1003
John XVIII, 1003-9
Sergius IV, 1009-12
Benedict VIII, 1012-24
[Gregory (VI), 1012]
John XIX, 1024-32
Benedict IX, 1032-44, 1045, 1047-8
Silvester III, 1045

Gregory VI, 1045-6
Clement II, 1046-7
Damasus II, 1048
Leo IX, St, 1049-54
Victor II, 1055-7
Stephen IX (X), 1057-8
[Benedict X, 1058-9]
Nicholas II, 1058-61
Alexander II, 1061-73
[Honorius (II), 1061-4]
Gregory VII, St, 1073-85
[Clement III, 1080, 1084-1100]
Victor III, 1086-7
Urban II, 1088-99
Paschal II, 1099-1118
[Theoderic, 1100-1]
[Albert or Adalbert, 1101]
[Silvester IV, 1105-11]
Gelasius II, 1118-19
[Gregory (VIII), 1118-21]
Callistus II, 1119-24
Honorius II, 1124-30
[Celestine (II), 1124]
Innocent II, 1130-43
[Anacletus II, 1130-8]
[Victor IV, 1138]
Celestine II, 1143-4
Lucius II, 1144-5
Eugene III, 1145-53
Anastasius IV, 1153-4
Hadrian IV, 1154-9
Alexander III, 1159-81
[Victor IV, 1159-64]
[Paschal III, 1164-8]
[Callistus (III), 1168-78]
[Innocent (III), 1179-80]
Lucius III, 1181-5
Urban III, 1185-7
Gregory VIII, 1187
Clement III, 1187-91
Celestine III, 1191-8
Innocent III, 1198-1216

The Church 257

Honorius III, 1216-27
Gregory IX, 1227-41
Celestine IV, 1241
Innocent IV, 1243-54
Alexander IV, 1254-61
Urban IV, 1261-4
Clement IV, 1265-8
Gregory X, 1271-6
Innocent V, 1276
Hadrian V, 1276
John XXI, 1276-7
Nicholas III, 1277-80
Martin IV, 1281-5
Honorius IV, 1285-7
Nicholas IV, 1288-92
Celestine V, St Peter, 1294
Boniface VIII, 1294-1303
Benedict IX, 1303-4
Clement V, 1305-14
John XXII, 1316-34
[Nicholas (V), 1328-30]
Benedict XII, 1334-42
Clement VI, 1342-52
Innocent VI, 1352-62
Urban V, 1362-70
Gregory XI, 1370-8
Urban VI, 1378-89
[Clement (VII), 1378-94]
Boniface IX, 1389-1404
[Benedict (XIII), 1394-1417]
Innocent VII, 1404-6
Gregory XII, 1406-15
[Alexander V, 1409-10]
[John (XXIII), 1410-15]
Martin V, 1417-31
[Clement (VIII), 1423-9]
[Benedict (XIV), 1425]
Eugene IV, 1431-47
[Felix V, 1439-49]
Nicholas V, 1447-55
Callistus III, 1455-8
Pius II, 1458-64

258 Appendices

Paul II, 1464-71
Sixtus IV, 1471-84
Innocent VIII, 1484-92
Alexander VI, 1492-1503
Pius III, 1503
Julius II, 1503-13
Leo X, 1513-21
Hadrian VI, 1522-3
Clement VII, 1523-34
Paul III, 1534-9
Julius III, 1550-5
Marcellus II, 1555
Paul IV, 1555-9
Pius IV, 1559-65
Pius V, St, 1566-72
Gregory XIII, 1572-85
Sixtus V, 1585-90
Urban VII, 1590
Gregory XIV, 1590-1
Innocent IX, 1591
Clement VIII, 1592-1605
Leo Xi, 1605
Paul V, 1605-21
Gregory XV, 1621-3
Urban VIII, 1623-44
Innocent X, 1644-55
Alexander VII, 1655-67
Clement IX, 1667-9
Clement X, 1670-6
Innocent XI, 1676-89
Alexander VIII, 1689-91
Innocent XII, 1691-1700
Clement XI, 1700-21
Innocent XIII, 1721-4
Benedict XIII, 1724-30
Clement XII, 1730-40
Benedict XIV, 1740-58
Clement XIII, 1758-69
Clement XIV, 1769-74
Pius VI, 1775-99
Pius VII, 1800-23
Leo XII, 1823-9

Pius VIII, 1829-30
Gregory XVI, 1831-46
Pius IX, 1846-78
Leo XIII, 1878-1903
Pius X, St, 1903-14
Benedict XV, 1914-22
Pius XI, 1922-39
Pius XII, 1939-58
John XXIII, 1958-63
Paul VI, 1963-78
John Paul I, 1978
John Paul II, 1978-2005
Benedict XVI, 2005-2013
Francis, 2013-Present
Source: J. N. D. Kelly, *The Oxford Dictionary of Popes*, Oxford, 1988.

Antipopes in square brackets.

Appendix III

GERMAN EMPERORS, KINGS OF FRANCE AND HOLY ROMAN EMPERORS

Carolingian Dynasty

d741	Charles Martel, Duke of the Franks
741-68	Pepin III, Mayor of Neustria from 752 King Pepin I of the Franks
741-54	Carloman, Mayor of Austrasia
768-814	Charles I the Great (Charlemagne*)
814-40	Louis I the Debonair of Aquitaine*
840-55	Lothair, King of Italy*
855-75	Lewis II, King of Italy*
855-76	Lewis the German of Bavaria, King of Germany
876-82	Lewis the Saxon
875-7	Charles II le Chauve, King of Neustria*
877-9	Louis II, King of France
879-82	Louis III, King of France
882-4	Carloman, King of France
882-5	Charles the Fat*
891-4	Wido of Spoleto*
893-928	Charles III the Simple, King of France
887-99	Arnulf, King of Germany*
896-9	Lambert of Spoleto*
901-5	Lewis, King of Provence*

KINGDOM OF FRANCE

928-54	Louis IV d'Outremer, King of France
954-85	Lothair, King of France
986-7	Louis V, le Faineant, King of France

Capetian Dynasty

987-96	Hugues Capet
996-1031	Robert le Pieux

1031-60	Henri I
1060-1108	Philippe I
1108-37	Louis VI le Gros
1137-80	Louis VII
1180-1223	Philippe-Auguste
1223-6	Louis VIII
1226-70	Louis IX, St.

Saxon Dynasty
918-36   Henry I, the Fowler, King of Germany

HOLY ROMAN EMPIRE
936(62)-73   Otto I,* The Great
973-83   Otto II*
983-1002   Otto III*
1002-24   Henry II*

Salian or Franconian Dynasty
1024-39   Conrad II*
1039-56   Henry III*
1056-1106   Henry IV*
1106-25   Henry V*
1125-37   Lothair II* of Saxony

Hohenstauffen Dynasty
1138-52   Conrad III
1152-90   Frederick I Barbarossa*
[1177-80   Rudolf of Swabia]
[1081-8   Hermann of Luxemburg]
1190-7   Henry VI*
1198-1218   Otto IV* of Brunswick (Guelph)
[1198-1208   Philip of Hohenstaufen]
1211-50   Frederick II*
[1246-50   Henry Raspe of Thuringia]
[1247-56   William of Holland]

KINGDOM OF FRANCE

1270-85	Philippe III le Hardi
1285-1314	Philippe IV le Bel
1314-16	Louis X
1316-22	Philippe V

Valois Dynasty

13228-8	Charles IV
1328-50	Philippe VI
1350-64	Jean Le Bon
1364-80	Charles V le Sage
1380-1422	Charles VI le Simple
1422-61	Charles VII le Bien Aimé
1461-83	Louis XI
1483-98	Charles VIII
1498-1515	Louis XII
1515-47	Francis I
1547-59	Henri II
1559-60	Francis II
1560-74	Charles IX
1574-89	Henri III

Bourbon Dynasty

1589-1610	Henri IV
1610-43	Louis XIII
1643-1715	Louis XIV
1715-74	Louis XV
1774-93	Louis XVI
1793-5	Louis XVII

Napoleonic Empire

1804-15	Napoleon I*

Bourbon Restoration
| | |
1814-24   Louis XVIII
1824-30   Charles X
1830-48   Louis-Philippe

Napoleonic Restoration
1852-70   Napoleon III*

HOLY ROMAN EMPIRE

1250-4   Conrad I
[1257-72   Richard of Cornwall]
[1257-75   Alfonso X of Castile]
1273-91   Rudolf I of Habsburg
1292-8   Adolph of Nassau
1298-1308   Albert I of Habsburg
1308-13   Henry VII* of Luxemburg
1314-47   Lewis IV* of Wittelsbach = Matilda of Habsburg
[1314-30   Frederick the Fair of Habsburg]

1346-78   Charles IV* of Luxemburg
[1349   Gunther of Schwartzburg]
1378-1400   Wenceslas of Luxemburg
1400-10   Rupert of the Palatinate
1410-37   Sigismund* of Luxemburg
[1410-11   Jobst of Moravia]

Habsburg Dynasty
1438-9   Albert II
1440-93   Frederick III

1493-1519   Maximilian I*

1519-56   Charles V*

1556-64   Ferdinand I*
1564-76   Maximilian II*
1576-1612   Rudolf II*

1612-37   Ferdinand II*
1637-57   Ferdinand III*
1658-1705   Leopold I*

1705-11	Joseph I*
1711-40	Charles VI*
1742-5	Charles VII* of Bavaria
1745-65	Francis I* of Lorraine = Maria Theresa, Habsburg
1765-90	Joseph II*

| 1790-2 | Leopold II* |
| 1792-1806 | Francis II* (Francis I) |

Habsburg Emperors of Austria

| 1804-35 | Francis I* |
| 1835-48 | Ferdinand I* |

| 1848-1916 | Francis-Joseph I* |

| 1916-18 | Charles I* |

Hohenzollern Emperors of Germany

1871-88	William I* of Prussia
1888	Frederick III*
1888-1918	William II*

* Crowned Emperors [ ] = anti-Emperors, or unconfirmed electees

Appendix IV

ARCHBISHOPS OF CANTERBURY

1	597	Augustine
2	604	Laurentius
3	619	Mellitus
4	624	Justus
5	627	Honorius
6	655	Deusdedit
7	668	Theodore
8	693	Berhtwald
9	731	Tatwine
10	735	Nothelm
11	740	Cuthbert
12	761	Bregowine
13	765	Jaenbert
14	793	Ethelhard
15	805	Wulfred
16	832	Feologeld
17	833	Ceolnoth
18	870	Ethelred
19	890	Plegmund
20	914	Athelm
21	923	Wulfhelm
22	942	Oda
23	959	Aelfsige
24	959	Brithelm
25	960	Dunstan
26	c.988	Ethelgar
27	990	Sigeric
28	995	Aelfric
29	1005	Alphege
30	1013	Lyfing
31	1020	Ethelnoth
32	1038	Eadsige
33	1051	Robert of Jumieges
34	1052	Stigand
35	1070	Lanfranc
36	1093	Anselm
37	1114	Ralph d'Escures
38	1123	William de Corbeil

39	1139	Theobald
40	1162	Thomas a Becket
41	1174	Richard (of Dover)
42	1184	Baldwin
43	1193	Hubert Walter
44	1207	Stephen Langton
45	1229	Richard le Grant
46	1234	Edmund of Abingdon
47	1245	Boniface of Savoy
48	1273	Robert Kilwardby
49	1279	John Peckham
50	1294	Robert Winchelsey
51	1313	Walter Reynolds
52	1328	Simon Meopham
53	1333	John de Stratford
54	1349	Simon Islip
55	1349	Thomas Bradwardine
56	1366	Simon Langham
57	1368	William Whittlesey
58	1375	Simon Sudbury
59	1381	William Courtenay
60	1396	Thomas Arundel
61	1398	Roger Walden
	1399	Thomas Arundel (restored)
62	1414	Henry Chichele
63	1443	John Stafford
64	1452	John Kempe
65	1454	Thomas Bourchier
66	1486	John Morton
67	1501	Henry Deane
68	1503	William Warham
69	1533	Thomas Cranmer
70	1556	Reginald Pole
71	1559	Matthew Parker
72	1576	Edmund Grindal
73	1583	John Whitgift
74	1604	Richard Bancroft
75	1611	George Abbot
76	1633	William Laud
77	1660	William Juxon
78	1663	Gilbert Sheldon
79	1678	William Sancroft

80	1691	John Tillotson
81	1695	Thomas Tenison
82	1716	William Wake
83	1737	John Potter
84	1747	Thomas Herring
85	1757	Matthew Hutton
86	1758	Thomas Secker
87	1768	Frederick Cornwallis
88	1783	John Moore
89	1805	Charles Manners-Sutton
90	1828	William Howley
91	1848	John Bird Summer
92	1862	Charles Thomas Longley
93	1868	Archibald Campbell Tait
94	1883	Edward White Benson
95	1896	Frederick Temple
96	1903	Randall Thomas Davidson
97	1928	William Cosmo Gordon Lang
98	1942	William Temple
99	1945	Geoffrey Francis Fisher
100	1961	Arthur Michael Ramsey
101	1974	Frederick Donald Coggan
102	1980	Robert Alexander Kennedy Runcie
103	1991	George Leonard Carey
104	2002	Rowan Douglas Williams
105	2013	Justin Welby

Source: Archbishop of Canterbury's Web site

268   Appendices

Appendix V

MONARCHS OF ENGLAND
after the act of Union in 1707 the king or queen is more correctly called
the monarch of Great Britain

Monarch	Reign
HOUSE OF WESSEX	
Egbert	802-839
Aethelbald	855-860
Aethelbert	860-866
Aethelred	866-871
Alfred the Great	871-899
Edward the Elder	899-925
Athelstan	925-940
Edmund the Magnificent	940-946
Eadred	946-955
Eadwig (Edwy) All-Fair	955-959
Edgar the Peaceable	959-975
Edward the Martyr	975-978
Æthelred II (Ethelred the Unready	979-1013 and 1014-1016
Edmund II (Ironside)	1016
DANISH	
Svein Forkbeard	1014
Cnut (Canute)	1016-1035
Harold I	1035-1040
Hardicnut	1040-1042
SAXONS	
Edward (the Confessor)	1042-1066
Harold II	1066
NORMANS	
William I	1066-1087
William II	1087-1100
Henry I	1100-1135
Stephen	1135-1154
Empress Matilda (Queen Maud)	1141
PLANTAGENETS	
Henry II	1154-1189
Richard I	1189-1199

John		1199-1216
Henry III		1216-1272
Edward I		1272-1307
Edward II		1307-1327
Edward III		1327-1377
Richard II		1377-1399
	HOUSE OF LANCASTER	
Henry IV		1399-1413
Henry V		1413-1422
Henry VI		1422-1461
	HOUSE OF YORK	
Edward IV		1461-1483
Edward V		1483
Richard III		1483-1485
	TUDORS	
Henry VII		1485-1509
Henry VIII		1509-1547
Edward VI		1547-1553
Jane Grey		1553
Mary I		1553-1558
Elizabeth I		1558-1603
	STUARTS	
James I		1603-1625
Charles I		1625-1649
	COMMONWEALTH	
Oliver Cromwell		1649-1658
Richard Cromwell		1658-1659
	STUARTS (restored)	
Charles II		1660-1685
James II		1685-1688
William III		1689-1702
Mary II		1689-1694
Anne		1702-1714
	HOUSE OF HANOVER	
George I		1714-1727
George II		1727-1760
George III		1760-1820
George IV		1820-1830
William IV		1830-1837
Victoria		1837-1901

SAXE-COBURG-GOTHA

Edward VII 1901-1910

WINDSOR

George V 1910-1936
Edward VIII 1936-1936
George VI 1936-1952
Elizabeth II 1952 - present

Index

A

Aachen 45, 64
Abbot Gregory 53
Abbot Hugh 73
Abelard, Peter 79
abortion 167, 228
Act of Settlement (1559) 141, 143, 171
Act of Succession 138
Act of Supremacy 138
Adam 36-7, 207, 225
Adrian VI (pope) 147
age of dogma and scholasticism 79
Age of Reason 159, 161-2, 242
aggiornamento 210
Aidan, St 56-7
Akinola, Peter 230
Alaric (king of Visigoths) 32, 38
Alban 27, 51
Albertus Magnus, St 80
Albigensians 49
Alcuin (missionary) 57, 63-4, 238
Aldersgate Street 168-9, 171
Alexander VI (pope) 150, 258

Alexandria 27, 30, 61, 68
Alexius I Comnenus 86
Alfred the Great 57
Ambrose of Milan 34
Anabaptist 127
Angles 52-3
Anglican Church *see* Church of England
Anglican Communion 131, 221, 226-7, 230, 234
Anglican Consultative Committee 226
Anglicanism 201, 224, 228
Anglo-Saxon Chronicle 54
Anglo-Spanish Treaty of 1499 132
annates 137
Anne (queen) 138, 173
Anne of Cleves 139
Anselm (Lombardian cleric) 79, 153, 265
Antioch 27, 68, 88
Apennines 41
Apocalypse of Peter 14
Apologia Ecclesiae Anglicanae (Jewel) 141

271

Apologists 25, 38
Apostolic Fathers 25
apotheosis 234
Appeal to the German Nobility (Luther) 125
Appeals Act 138
Aquinas, Thomas 9, 80, 83, 153, 155, 158, 223, 228, 239
Aristotle 80, 155
Arius (theologian) 30, 236
Armenia 109
Artemidoras (presbytera) 225
Arthur (prince of Wales) 131-2, 135, 138
Asia Minor 20, 30, 62, 87-90, 109-10
assumption of Mary 200 *see also* Virgin Mary
astronomy 92, 156
Athanasius (bishop of Alexandria) 30
Athenagoras (patriarch) 216
Athens 114, 244
Athos, Mt 110
Augustine, St, of Hippo 32, 34-40, 49, 54-7, 77, 153, 200, 237
Ausculto Fili (Boniface) 98
Austen, Jane 194
Auvergne 85
Avignon 96, 99-102, 104, 239

B

Babylonish captivity 96, 125
Bacon, Francis 160
Bainton, Roland 118
Baldwin (Godfrey's brother) 88
baptism 34-5, 82, 127, 168, 173, 212
Barberini, Maffeo 158
Barbican Centre 168
Barclay, William 17
Barth, Karl 210, 244
Basil (emperor) 68
Basil of Caesarea 31

Basilica Church of San Lorenzo 33
Basilica of Santa Maria Sopra Minerva 154
Basilica of St John Lateran 81, 100
Battle of Lechfield 75
Battle of Manzikert 109
Battle of Milvian Bridge 23, 28
Beagle 162
Becket, Thomas à 140
Bede (historian) 53, 55, 57
Beethoven, Ludwig van 190
Bellarmine, Robert 158
Benedetti (count) 195
Benedict, St 42-5, 50
Benedict, St, rule of 43-5, 48
Benedict IX (pope) 98, 255, 257
Benedict XI (pope) 95
Benedict XIII (pope) 101-2, 258
Benedict XV (pope) 203, 259
Benedict XVI (pope) 227, 259
Bentham, Jeremy 163
Bergamo 206, 217
Bernard of Clairvaux 79, 89, 239
Bernini (Italian sculptor and architect) 21, 122, 208, 210
Bertha (Ethelbert's wife) 54, 56, 224
Betjeman, John 130
biblical criticism 79, 114
Bill of Rights 173
Bindoff, S. T. 9, 132, 241
Bischofshof 118, 129
Bismarck, Otto von 192, 195-6, 203
Black Christmas 218
Black Death 104, 110
Black Friars *see* Dominican Order
Blake, William 180
Blitz of 1940 168
Bohemund of Apulia 88
Böhler, Peter 171
Boleyn, Anne 134-5, 137-9, 173
Bologna 80, 189
Bonaparte, Napoleon 182-3, 185, 189-93, 195-8, 202, 243
Bonhoeffer, Dietrich 204, 209

The Church 273

Boniface, St 57, 63
Boniface VIII 47, 82-3, 97, 211, 257
Book of Common Prayer 173
Book of Kells 56
Booth, William 225
Boris I (king) 70
Bosphorus 90, 106, 108
Brahe, Tycho 156
Bramante, Donato 21, 122
Briand, Aristide 192, 202
Brief History of Time, A (Hawking) 166
Britain 12, 27, 51-2, 55-6, 131, 169, 179-80, 218, 241-2, 245
Brown, Antoinette 225
Brunelleschi's Dome 112
Bruno, St 46
Bultmann, Rudolph 165
Burgundy 46, 74, 81, 118, 146
Burke, Edmund 185
Butterfield, Herbert 155, 164
Byzantium 30, 61, 63, 67, 70, 86-7, 89, 103, 106, 109-10, 240

C

Caesar Augustus 14-15
Caesarea Philippi 13, 15, 234
Cajetan (papal legate) 124
Caligula (emperor) 247
Calixtus II (pope) 78
Calvin, John 128, 240
Calvinism 128
Canisius, Peter 150
canon 31 *see also* New Testament; Old Testament
Canossa 72, 78-9, 82-4, 86
Canterbury 55-6, 80, 82, 139-40, 237
Canterbury Cathedral 216
Cape of Good Hope 115
Carafa *see* Paul IV
Cardinal Cesarini 110
Cardinal Contarini 148, 151

Cardinal Humbert 67, 71, 238
Cardinal Montini *see* Paul VI (pope)
Cardinal Ratzinger *see* Benedict XVI (pope)
Cardinal Wolsey 133, 135
Carlstadt (radical preacher) 126, 188
Carmelite friars 49
Carthage 31, 61
Carthusian Order 46
Cassino 43 *see also* Monte Cassino
Castel de San Angelo 78, 147
Castel Gondolfo 204
Castle Church of Wittenberg 123
Cathari *see* Albigensians
Cathedral at Amiens 81
Cathedral of Notre Dame 181, 188
Cathedral of Santa Maria de Fiore 112
Cathedral of St Paul 168
Cathedral of St Sophia 67, 107-8, 110
Catherine of Aragon 131, 140, 147
Catherine of Siena 100, 224
Catholic Church *see* church
Catholic Institute for International Relations 215
Catholic Reformation 49, 143, 150, 158, 241
Catholicism 46, 89, 123, 127, 164, 173, 190, 203-4, 208, 212, 215-16, 227
Cavour, Camillo 197-8
Celestine V (pope) 99
celibacy 71, 76, 83, 176
Central Italy 41, 146, 197-8
Chardin, Teilhard de 213
Charlemagne *see* Charles V (holy Roman emperor)
Charles I (king) 172, 260, 264, 269
Charles II (king) 172, 260, 269
Charles IV (emperor) 100, 262-3
Charles V (holy Roman emperor) 59-60, 63-5, 68-9, 73-4, 123, 127, 146-8, 151, 190-1

Chartreux 46
chastity 44, 47-8
Chaucer, G. 122, 142
chemistry 160
chi-rho 24
Chinese Cultural Revolution 220
Chirst *see* Jesus
Christian monasticism *see*
    monasticism
Christmas Day 59, 61, 218
Chrysostom, John 225
church (*see also* Eastern Church;
    Western Church) 62, 79, 119,
    124, 129, 133, 145, 150-1, 166,
    181, 183, 199, 203-4, 206, 213-
    14
  fortunes of 23, 27, 130, 147, 169
  four notes of 21
  invisible 36
  nature of 20, 22
  universal 61
  visible 36, 242
Church of England 53, 57, 129, 131,
    138-9, 141-3, 170-1, 173-4, 176,
    178-80, 216-17, 219-22, 224-30,
    234
Church of Our Lady 117
Church of Rome 36, 147, 149, 151,
    161, 189, 196
Church of Santa Croce 159
Church of St Francis 112
Church of St Sernin 80
Church of St Sophia 67
Church of the Holy Sepulchre 47
Churchill, Winston 219
Cisneros, Xavier 145
Cistercians 46, 81, 96
Cîteaux 46
Civil Constitution of the Clergy 187,
    190
civil rights 171, 186, 226
Clarendon Code 172
Clemenceau, Georges 192, 202
Clement of Alexandria 26, 225
Clement III (pope) 77, 256

Clement V (pope) 47, 96, 99, 240,
    257
Clement VI (pope) 100, 257
Clement VII (pope) 101, 114, 134,
    146-7, 156
clerical marriage 78
Clericis Laicos (Boniface) 98
Clermont 85, 87, 93-4
Cluniacs 45-6, 96
Coke, Thomas 176
cold war 111, 205, 208
Colet, John 141
College of Cardinals 75, 95
Colonna, Odo *see* Martin V (pope)
Colonna, Sciarra 98
Colonna family 97-8
Columba 56
Combes, Emile 192, 202
communication, art of 12
Communion 73, 124, 128, 131, 176,
    201, 212, 216, 220-1, 226-7, 230,
    234
communism 28, 204-5, 209, 216
Compostela 80, 94
Conciliar Movement 80, 104
Concordat 118, 189-90, 192, 204,
    243
Concordat of 1801 189-90, 192
Concordat of Worms 78, 118
Conrad III 89, 261
Constantine (emperor) 23-5, 28-31,
    33, 38, 41, 60, 62-4, 67-8, 107-11,
    113, 116
Constantine XI Palaeologus 107,
    109
Constantinople 32, 62-3, 67-71, 88,
    90, 107-11, 113, 115, 224, 240
Constantius (coemperor) 23-4,
    248
constitutionalism 197, 199, 240
Contrat Social (Rosseau) 164
Copernicus, Nicholas 115, 155-8
Coptic tradition *see* Monophysite
Cornelius (pope) 252

The Church 275

Cosimo II (Tuscany's grand duke) 158
Council of Carthage 31
Council of Chalcedon 69, 225
Council of Constance 102, 104, 145
Council of Constantinople 70
Council of Hippo 31
Council of Laodicea 225
Council of Nicaea 30
Council of Pisa 101-2
Council of Rome 31
Council of the Marches 131
Council of Trent 143, 148-50
Council of Vatican:
   I 201-2, 205, 210, 212
   II 205, 210, 212, 214-17, 244
counterreformation 149
Couthon (radical politician) 185
Cranmer, Thomas 136-41, 241, 266
Cromwell, Oliver 143, 168, 269
Cromwell, Thomas 136
Crusade: First 78, 87
Crusade: Second 89
Crusade: Third 90
Crusade: Fourth 90, 109
Crusade: Children's 91
Crusade: People's 88
Cuban Missile Crisis of 1962 214
Curia 101, 147, 200, 204, 213-15, 227-8
Cyprus 110

D

Damascus 62
Damasus (pope) 31, 253
Dan 15
Dante (Italian poet) 98, 100, 112, 207
Danton (radical politician) 188
Danube 227
Darwin, Charles 162-4
Dauphiné Alps 46
David, Jacques-Louis 182
Davies, Norman 59, 64

Day of Infamy 219
De Civitate Dei (Augustine) 38
De Revolutionibus Orbium Coelistium (Copernicus) 155, 158
Dead Sea Scrolls 14
December Solstice 55
Decline and Fall of the Roman Empire, The (Gibbon) 164
Dei Filius 201
Dei Verbum 212
Deira 52-3
deists 164
Descartes, René 160
Dialogo del Due Massimi Sistemi del Mundo (Galileo) 158
Dialogues Concerning Two New Sciences (Galileo) 159
Diaz, Bartholomew 115
Dictatus Papae (Gregory VII) 77, 82
Dignitatis Humanae 212
Diocletian (emperor) 28, 51
Divine Comedy (Dante) 112
Divine Office 44, 46
Dollinger, J. 201
Domesday Survey 48
Dominican Order 48, 135, 237
Donatello (Florentine sculptor and painter) 112
Donation of Constantine 63, 113
Donation of Pepin 63
Donatists 35-6
Duc of Gramont 196
Duke of Aquitaine 62
Duns Scotus, Blessed 80, 199
dynamics, theory of 159

E

Easter 57, 71, 131
Eastern Church 27, 61, 70
Eck, Jan van 119, 124
economic determinism 163
Eddy, Mary Baker 226
Edessa 88-9
Edict of Milan 28, 33, 202

276 Index

Edict of Nantes 185
Edict of Worms 120
Edward VI 139, 188
Edwin (king of Northumbria) 56
Egypt 15, 90
Eiffel Tower 181, 193
Einstein, Albert 160, 166
Elizabeth I (queen) 138-9, 141, 143, 171
Elizabeth II (queen) 216
English Church see Church of England
English Civil War 143, 172
Enlightenment 161, 193, 199
Eostre 55
Epiktas (presbytis) 225
episcopal collegiality 212
Erasmus, Desiderius 114, 120, 125, 142, 145
Eternal City 38, 52
Ethelberga (Ethelbert's daughter) 56
Ethelbert (king of Gaul) 54-6, 224
European Renaissance see Renaissance
European Union 208, 216
Eusebius (Constantine's biographer) 19, 24
euthanasia 167, 228
Eve 36, 225
Exodus 15

F

Far East 115
Farnese, Alexander 147
Fascism 209, 244
female ordination 226-8
feminist movement 226
Ferdinand (king of Spain) 132, 145
final judgement 207
Fisher, Geoffrey 216, 220
Fisher of Rochester 138
Fleming, Alexander 162

Fouché 184, 188
Fox, George 173
France 47, 49, 74, 128-9, 146, 179, 182-6, 188-90, 192-3, 195, 197-8, 200, 202, 240, 243
Francis I 146, 148, 151
Francis II 190-1
Francis of Assisi 48
Franciscan Order 48, 237
Franco-Prussian War 201-2, 243
Frederick I 79, 90
Frederick II 91, 261
Frederick the Wise 124-5
French Revolution 183, 243

G

Galileo 115, 153-61, 166-7, 242
Gama, Vasco da 115
Garibaldi, Giuseppe 197-8
Gaudium et Spes 211
Gaul 24, 27, 54, 61-2
Gay and Lesbian Movement 229
German Diet 118-19, 127
Germany 74, 117, 120, 126-8, 146-7, 196, 201-4
Gerson, Jean 102
Gibbon, E. 28, 33, 100, 108, 164
Giberti of Verona 146, 151
Gibraltar 61
Giles of Viterbo 147
Giustiniani (lieutenant) 108-9, 115
Gnostic Gospels 14, 236
Gnosticism 25
Godfrey of Bouillon 88-9
Golden Horn 108
good works 121, 149
Got, Bertrand de 95, 105
grace, theology of 36
grand design, theory of 75, 161
gravitation, universal law of 160
Gregory I (pope) 53-6, 76
Gregory II (pope) 69, 254
Gregory VII (pope) 72, 75, 81-2, 85-6, 98, 239

The Church

Gregory XI (pope)   100, 257
Gregory XII (pope)   101-2, 257
Gregory XIII (pope)   151, 258
Grey, Jane   140, 269
Grey Friars *see* Franciscan Order
Gutiérrez, Gustavo   164, 215
Guzman, Dominic de   48

H

Habsburg Empire   197
Hadrian's Wall   51
Hall, Ronald   9, 219-21, 226, 231
Hampson, Michael   229
Hampton Court Conference   172
Harvey, William   162
Hattersley, Roy   179
Hawking, Stephen   166
Helena (Constantine's mother)   28, 224
heliocentricity   154, 160
Hella (Angle-land's king)   53
Helwys, Thomas   173
Henrician Reformation   141
Henry the Navigator   115
Henry II   82, 261, 268
Henry III   75, 261, 269
Henry IV   72, 75-6, 82, 86, 239
Henry V   78, 261, 269
Henry VII   132, 263, 269
Henry VIII   47, 80, 133, 135, 147, 241
heresy   21, 25, 36, 66, 70, 154-5
Hermon, Mt   15
Herod the Great   14-15, 91
High Middle Ages   79, 83
High Renaissance   114 *see also* Renaissance
Hildebrand *see* Gregory VII (pope)
Hill, Jonathan   167
Hippo   35, 39, 61
Historia e Dimostrazioni Intorno Alle Macchie (Galileo)   158
Hitchens, Christopher   31, 230
Hitler, Adolf   204

Hobbes, Thomas   163
Holy Club *see* Methodist movement
Holy Land *see* Jerusalem
Holy Office of the Inquisition   154
   see also Papal Inquisition
Holy Roman Empire   104, 118
Holy Sepulchre   47, 86-7, 89
Holy Spirit   17-18, 70, 127, 174, 176, 201, 208, 210, 222
Holy Trinity   31, 37, 39
Holy Truth   212
Homo sapiens   162
homosexuality   228-9
Hong Kong   218-21, 226, 244-5
Honorius (emperor)   38, 249, 253, 256, 265
Hooker, Richard   141, 241
Humanae Vitae   166, 214
Humber   54
Hume, David   165
Hundred Years' War   100
Huss, Jan   103, 125
Hutten, Ulrich von   126

I

iconoclasm   69, 238
iconodules   70
Ignatius (church father)   19, 27, 222
Ile de la Cité   181
Immaculate Conception   199-200, 243
Index of Forbidden Books   151, 158, 164
indulgences   87, 122-4, 149-50, 174
Industrial Revolution   161, 177
Ineffabilis Deus   199-200
Innocent III (pope)   48, 73, 81, 83, 91, 98, 239
inquisition *see* Papal Inquisition
Institute of the Christian Religion 128
Iona   56-7, 238
Ireneus (bishop of Lyons)   14

Isabella (queen of Spain) 132, 145
Islam 46, 61-2, 68, 90, 115, 217
Israelites 15
Istanbul 106, 240
Ituraea 14
Ivan III 111

J

Jacobins 184
Janissaries 107
Jenner, Edward 162
Jerome (church doctor) 31, 114,
    134, 149
Jerusalem 14, 17-19, 22, 25, 28, 47,
    86-91, 93
Jesus Christ: life of 25
Jesus Christ: Spirit of 16, 120, 145
Jesus Christ: spiritual pre-eminence
    of 38
Jewel, John 141
Jewish Diaspora 19
jihad 61
John, Jeffrey 230
John of the Cross 151
John Paul II (pope) 167, 205, 215-
    16, 227, 259
John XII (pope) 75, 255
John XXIII (pope) 102, 206-8, 210,
    213, 216-17, 244, 259
Jordan, river 15, 19
Joseph II (emperor) 191, 264
Josephine (Napoleon's first wife)
    182, 191
Josephus 15
Josiah (king of Judah) 136
Journey of a Soul (John XXIII) 208
Julius II (pope) 114, 133-4, 138, 150,
    258
Julius III (pope) 150, 258
Justin Martyr of Palestine 26-7
Justinian (emperor) 64, 67-8, 107,
    238, 249

K

Kairuan 61
Kant, Emmanuel 165
Kent 52, 54, 57, 224, 244
Kepler, John 115, 156-7
Kingswood School 178
Knights Hospitallers 47, 89-90
Knights Templars 47, 89-90, 97, 99,
    239
Knox, John 128
Koestler, Arthur 159
Kolbe, Maximilian 204, 209
Koran 61
Kossovo 110
kulturkampf 192, 202
Küng, Hans 211

L

la Cruzada *see under* Crusade
Ladislav (king of Poland) 110
Lahn River 194
Lambeth Conference:
    1948 221
    1968 226
    1978 227
    1998 230
Lamennais, Hugues Félicité Robert
    de 164
Langton, Stephen 82, 266
Lateran Council: Fourth 82
Lateran Council: Fifth 145
Lateran Treaties of 1929 204
Law of Guarantees 198
Law of Separation (1905) 192, 202
lay investiture 77-9
League of Cognac 146
League of Nations 203-4 *see also*
    United Nations
legions 23, 51-2, 224
Lent 57
Leo 59-61, 64, 67, 69, 71, 75, 114,
    123, 146, 202, 238
Leo III (emperor) 69

Leo III (pope) 59
Leo IX (pope) 67, 71, 75, 256
Leo X (pope) 114, 123, 146, 258
Leo XIII (pope) 202, 259
Leonardo *see* Vinci, Leonardo da
Li Tim-Oi, Florence 220-1, 226-7, 231
liberalism 197, 199-201
liberation theology 164, 215, 244
Liberty of the Christian Man, The (Luther) 125
Licinius (Constantine's coruler) 28-9, 248
liebfraumilch 117, 129
life, sanctity of 214, 228
Lindisfarne Gospels 56-7
Linnaeus, Carl 162
Locke, John 163
Lombard, Peter 82
Lombardy 33, 75, 198
Louis VII 89, 261
Louis IX 91, 97, 261
Louis XIV 161, 185, 262
Louis XVI 183, 193, 262
Loyola, Ignatius 150-1
Lumen Gentium 211
Luther, Martin 118-29, 133, 148-9, 154, 156, 169-71, 240-1
Lutheranism 127-8, 146

M

Macao 219-20
Machiavelli, Niccolò 114, 159
McIlroy, David 32
MAD (mutual assured destruction) 208
Manichaeism 37
Marie-Antoinette 184
Marie-Louise 191
Marsilius of Padua 136
Martel, Charles 62-3, 260
Martin V (pope) 103, 257
Marx, Karl 163
Mary (Catholic queen) 9, 139, 141-2

Mary Magdalene 223
mass 36, 45, 59, 82, 212, 214-15, 224, 227, 242
Matilda (countess of Tuscany) 72-3, 263
Maxentius (Constantine's rival) 23-5, 248
Maximilian (emperor) 123, 133
Mayflower 172
Mazzini, Giuseppe 197
Medieval Classicism 80
Melanchton, Phillip 127
Methodist Church of Great Britain 179
Methodist movement 170, 174, 176-80, 234
Methodist New Connexion 179
Metternich (prince) 191, 197
Michael I Cerularius 67, 71
Michelangelo (Italian sculptor, painter, and architect) 21, 114, 123, 159, 207
Middle East 30, 90, 92
Middle Franks *see* Burgundy
Middle Way 171
Middles Ages 41
Milan's Academy 34
Mill, John Stuart 163
Milton, John 169
Milvian Bridge 24, 31
Mohammed 61, 63
Mohammed II 107
Molay, Jacques de 47, 99
monastic orders 41, 48-9, 71
monasticism 29, 41-6, 48, 50, 54, 56-7, 69
Monica (Augustine's mother) 34, 224
Monophysite 68
Monte Cassino 41, 43-5, 50
More, Thomas 114, 138
Mother Teresa 216
Muntzer, Thomas 126, 161
Museum of London 169
Mussolini, Benito 203

N

Nag Hammadi 14
Nag Hammadi Gospels 223
Naples 43, 99, 118, 198
Napoleon III 195-6, 263
Nash, Beau 176, 194
natural law 80, 160, 228
Nazism 204, 209
Nero (emperor) 20
New Testament 13, 17, 19-20, 31, 124, 222, 229
Newton, Isaac 159-60
Nicea 30-1, 69, 88, 90, 110
Nicene Creed 30-1
Nicholas I (pope) 70, 74, 254
Nicholas V (pope) 111, 113-14, 257
Ninety-Five Theses (Luther) 123
Nogaret, William de 98
nonconformity 174, 180, 192
North Africa 34-5, 40, 91
Northern Italy 24, 98, 109, 111, 113, 146, 148, 198
Nursia 42

O

obedience 44, 47-8, 81, 99
Obedience of a Christian Man, The (Tyndale) 135
Of the Laws of Ecclesiastical Polity (Hooker) 141
Old Testament 69, 97, 136, 221, 229
Old World 115
On the Babylonian Captivity of the Church (Luther) 125
Ordinatio Sacerdotalis 227
Organic Articles 190
Origen of Alexandria 26
Origin of Species (Darwin) 162, 164
original sin 37, 39, 120, 200, 207
Orthodox faith 67, 70, 90, 107, 110-11, 192
Oswald (king of Northumbria) 56-7
Otto I (emperor) 74, 261

Otto II (emperor) 75, 261
Otto IV (emperor) 81, 261
Ottomans 110, 113, 192
Oxford Dictionary of the Christian Church, The 81

P

Pacem in Terris 213
Padua 80
Palais de Justice 181
Palestine 88-90
Paley, William 161
Palmieri (writer) 112
papal infallibility 201, 215
Papal Inquisition 48, 151, 154
Papal States 63, 97, 100, 146, 191-2, 197-8
Papal Volunteers to Latin America 215
Paris Peace Conference 203
Parish Church of St Laurence 130
Parthenon of the Florentines 159
Pascal, Blaise 164
Pastor Aeternus 201
Patricius (Augustine's father) 34
Paul III (pope) 138, 147, 150
Paul IV (pope) 150-1, 258
Paul V (pope) 158, 258
Paul VI (pope) 166, 211, 214, 216, 259
Paulinus (missionary) 55
Pax Romana 51
Payens, Hugues de 47
Peace Settlements 203
Peasants Revolt 126-7
Pelagians 36-7
Pella 19
penicillin 162
Peninsula Hotel (Kowloon) 218, 230
penitential Psalms 159
Penn, William 173
Pentateuch 134
Pentecost 17

The Church

281

Pepin (Martel's son) 62-3
Peter the Hermit 88
Petrarch (Italian poet) 96, 100, 112
Petrine City 104
Philip Augustus 82
Philip II 90, 151
Philip IV 99, 105
Philip Neri 151
Philip the Fair 47, 95-9
Photius (layman) 70
Phranza (historian) 108
physics 159-60
Pilgrim Fathers 172-3
Pilgrimage of Grace 142
Pink Bishop *see* Hall, Ronald
Pirenne, Henri 63
Pisa 87, 101, 111, 154, 156
Pius IV (pope) 150, 258
Pius V (pope) 151, 216
Pius VI (pope) 187, 189, 258
Pius VII (pope) 182, 189, 191, 202, 258
Pius IX (pope) 196-7, 200, 202-5, 208, 243, 259
Pius X (pope) 203
Pius XI (pope) 203-4
Pius XII (pope) 21, 200, 204, 206, 209, 243
Plymouth Colony 172
Po Valley 72
Pole, Reginald 140, 149, 266
Poor Clares 48
poverty 44, 47-8, 87, 164, 166
praemunire 137
pragmatism 55, 123, 157
Prayer Book (1559) 141
Preaching Friars *see* Dominican Order
predestination 37, 39
Primitive Methodist Church 179
Prince, The (Machiavelli) 114
Protestant Reformation 37, 82, 84, 116, 134, 137, 139-41, 143-4, 149, 161-2, 164, 171-4, 211, 213, 215-16

Ptolemy 115, 155
purgatory 45, 122, 149
Pyrenees 61

Q

Quanta Curia 200

R

Rahner, Karl 211, 215, 244
Raphael (Italian painter) 114, 123
Raymond (count of Toulouse) 88
realpolitik 70
reason 40, 48, 159, 161-2, 165, 182, 184
Red Hats 206
Red Shirts 198
Reformation Parliament 138
reformers, sixteenth-century 31
Reichskonkordat 204
renaissance 111, 113-16, 147, 238, 240
Rensuke Isagai 219
Reuchlin (Christian humanist) 114
Rhine 117, 194, 196
Rhone Valley 96
Ricci, Matteo 150
Richard I (Lionheart) 90, 92, 268
Risorgimento 196, 199
Robert (duke of Normandy) 88
Robespierre (radical politician) 185, 188-9
Robinson, Gene 230
Robinson, John 165, 172, 239, 244
rock *see* Simon Peter
Rock of Gibraltar 17
Roman Church of St Martin 55
Romanism 173
Romero, Oscar 216
Roncalli, Angelo Giuseppe *see* John XXIII (pope)
Roper, Trevor 46
Rousseau, Jean-Jacques 163-4
Runcie, Robert 216

Russia 66-7, 111, 192
Rutherford, Ernest 166

S

Sack of Rome 135, 144, 147, 152
Sacrosanctum Consilium 212
St Jean d'Angély 95, 99, 105
Saint-Just 185
St Martins-le-Grand 168
St Peter's Basilica 198, 204, 208, 210
Saladin (sultan of Egypt) 90, 92
salvation 36-7, 77, 87, 98, 124, 169, 171, 211-12
San Benedetto 42
Santiago de Compostela 94
Saxa Rubra 24
Scarisbrick, J. J. 138
schism 21-2, 64, 66-7, 85, 104-5, 109
Schweitzer, Albert 165
Scientific Revolution 155
Scotland 56-7, 101, 128
Seljuk Turks 86, 109
Seymour, Jane 139
Shennan, J. H. 185
Shrine of Our Lady 200
Sicut Universitatis Conditor (Innocent III) 81
Siderius Nuncius (Galileo) 157
Sigismund (emperor) 102, 104
Simon Peter 13-22, 97-9, 101, 103-5, 206-8, 210
simony 77-8, 103
Sisters of Charity 49, 216
Sistine Chapel 114, 206
Sixtus V (pope) 151
socialism 200, 205
Society of Jesus 150
Sodom and Gomorrah 229
Solidarity Movement 216
Solomon (king of Israel) 42, 47
South Africa 28
Soviet Union 203-4, 208
Spiritual Exercises (Loyola) 150

spiritual renaissance 64, 217
Sputnik 208
Stalin, Joseph 204
Staupitz (Luther's superior) 121
stem cells 167
Stephen IV (pope) 74, 254
Sweden 161
Syllabus Errorum (Pius IX) 200
Synod of Whitby 57

T

Tacitus (Roman historian) 113
Takashi Sakai 219
tax relief 28
Temple, William 220, 244, 267
Temple of Reason 188
temporal state 38, 77
Tertullian of Carthage 26, 223, 225
Test and Corporation Acts 179
Tetrarch Philip 14-15
Tetzel, Johann 122
Teutonic Knights 89
Theodora (empress) 70
Theodore (monastic activist) 41, 254, 265
Theresa of Avila 151
Thirty Years' War 151, 158, 161, 242
Tiber River 21, 24, 74
Tiberius (emperor) 14
Tillich, Paul 165
Titus (Roman general) 19, 53
Toleration Act of 1689 173
Torres, Camillo 215
Trachonitis 14
Trade Union Movement 179
Trajan (emperor) 53, 247
Transcendent Being 163
Treason Act 138
Treaty of Campo-Formio 189
Treaty of Rome 208
Treaty of Verdun 74
Treaty of Vienna 191
Trevor-Roper, Hugh 93

Tridentine Decrees   149-51
Tunis   91
Turkey   106
Tyndale, William   135

U

ultramontanism, theory of   201
Unam Sanctam (Boniface VIII)   82, 98, 211
Unitarian movement   165
United Church of Canada   226
United Nations   205
United Reformed Church   216
Universal Church   52, 61, 67, 118-19, 201
University of Cambridge   80, 166, 236-45
University of Padua   157
University of Pisa   157
University of Prague   156
University of Tübingen   215
University of Wittenburg   120
Urban II (pope)   78, 85, 89-91, 256
Urban V (pope)   100
Urban VI (pope)   100, 257
Urban VIII (pope)   158, 258

V

Valla, Lorenzo   112
Vatican Library   113
Venice   87, 90
Vespasian (emperor)   19, 247
Victor Emmanuel (king)   196, 198
Victoria Harbour   219
Vinci, Leonardo da   114, 240
Viollet-le-Duc, Eugène   182
Virgin Mary   108, 125, 149, 199, 213, 225
Virginia (Galileo's daughter)   159
Voltaire (French writer)   161, 164, 183, 241
Vulgate   114, 134, 149

W

Wall Street Crash   204
Warham (archbishop of Canterbury)   137
Wartburg Castle   126
Weimar Republic   203
Wesley, John   168-9, 176, 179, 242
Wesley, Samuel   169
Western Church   12, 35, 37, 49-50, 61, 65, 83-4, 96, 101, 153, 183, 219, 239
Western Franks *see* France
Western monasticism   42-3 *see also* monasticism
White, Ellen   226
White Friars *see* Carmelite Friars
Whitefield, George   170, 175, 242
Wilberforce, William   178
William I of Prussia   194
William III   173, 269
William of Occam   80
Williams, Rowan   230
Wilson, David Dunn   10, 224
Wittenberg   118, 123, 126, 188
Wong Nai Chung Gap   219
Worker Priest Movement   209
World Council of Churches   209, 214
World War I   192, 203
World War II   41, 203-4, 209
Worms   117, 154
Wycliffe, John   103, 142

X

Xavier, Francis   150

Y

York   23, 55
Young, Mark   218-19, 221, 230
Yuletide festival   55

Z

Zachary (pope) 63
Zwickau 126
Zwingli (religious leader) 128, 161,
    240

Lightning Source UK Ltd.
Milton Keynes UK
UKOW050423290613

212987UK00001B/10/P